SUPER SKILL

Why STORYTELLING Is the Superpower of the AI Age

JOE LAZER

Prospecta Press

Hardcover 978-1-63226-172-4
eBook 978-1-63226-173-1

Published by
Prospecta Press
PO Box 3131
Westport, CT 06880

Prospectapress.com
Book and cover design by Alexia Garaventa

*For Max—Thank you for transporting
me to Neverland every day.*

CONTENTS

PART III: UNLEASH

PART IV: UPGRADE

INTRODUCTION

On December 22, 2022, my son Max was born.

It had been a complicated birth. Max came out ghost-white and not breathing. The world stopped, the tiny pixels of the operating room shattering all around me. Doctors pumped air into his tiny lungs. When he let out his first cry and the doctor put him in my arms, I sniffed his head greedily. Prospective parents hear about that newborn baby smell all the time, but then you actually smell it. It's intoxicating. My brain flooded with oxytocin, nature's love drug. And the pixelated world merged back together, bright and new.

We spent Christmas in our tiny, fluorescent hospital room. Like a good Jewish boy, I ventured out for Chinese food. The restaurant was so crowded that I accidentally hip-checked my wife's anesthesiologist into the takeout counter.

I never felt more like a primate, slinging my perfectly healthy son at my side as I walked him back and forth across the 10x10 hospital room, a spring roll dangling in my mouth like a celebratory cigar. After five days, we headed back to our apartment in Brooklyn. I had a four-week paternity leave from my job at a red-hot AI startup called A.Team, fresh off $50 million in funding. Without a constant barrage of work emergencies battering my brain, I developed two big obsessions:

The first was keeping Max alive.

The second was ChatGPT.

The AI tool was swarming the world and inviting prophesies that writers like me would soon go extinct. I stayed up late at night, worrying about what ChatGPT meant for me and my newborn son. The only reason anyone paid me enough to afford our bougie Brooklyn apartment was because I was a strong writer and leader of creative marketing teams. Was my career over? Would I no longer get to do the thing I loved the most? And what about Max? Would my son grow up in a beige world with little regard for human storytellers?

Four weeks earlier, OpenAI had launched ChatGPT as a small research experiment to test its latest GPT-3.5 model. OpenAI's CEO, Sam Altman, hoped they could attract 10,000 users for the tool. Enough for decent feedback.

I heard about ChatGPT almost immediately, but that wasn't surprising. A.Team was an AI company, and our Slack was a constant stream of the latest tech news and coolest new products. But it did surprise me when my mom called me about it. This is a woman who still has the @verizon.net email address that came with our dial-up internet.

"Have you heard of this ChadGBT?" she asked. "All of the kids at work are talking about it."

Then ChatGPT was in my group chat. Moments later, it was everywhere. It was like aliens had landed on Earth, and they were eager to write blog posts for you. On LinkedIn, everyone speculated that writers were cooked. All this played out just as my newsletter passed 100,000 subscribers and a TV pilot I co-created with my writing partner, Shane Snow, started filming in Chicago. I had accomplished my high school dream to carve out a career as a writer and storyteller. Would AI end all that?

I'd been writing about tech since I was twenty-one, and ChatGPT was the most explosive technology I'd ever seen. It grew to 57 million users in the first month. By comparison, Facebook took over three years to surpass 50 million users. A consensus emerged: Humans were fucked. Analysts were tripping over each other to declare that AI would put anyone with a humanities degree or a creative job out of work. Goldman Sachs predicted that 300 million creative jobs would soon be lost. McKinsey projected that generative AI was poised to add $2.4–$4.4 trillion to the global economy—more than the GDP of the United Kingdom—and that AI would replace the content creation function within the marketing teams of most companies. Mira Murati, the young superstar CTO of OpenAI, declared that "some creative jobs will go away, but maybe those jobs shouldn't have existed in the first place." Jason M. Allen, who won a prominent photography competition by submitting an undisclosed AI-generated photo, declared, "Art is dead, dude. It's over. AI won. Humans lost."

On LinkedIn and X, the swindlers and zealots preached the AI dogma with an intensity not seen since they were sending Dogecoin to the moon. Creatives were dead, and only the true believers would survive. Prompt or perish. Staring at my newborn son as he nuzzled to sleep in the early morning light, I wondered: What if they're right? And even if they're not, what skills would he need to thrive in a world remade by a tech tsunami? More urgently, what skills would I need?

In the tech and business world, a new mantra emerged: "AI won't replace you. Someone using AI will replace you." You might not have a job as a writer, strategist, or designer anymore, but if you get good at using AI, you'll have career security. As I write this, nearly three years after the launch of ChatGPT, this mantra is more prevalent than ever. It's catchy. It's also wrong.

Why I wrote this book

I've spent my career at the intersection of storytelling, the future of work, and technology—in particular, AI. In college, I helped found *The Faster Times*, a digital media startup, and over the next four years, despite being twenty-three and having little idea of what I was doing, grew it into a profitable business as the Chief Creative Officer. I then joined the founding team of Contently, a tech company that pioneered the content marketing industry, building on-demand content teams for brands through an elite network of 200,000 journalists, and filmmakers. We built an ecosystem where freelance creatives could make hundreds of thousands of dollars a year telling stories on behalf of brands, helping Fortune 1000 companies become publishers. At Contently, I conducted myriad neuroscience and behavioral science research initiatives—from scanning voters' brains while they watch political ads to tracking readers' eyes as they read branded content in the *New York Times*. I also wrote a best-selling book on the art and science of business storytelling, *The Storytelling Edge*, with my writing partner, Shane Snow.

In other words, I'm obsessed with new technology trends and how they transform the skills and tactics we need to be successful. I've spent the past three years studying and writing about AI and the future of work in my newsletter, which has grown to nearly 200,000 subscribers across Substack and LinkedIn. This was also part of my day job. A.Team is an AI future-of-work company, and as head of marketing, part of my job was to figure out how AI would change the way we work—and which skills would matter most.

Starting in early 2023, I dug deep into AI use cases and research. I hosted a monthly AI Salon at A.Team's downtown New York offices, interviewing AI and future of work leaders. I tried out all the tools with my team. I texted an annoying number of questions to my brother-in-law, who was in the process of starting one of the hottest AI research labs in Silicon Valley. I used ChatGPT constantly and observed my direct reports, who were voracious early adopters of generative AI. I quickly noticed one area where AI couldn't help them. While AI thrives at technical tasks, it doesn't help with the hardest, most human part of work—the "soft skills" that allow you to actually get things done by building relationships and cajoling stakeholders to rally around your plan.

I began to have a revelation. The key decision isn't whether you'll invest in your AI skills. *It's whether you'll invest in your humanity.*

Who this book is for

As I write this, the majority of US workers are worried about how AI will affect their careers. I don't blame them. We've invented a technology modeled after our brains that can think and perform tasks 1,000 times faster than we can. Every day, we're confronted with another headline warning that AI is coming for our jobs and that we need to level up or else.

Naturally, this gives people a sense that they lack agency. A feeling that there's a wave on the horizon, building slowly to a tsunami, and they're on the shore with nowhere to run.

This is a book for people who want to get their agency back. People who want to take control of their destiny and question the self-serving advice of our Silicon Valley overlords. People who want to stand out by embracing what makes them most human.

This is a book for people who want to tap into their most human superpowers and future-proof their careers.

What this book is about

As AI and other advanced technology can do most technical skills better than us, we need to ask a simple question: "What's our most human ability—the thing AI won't be able to replicate, even if it gets 100x better?"

The answer is storytelling. If you invest in one core skill in the AI age, it should not be prompt engineering. It should be storytelling. Those who invest in storytelling will outperform the competition in all the "soft" skills that matter in the new age of work: Communication. Leadership. Empathy. Critical thinking. Collaboration.

Storytelling is humanity's greatest cognitive superpower. It's how we transformed from a mid-rate species with few dominant traits into ultra-social learning machines that rose to conquer Earth. It's how we've forged bonds, passed down lessons, and taught each other to survive and thrive. The ability to tell great stories separates the bankrupt startup founders from the serial unicorns, the CMO from the middle manager. Stories are how we persuade, influence, and lead other people. They're the super skill that powers all of the soft skills that matter. In a world in which AI can do most technical tasks better and faster than us, those soft skills will be 95 percent of what matters at work. Get better at storytelling, and you'll get better at all of them.

THE SUPER SKILL OF THE AI AGE

This breaks against the conventional wisdom today, which says that if you want to succeed in the next age of work, all you need to do is learn how to use AI. LinkedIn influencers are demanding that we put AI tools in the hands of kindergarteners, lest we fall behind China. Attention-seeking founders are bragging about firing everyone who doesn't adopt AI fast enough. We've lost the plot. Yes, AI is a transformative technology for the next age of work. But generative AI is an amplifier of human abilities, not an endpoint. You will not future-proof yourself by simply using ChatGPT for every task and becoming a "prompt engineer." You won't be able to discern good ideas from bad ones or have the skill to sell any of those ideas internally. That "swipe file" of go-to prompts from a LinkedIn influencer will not save you. Make AI your primary skillset, and before long, your communication and critical thinking skills will atrophy. AI won't be working for you; you'll be working for AI.

We're already seeing this happen. Neuroscience research from MIT shows that overreliance on AI shuts off parts of our brains, and college students who depend on AI are seeing their communication and critical thinking skills decline. Researchers also found that if you think and write on your own *first*, and then use AI as an amplifier, you can reach a new, higher level of cognitive engagement.

My argument here is simple: If you want to win the new world of work in which AI can do most technical skills better than us, invest heavily in unleashing your human storytelling superpowers *first*, then use AI as an amplifier on top of it. While everyone else is zigging by outsourcing their critical thinking to ChatGPT, you zag. Do it well, and I promise you'll find yourself leading the race.

This book is structured to help you do that. The first parts reveal the secret science of storytelling, and how to apply those lessons to lead, persuade, and build trust. With that foundation in place, the final section reveals how to use generative AI to upgrade your storytelling skills.

As we begin, I have great news for you: You are already a storyteller. We all are. As children, we lived in a world of stories. When we go to sleep, our minds dream in stories to prepare us for the day to come. We lose confidence in those skills as we grow older and doubt ourselves, but you are already more of a storyteller than you realize. Pay close attention to every interaction you have for the next twenty-four hours; if you're like most people, you spend 75 percent of your waking hours consuming, exchanging, or daydreaming in story. For us humans, storytelling is as natural as breathing, and we need it almost as badly as air.

What you'll get out of this book

My goal in writing this book is to put you back in control. By the end, you'll know how to tap into your innate human storytelling superpowers, future-proof yourself against the technological chaos, and become irreplaceable.

In Part I, I'll reveal the mind-bending science of storytelling and how it became our superpower, helping us become ultra-social learning machines that rose to conquer the Earth. You'll learn how stories transform our brain and why storytelling has such a profound and underrated power in business—determining what we buy, who we follow, and why some companies and leaders succeed while others crash and burn. I'll also reveal why we're quickly shifting from the code economy that's dominated the last twenty years into a new storytelling economy where narrative is power, and the ability to craft and share stories determines success.

The final three sections of this book will reveal fifteen principles to hone your storytelling superpowers and win the AI age, nestled within a simple, proven framework: **Unlock. Unleash. Upgrade.**

Part II (Principles 1–6) covers **Unlock.** We all have innate storytelling superpowers, but we need to constantly rediscover and hone them. These principles are your storytelling foundations. As most people's communication and storytelling skills will atrophy from overreliance on AI, these principles will give you a massive advantage in the workplace. You are a storytelling animal; you just need to unlock your sixth sense for stories. You'll master the four elements of great storytelling and the shapes of addictive narratives. You'll learn how to build trust through active listening, identify your muse, and develop taste that will make you stand out from the crowd—plus, you'll learn a little-known hack for unlocking your creativity and developing quick-twitch storytelling muscles, tapping into what neuroscientists call "multimodal encoding" and visuospatial processing.

In Part III (Principles 7–11), we'll progress to **Unleash.** You'll learn how to build upon your storytelling foundations and deploy your storytelling skills strategically across every aspect of your professional life—leading teams, selling ideas, building your personal brand, strengthening relationships, and crafting the Big Idea that makes you stand out. You'll discover genius techniques for telling resonant stories from some of the greatest storytellers of the modern age: cultural icons like David Sedaris, Kevin Hart, and Steve Jobs; coaches like Bill Cowher; and entrepreneurs like Sara Blakely and Sam Altman.

Finally, in Part IV (Principles 12–15), we get to **Upgrade.** With your storytelling mastery in place, we'll explore how to use AI to develop and hone your storytelling skills. I'll show you how to avoid the dreaded AI "Vortex of Mid," the powerful force that sucks your content into a black hole of mediocrity, atrophying your storytelling and communication skills in the process. Through the stories of Louis-Jacques-Mandé Daguerre, Holly Herndon, and a band of AI filmmaking rebels, I'll reveal the three levels of storytelling innovation and how to apply them.

By the time you read this book, the pace of AI innovation will have changed from when I'm writing it, and that's okay. I've designed the principles of this book to be timeless. For 100,000 years, stories have dominated the lives and tribes of Homo sapiens, and that's unlikely to change in the next 100,000 years.

So let's start by truly understanding the power of storytelling in work and life.

Part I:
THE STORYTELLING ECONOMY

If I could give my 13- and 16-year-old one competence
that I think would stand the test of time,
it'd be storytelling.

— Scott Galloway

Chapter 1

STORYTELLING SAPIENS

Picture a Neanderthal in your mind. Close your eyes. Imagine every detail of his body—his face, his calves, his toes.

If you're like most people, you imagined a hairy, hunched, dim-witted brute. And he's carrying a giant club, right? That's the popular depiction of Neanderthals—our hominid cousins who were just too dumb to survive.

But what if I told you that Neanderthals were superhuman? Over the past few decades, research has revealed that Neanderthals were not only much stronger than Homo sapiens, they also may have been smarter. Their brains were 15 percent larger. They built fires, cooked food, made clothing, and drew cave paintings. They were like the hairy lost Hemsworth brother who eschewed Hollywood for MIT.

As Rutger Bregman explains in his book *Humankind*, "We may boast a superbrain, but they packed a gigabrain. We have a MacBook Air, and they got the MacBook Pro." Neanderthals and Homo sapiens coexisted with each other for thousands of years. So if they were so much bigger and smarter, how did humans become the dominant species on Earth?

It's tempting to imagine a *300*-style showdown, in which the underdog humans banded together to win a great battle against all odds. But the real answer is far less dramatic, yet far more meaningful. It all started with one little evolutionary quirk.

For millennia, humans survived with few dominant traits. Compared to our Neanderthal cousins, we had tiny brains and smaller muscles. If prehistoric bookies were placing odds on which species would rise to conquer the Earth, Homo sapiens would have been the ultimate longshot. But then, something magical happened. As Yuval Noah Harari writes in his seminal book *Sapiens*, there was a surprise evolution in the DNA of Homo sapiens between 70,000 and 200,000 years ago. Suddenly, humans had a unique vocal range, which allowed for distinct vowels, consonants, and syllables and quickly progressed into the capacity for syntax and language. Harari calls this the start of the "Cognitive Revolution." But this revolution didn't mean we were suddenly smarter than our primate cousins at everything. It simply meant we had one special skill that made all the difference.

Ultra-social learning machines

In the mid-2000s, a team of German researchers conducted a set of thirty-eight tests to compare the intelligence of chimpanzees and orangutans with human toddlers because . . . why not? The beauty of science is that you can ask yourself, "Who's smarter, a chimp or my two-year-old?" and then get funding to find out the truth.

The tests were based on the highly regarded Primate Cognition Battery Test, which measures the core components of social and physical cognition, like spatial understanding, calculation, and causality.

I have a toddler, and while he makes some truly bizarre decisions—like smashing peaches into toy convertibles and trying to plug his Elizabeth Warren action figure into the outlet—I would have bet that he's smarter than an orangutan and chimpanzee.

Surprisingly, though, the human toddlers didn't score much better than the orangutans and chimpanzees. Across every test, the chimps beat or tied us, and the orangutans got extremely close.

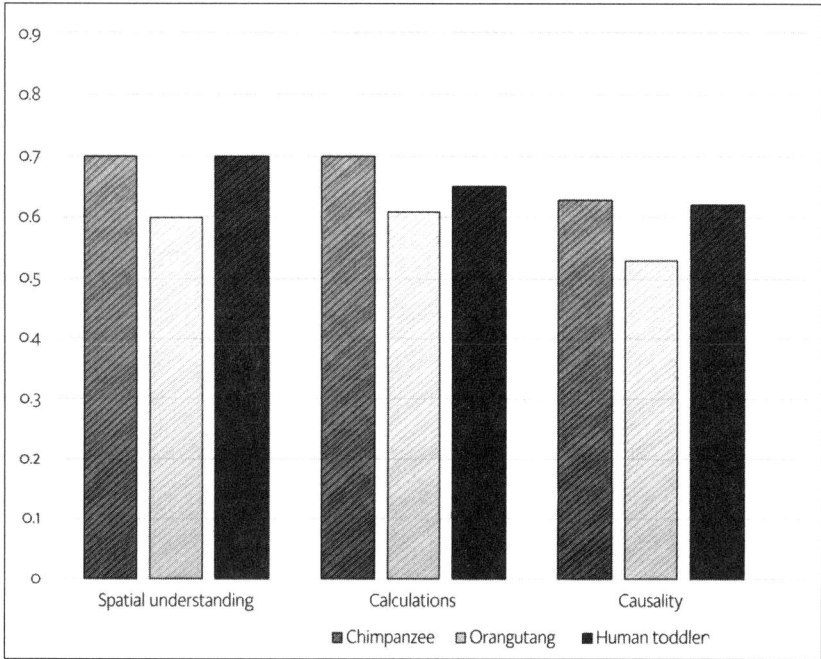

But then the researchers tested a fourth skill: social learning. And we Homo sapiens *dominated*.

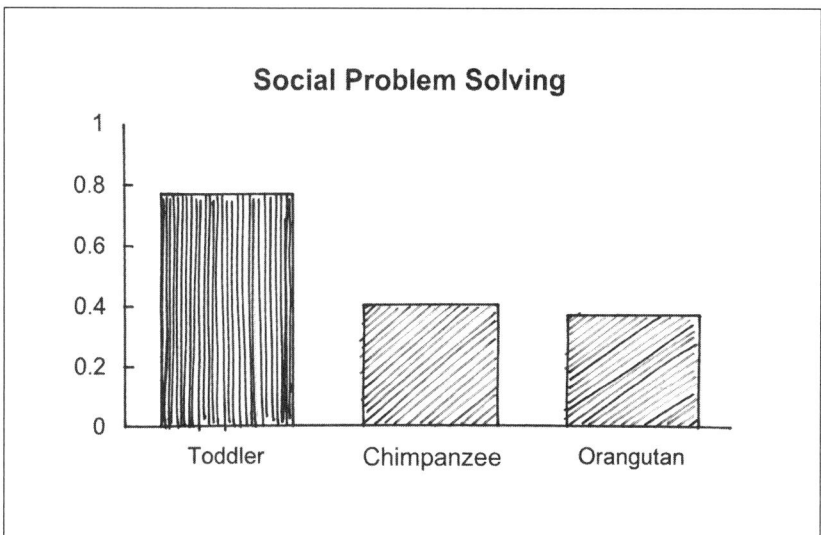

As Bregman explains, human beings are "ultra-social learning machines," built with unique features that make it easier for us to trust others and form teams:

- We blush, which shows others what we think and builds trust.

- We have whites in our eyes, which lets others follow our gaze, making us an open book.

- We have a smooth forehead, allowing for subtle nonverbal communication via our eyebrows.

- Most important, we can build trust and pass down lessons to each other through stories.

This social learning dynamic is why parenting a newborn is so freaking hard. If you're someone who watches *Planet Earth* while eating an entire bag of Doritos at 1 a.m., you already know that many mammals—elephants, giraffes, wildebeests—can walk within a couple of days of being born. Human babies, by contrast, typically don't walk until they're one year old. They're terrifyingly helpless. As I discovered with horror when preparing to become a father, their skulls *aren't even fully formed.*

You might think that's an incredibly stupid way to evolve. Your offspring can't walk? Or protect themselves? They can barely eat? *Their skulls are squishy?* Sounds like a recipe for going extinct, just like 99 percent of species that have tried to make it on this big blue ball we call Earth. Yet somehow, here we are—eight billion strong, spread out across every corner of the planet, doing crazy things like building robot dogs and sending Katy Perry into space.

It turns out there are benefits to being born underdeveloped that are unique to humans. At birth, our brains have a high degree of neural plasticity, meaning we're adaptable. Because we're helpless as babies, we receive constant care from adults. What are those adults doing while they're caring for us? Chugging coffee and trying to keep from going insane from sleep deprivation, mostly. But what else are they doing while mainlining caffeine? They're immersing us in a world of language and stories. At a time when most mammals are still gestating in the womb, we're out there developing the capacity for language. While they're nestled in embryonic fluid, we're learning how to survive and thrive in our environment, our brains reorganizing their neural pathways and connections every time we learn something new.

This knack for social learning gave us a key advantage over our stronger and smarter Neanderthal cousins, and the following thought experiment from famed anthropologist Joseph Henrich shows us why.

Storytelling and teamwork

Imagine a scenario in which there's a tribe of humans and a tribe of Neanderthals. For dramatic effect, let's say one in ten Neanderthals had serious Steve Jobs energy and were likely to invent something important, like a fishing rod, on their own. Meanwhile, only 1 in 1,000 humans could do the same. When it comes to inventing things, the Neanderthals are 100 times smarter.

But then let's say each Neanderthal only has a social group of one to teach how to fish. Despite their impressive capabilities, each Neanderthal only talks to their cavemate, Steve. On the flip side, each human is part of a social group of ten that they can teach to fish. By Henrich's calculations, only one in five Neanderthals would learn how to fish in a lifetime. But 99.9 percent of humans would learn the skill, eventually picking it up from someone else.

Our ability to work in teams provides a remarkable advantage. Hunter-gatherer tribes of 500 typically roamed in teams of twenty-five people. As a result, we commonly came across other groups and shared knowledge. As Bregman writes in

Humankind, this teamwork likely allowed us to survive the last Ice Age, sharing resources and spreading survival lessons, while Neanderthals became extinct.

How exactly did we pass along information so well from generation to generation? After all, the earliest writing didn't appear until 5,500 years ago in Mesopotamia. Literacy only became common in the last few hundred years. Most people weren't learning from textbooks and memos. It all comes back to that deluxe feature of Homo sapiens: our special vocal range. This gave us access to distinct vowels, consonants, and syllables, which led to our greatest cognitive technology: storytelling.

We've innately understood how stories pass on information for hundreds of thousands of years, but the last fifty years has ushered in a wave of research that shows how powerful they really are. A 1969 Stanford study found that students remembered six to seven times more words when those words were embedded in a story. Over the past fifteen years, neuroscience research has shown that immersive stories trigger long-term memory encoding.

Telling stories around the campfire was how we relayed lessons about fishing, agriculture, hunting, gathering, and being good members of our tribe. Bregman likens our built-in technology of storytelling and social learning to Wi-Fi. A Neanderthal may have been a state-of-the-art, super-fast computer while we were a slower PC with less RAM, but we were connected and could learn from one another, and that made all the difference.

Gossip and gods

As humanity evolved, storytelling became our greatest cognitive technology, allowing us to accomplish incredible feats as a species. The first great unlock was the ability to work together in large groups.

In the early 1990s, British anthropologist Robin Dunbar made a compelling case that humans can only comfortably maintain stable relationships with about 150 people, a phenomenon famously known as "Dunbar's number." After that, things get dicey. But if that rule were hard and fast, we'd still be stuck in hunter-gatherer tribes. We wouldn't have countries of hundreds of millions or societies of billions. We would never have rallied people together for fantastical adventures like going to the moon. So what happened? Our early storytelling capabilities took a series of small leaps.

The first was our one true storytelling love: gossip. We told stories about each other as a means of societal regulation. It set standards and consequences for what it meant to be a good member of the tribe, while also serving as a key form of social bonding. (What would friendship be if we could never talk shit about other people?) Anthropologists now believe that the earliest form of storytelling was gossip. We naturally progressed from communicating, "This is where you'll find bison" to "Did you *hear* about what happened on the hunt?!" If you weren't contributing enough and being a good member of the tribe, gossip was a way to keep you in check. We see this evolutionary instinct in full force today. Gossip is how we regulate behavior in our friend groups and communities, and it shapes our reputations at work.

Once gossip emerged, we were hooked on stories. The next great innovation was myths: stories of the heavens and earth, of the clouds and sea. These stories formed a prehistoric religion that anthropologists call "Paleolithic Animism," a spiritual belief that every visible force (plants, animals, rain) and invisible force (wind, heat, cold) had agency. Around 30,000 years ago, we began recording these stories through intricate cave paintings. We can't know the exact stories our ancestors told then, but there is one crucial clue that still exists today.

Storytelling, sex, and social cohesion

In 2017, researchers from UCLA's Department of Anthropology traveled to the Luzon Islands in the Philippines to study the

Agta, a remote hunter-gatherer tribe that chooses to live the same way its ancestors did 35,000 years ago. The Agta were an ideal case study for understanding the traits and skills most important to our evolution—and what we value most as human beings.

The UCLA researchers found that skilled storytellers—those voted as the best storytellers by tribe members—were most sought after as mates. They had the greatest reproductive success, producing an additional 0.53 living offspring compared to non-skilled storytellers. But that's not all. They also found that skilled storytellers were the most sought-after social partners. The researchers asked 291 Agta people across eighteen camps whom they would most like to live with, and they were twice as likely to nominate a skilled storyteller. In fact, skilled storytellers were more attractive and more popular than even the top foragers, hunters, and fishermen.

Yes, this means that if you can tell great stories, everyone will want to have sex with you and be your friend. And they'll want to work with you, too.

But this begs a question: *Why* would you prefer to mate with someone great at telling stories rather than someone skilled at supplying food? Wouldn't the latter be way more valuable?

We can find a big clue in the stories they told. Over the course of three nights, the UCLA researchers asked the most skilled elders to tell them the stories they usually tell children and each other. They write:

> All stories conveyed norms and principles regu-
> lating cooperation and social behaviour, specif-
> ically sex equality ("The sun and the moon"),
> social egalitarianism and friendship ("The wild
> pig and the seacow"), group cooperation ("The
> monkey and the giant") and group identity and

social acceptance ("The winged ant"). In these stories, the ending reflects a reconciliation of individual interests and differences, while also exemplifying various mechanisms of social norm enforcement, such as emphasising the benefits to cooperation over competition, examples of punishment for breaking norms, and reverse dominance hierarchies to prevent individual accumulation of power.

Like gossip, these proto-religious myths served an important purpose: social cohesion. When the researchers expanded their study to examine eighty-nine stories from seven Agta hunter-gatherer tribes, they found that 70 percent of the stories told were designed to regulate social behavior. This shows us why skilled storytellers were so sought after as mates and members of the tribe. Like a conductor, a storyteller orchestrated the cooperation of the tribe. The researchers found that camps with more skilled storytellers worked together better. A skilled hunter or forager who could generate 15 percent more food than the average individual member of the tribe was good. But a skilled storyteller who could bring the tribe together as a team and increase everyone's knowledge and productivity by 20 percent was much better.

From the dawn of human history, great leaders have had one thing in common: They're great storytellers.

Storytelling and society

Around 15,000 years ago, the last Ice Age began to end, and our ecology changed, giving birth to lush woodlands with plentiful food. In areas like the Fertile Crescent, humans began settling in one place for the first time. As human society exceeded Dunbar's Number—that 150-member threshold—we needed a way for everyone to feel connected and trust one another. Our great cognitive technology—storytelling—needed to take another leap.

In hunter-gatherer tribes, storytelling served the purpose of direct social regulation within the small group of people we knew, the equivalent of the stories we tell our kids to teach them proper social behavior. But as our societies expanded to the thousands, we needed a new storytelling system if we wanted to work together in large numbers. Yuval Noah Harari explains in *Sapiens* that this new system was fiction. "You could never convince a monkey to give you a banana by promising him limitless bananas after death in monkey heaven," he writes. But with Homo sapiens? It works beautifully.

The ability to learn from each other through stories gave us a leg up on Neanderthals and allowed us to survive the last Ice Age. We were the equivalent of the close-knit team weathering the economic depression together while our competitors went out of business. And now, with the power of fiction and great myths in our hands, we could rally an enormous number of strangers together to accomplish a shared goal—something no other animal could do. We think of fiction only as novels, TV shows, and films, but as Harari explains, the human system of fiction is even more elaborate. Religion, laws, nationality, and currency are all "common myths that exist only in people's collective imagination. . . . Two lawyers who have never met can nevertheless combine efforts to defend a complete stranger because they both believe in the existence of laws, justice, human rights, and money paid out in fees."

Our society is literally constructed of stories. Shared myths allowed us to band together to build the walls of Jericho—one of our first major cities in the Fertile Crescent—something a hunter-gatherer tribe of 150 could never accomplish, but a larger group of 1,000 could. Ten thousand years later, Winston

Churchill would tell a story of Britain as a beacon on a hill, rallying an entire nation to endure the German Blitzkrieg. Martin Luther King Jr. would tell a vivid story of his dream of equality, and inspire people across the nation to put their lives on the line for civil rights. John F. Kennedy would tell the story of a sci-fi future and inspire thousands of people to rally together to put a man on the moon.

The atomic particle of power

Stories inspire and terrify us; they tell us who we fear and who we follow. Storytelling is the atomic particle of power. Power does not exist without a story that makes people believe in it. We follow dictators and authoritarians because of the stories of their divine appointment and the tales of what will happen to us if we don't play by the rules. We follow business leaders because they inspire us with a vision of what we can accomplish together. We follow religious leaders because of their stories of how life came to be, and what comes after it. We live in a capitalist society because we accept the shared fantasy of money, and we obey the law because we all believe that a country with invisible boundaries exists. We learn how to exist in the world through stories. Researchers have even found that reading fiction turns us into more empathetic and socially adept humans.

Once you see the power of stories, you can't unsee it. Stories play a central role in your day-to-day life and major events in the world. They transformed us from a middling species with barely more significance than baboons into ultra-social learning machines that rose to conquer Earth. And that power has been growing exponentially.

Today, a great storyteller can reach billions of people worldwide in seconds. They can tell the story of a new company and, without a single customer, it'll be worth billions. Sam Altman's ability to tell the brilliant story of AI's sci-fi future has OpenAI valued at $500 billion, even though OpenAI's business *loses* $5–$15 billion annually. In April 2025, Altman bought famed Apple designer Jony Ive's design company, IO, for $6.5 billion—even though Ive's company was little more than a fiction incorporated. It didn't have a single product or customer. By all accounts, Altman did it for the plot. The acquisition washed Google I/O—the flagship AI event of OpenAI's biggest competitor—out of the news.

But stories are far more than power. They're joy. I didn't fall in love with Kurt Vonnegut at sixteen because of a quest to be king. It was because our brains are programmed for stories. They give us incredible joy, lighting up the brain's pleasure sensors. They're at the core of our friendships, love, and loyalty. It's our most human trait, and it's only growing more powerful each day as AI takes over the new world of work.

To truly understand why, we need to look deep inside the human brain.

Chapter 2

THE NEW SCIENCE OF STORIES

In early 2005, a 6'5" man with broad shoulders and a chiseled jaw boarded a cross-country flight. If you were on that plane, you might have mistaken Dr. Paul Zak for an NFL quarterback. He was actually a neuroscientist, still buzzing from having presented groundbreaking research on a mystical neurochemical called oxytocin at a big conference.

Dr. Zak had two young daughters whom he hated to be away from. So as he squeezed into his economy seat, he pulled out his laptop, eager to finish his work so he could focus on his family once he landed.

Dr. Zak scrunched over, typing like a pterodactyl from *Jurassic World 7: IT Department*. Suddenly, turbulence hit. Dr. Zak's knees bucked the keyboard; his stomach shot into his throat. He could barely keep his laptop on the tray table, never mind type. He needed to distract himself, so he turned on a movie—*Million Dollar Baby*, which had just won the Oscar for Best Picture.

If you haven't seen *Million Dollar Baby*, it tells the devastating story of Maggie Fitzgerald (Hilary Swank), a thirty-one-year-old waitress from Missouri's Ozarks who dreams of becoming a professional boxer. She wanders into a rundown boxing gym and tries to convince the grizzled head trainer, Frankie Dunn (Clint Eastwood), to train her. He initially says no but reluctantly accepts after his prize fighter leaves him.

Maggie defies everyone's expectations. She's nimble and fierce. She wins fight after fight, bonding with Frankie, who fills the void of Maggie's dead father, while Maggie fills the void of Frankie's estranged daughter. Before long, Maggie earns a shot at $1 million and the welterweight championship belt in Las Vegas, but then, tragedy strikes. In the title match, Maggie's arch-rival sucker-punches her from behind. Maggie crashes on her corner stool, breaking her neck. She wakes up as a ventilator-dependent quadriplegic. In the hospital, Maggie is left with one last mission: to convince her found-father Frankie to kill her out of mercy.

As Dr. Zak watched this tragic father-daughter tale, the world around him melted away. Before he knew it, the movie was over, and he felt someone shaking him on the shoulder, asking, "Are you okay? Are you okay?"

Dr. Zak turned. It was his seatmate. *What was this weirdo talking about? Why the hell was he shaking him?* And that's when Dr. Zak realized he'd been sobbing uncontrollably. "Gobs of goop were coming out of every orifice in my face," he told me.

When Dr. Zak returned to his lab the next day, he told a psychologist in his lab about his strange reaction. "That's no surprise," she said. "Psychologists use video to change people's moods all the time."

The morality molecule

For as long as he could remember, Dr. Zak had been obsessed with morality. As a kid, he noticed that both religious and non-religious people were equally fixated on morality—doing the right thing and caring for others—and wondered if there was some biological human basis for it. As he became an established researcher at

Claremont Graduate University, Dr. Zak decided to pursue a wild hunch: What if a mysterious neurochemical he'd been studying, called oxytocin, was secretly the morality molecule?

In the early 2000s, researchers didn't know much about oxytocin. They'd discovered that it caused rodents to care for their offspring and tolerate burrow mates, and that in human beings, it spiked among mothers during childbirth and breastfeeding, and in both men and women during sex. Beyond that, oxytocin was a minor scientific mystery.

But how do you measure morality? It's a question that has perplexed philosophers since Plato. So Dr. Zak and his team decided to focus on a single virtue: trust. Research had just come out showing that the proportion of trustworthy people in a nation was correlated to its economic performance. Countries and businesses that operated with a greater degree of trust tended to thrive.

Dr. Zak's initial research indicated his hunch was right: oxytocin is directly related to trust. When we perform a "trustworthy" action, like giving up resources or helping another person, the oxytocin levels spike in the brains of the giver and receiver, indicating that oxytocin plays a crucial role in human cooperation and connection. If you want to build stronger relationships and teams, raising oxytocin levels is key.

The big question for Dr. Zak was *how* you boost oxytocin levels. Dr. Zak's experience on the plane gave him an idea: What if the production of oxytocin wasn't just triggered through physical interaction but also through stories?

Luckily for Dr. Zak, a secretive US military agency was also interested in this question.

Narrative networks

In 2011, DARPA—the semi-secret agency inside the US Department of Defense—released a rare call for research proposals. Ten years in, the war in Afghanistan was a disaster.

Attacks from the Taliban, Al-Qaeda, and other insurgent groups persisted, forcing President Barack Obama to deploy 100,000 additional troops.

Critically, the United States was losing the recruiting battle for informants. The Taliban and Al-Qaeda were savvier at recruiting civilians to their side; the leaflets the US military dropped from the sky just weren't cutting it. So DARPA wanted to know if there was a way they could peek inside people's brains and figure out which stories and messages built trust and influenced people.

DARPA put out a call for research proposals to America's neuroscientists. Did any of them have a way to do this? Could they develop a device to analyze people's neurological responses in the field and help the military figure out the most effective messages for countering terrorist propaganda and recruiting Afghani villagers to their side? DARPA called the initiative the Narrative Networks Project.

Does this sound like something out of an episode of *Black Mirror*? Absolutely. But for Dr. Zak, it also presented an opportunity. He applied for DARPA funding and got it. With these resources, he could finally study if emotionally resonant stories were the key to unleashing oxytocin and scaling trust.

To test his theory, Dr. Zak and his team edited two videos from St. Jude's Research Hospital and showed them to participants. As Dr. Zak writes in a 2015 paper, the first video was "high in tension and emotional resonance." It tells the story of a father whose two-year-old son, Ben, is stricken with terminal brain cancer. The father wants to connect and play with his son, but it's a devastating situation. He knows Ben only has a few months to live. After a struggle, the father finds the strength to stay close to his son "until he takes his last breath."

As a control, subjects watched a second video, which included the same father and son, but deliberately lacked any real story. It showed the two spending a day together at the zoo. The boy is bald from chemotherapy and is called "miracle boy," but there's no narrative.

Since oxytocin is released in both the brain and the blood, Dr. Zak's team was able to study oxytocin levels by analyzing blood samples of research subjects. Participants who watched the video with a strong narrative arc had higher oxytocin levels; they were also more empathetic and willing to donate money to a stranger in the study afterward. In experiment after experiment, this phenomenon held true. When people in the United Kingdom watched public service announcements with a strong narrative arc, their oxytocin and attention levels spiked, and they were 261 percent more likely to give to charity than if they watched a video with a weak narrative.

How stories change our minds

With this research, Dr. Zak scientifically proved what politicians, artists, and business moguls had intuitively known for centuries—that great stories build trust and empathy, transforming people's behavior. If you want people to trust you and rally around you, you need to tell a great story.

This is why the master storytellers from the hunter-gatherer tribes we met in chapter 1 were much more sexually and socially desirable than even the best hunters. Their stories spiked oxytocin in the brains of others in their tribes. That's also why teams who share stories collaborate and adapt more effectively.

Dr. Zak had also done something revolutionary: He'd found a way to identify *which* stories change people's minds. Not all stories are created equal; the weak narratives he tested fell flat. Only stories high in tension and emotional resonance changed people's minds. But Dr. Zak's work wasn't finished. Analyzing which messages work best was just part one of DARPA's Narrative Networks Project. Next up was figuring out how to test which stories change our brains at scale.

"We had to get away from blood draws," Dr. Zak told me. After all, it was impractical—and deeply dystopian—for the military to take Afghan villagers' blood samples after listening to propaganda messages. That truly would be some *Black Mirror* shit.

For part two of the DARPA project, Dr. Zak's team developed a brilliant innovation: a tiny neurosensor that fits on the inside of your wrist to measure attention via heart rate and oxytocin release via the vagus nerve. They also built a machine-learning algorithm based on data from past experiments to interpret the results, creating an "immersion score" that quantified how engaged people's brains were with a story. "It was a really noble goal," Dr. Zak explained. "How could we train soldiers to use words rather than weapons to help reduce conflict in areas around the world?"

Suddenly, Dr. Zak had a way to measure which stories change our minds *in real-time*. Back home in the United States, this would have enormous implications for the business world.

Storytelling and sales

Dr. Zak's deal with DARPA allowed him to apply his technology to commercial uses. The logical avenue was advertising. Advertising creatives had long believed that a great story was the key to convincing someone to buy a product, but there had never been a reliable way to predict which stories would have the biggest impact on people. Focus groups to test commercials were notoriously flawed, sabotaged by subjects' bias toward telling researchers what they want to hear. Even Don Draper didn't have a 100 percent hit rate. One day he was pitching Lucky Strike with "It's Toasted," the next day, he was tanking his career by pitching Hershey's with a story of eating a chocolate bar in a brothel.

Dr. Zak and his research partner, Dr. Jorge Barraza, spun their technology into a new company, Immersion Neuroscience, and applied it to advertising. They quickly proved that Don

Draper was right: Great stories—not a list of features or "proof points"—make people's brains want to buy. In a study with the ad agency BBDO, they could predict which commercials would lead to sales with 83 percent accuracy based on how immersed the subjects became in the story of the commercial.

One of the best ads they ever tested, for instance, was a spot called "Empty Chair" for Guinness. A bartender at a pub repeatedly sets aside a pint in front of an empty chair—during football match celebrations, a bachelorette party, and the holiday season. A patron tries to take the chair, and the bartender rebukes him with a stern shake of the head. Finally, we get the payoff: A soldier returns home, and the pint of Guinness and chair is there waiting for him. The entire bar raises their pints in tribute. It exemplified all of the best-performing branded content that Dr. Zak's team had tested.

"You've got to build tension," explained Dr. Zak. "First thing—you've got to capture my attention, say with a hot open, just something that's mysterious or unusual or odd. Once you have my attention, you need to make me care about it by having some human conflict or drama."

There are two big reasons for this. The first is trust. Great stories trigger the production of oxytocin, which makes people trust you or your brand more. The second reason is the strong link between stories and memory; if you want people to buy something from you, they need to remember you.

Neuroscientists have a saying: "Neurons that fire together, wire together." When we hear a great story, the neural activity in our brain spikes. It's like someone flipped on a switchboard, illuminating the city of our mind. This is why we're much more likely to remember something when it's told to us through a story versus a memo or fact sheet. As all those neurons fire together, they wire together into neural pathways, and we're much more likely to remember the message later on.

Stories at work

As Dr. Zak's work shows, the power of storytelling pervades every aspect of our work lives. It's the meta super skill that powers all the soft skills that matter most at work.

Want to build trust with your colleagues and direct reports? Start by telling a compelling story of who you are and what you care about. Want your team to work better together? Share stories about your lives. Want to sell a new idea to your boss, colleagues, or potential investors? Lead with a story, not facts and figures. Want to persuade someone to buy something from you? Tell the story of how your product changed a customer's life.

Stories make us remember. They make us care. And most crucially for most of you reading this book, stories make our brains want to buy. If you want someone to collaborate, help, or do business with you, the formula is simple: You need to start by telling a great story.

The only problem? For the past two decades, we've systematically neglected our storytelling superpowers.

Chapter 3

WELCOME TO THE STORYTELLING ECONOMY

In February of 2025, OpenAI cofounder Andrej Karpathy tweeted about his experiments with "vibe-coding" that had been made possible by large language models (LLMs) getting "too good" at generating code. "I'm building a project or webapp, but it's not really coding—I just see stuff, say stuff, run stuff, and copy paste stuff, and it mostly works."

A few weeks later, *New York Times* tech columnist Kevin Roose published a column about his vibe-coding experiments. Despite not knowing how to code, he'd built a podcast transcription tool, a searchable database for his social media bookmarks, and an app called Lunchbox that told him what to pack for his son's lunch based on what was in his fridge. To Roose, it felt "like sorcery."

The column went viral. "Vibe coding" soon became a cultural phenomenon, with knowledge workers across LinkedIn, Reddit, TikTok, and YouTube sharing viral videos of what they'd built. Almost every major media outlet, from the *Guardian* to *Ars Technica* to *Forbes*, covered the phenomenon. For most, vibe coding felt like it came out of nowhere, but it reflected a trend that was years in the making.

If we want to understand how generative AI will change the future of work, we need to figure out where it's headed, what it excels at, and where we'll fit in. The good news: Three years after the release of ChatGPT, we now have strong trend lines. And the truth is different than the conventional wisdom you hear on LinkedIn.

Anchoring bias and the future of AI

Have you ever been shopping online and seen an item that was marked down from $100 to $59.99? What was your first thought? That's a damn good deal, right?

At that moment, you're a victim of anchoring bias, one of advertisers' favorite psychological tactics. Humans have a common inclination: We form opinions and make decisions based on the first piece of information we receive. This is why when advertisers show us the original price of an item ($100) and then the discount price ($59.99), we're more likely to think we're getting a good deal. Our perspective anchors to the original price, even if it's total BS.

The same dynamic plays out with explosive new technology like generative AI.

Starting in 2021, anyone could use OpenAI's GPT-3 model to generate ad copy or blog posts through OpenAI's research playground. Few did. That's why OpenAI built ChatGPT. They wanted to attract users to get faster feedback on their latest model, GPT-3.5. The development of AI models is terrifyingly opaque, and for whatever reason, GPT-3.5 made a significant leap in writing ability. GPT-3 was like Steve, a C-minus freelance copywriter you'd probably fire after two or three jobs. ChatGPT was like Ted, a B-minus copywriter with tons of ideas and the capacity for the occasional flash of brilliance. We've all had Teds on our team and thought, "Yeah, he's solid." So once AI crossed the Ted Chasm, people lost their fucking minds.

ChatGPT grew to a million users in five days and 100 million in two months. On social media, millions of people shared examples of ChatGPT's writing ability.

Because writing was the first major use case that most people experienced with generative AI, an anchoring bias took hold: AI is great at writing, posing a big threat to writers and creatives.

It seemed logical. Ever since the Great Recession, coding had been on an upswing while the humanities were in decline. Between 2012 and 2022, the percentage of students studying the humanities plummeted 24 percent, even as overall enrollment increased. The University of Wisconsin, for instance, awarded 30 percent more degrees in 2023 than 2008, but despite this overall increase, humanities degrees dropped by nearly 60 percent. Meanwhile, engineering degrees skyrocketed 57 percent over a similar time period. It was ironic. At the same time that Dr. Zak and his team were discovering the incredible power that storytelling wielded in the world of work, students were fleeing the programs that would hone their soft skills.

Through the 2010s and early 2020s, coding dominated the economic and cultural zeitgeist. In major hubs like New York and San Francisco, WeWork-sponsored open bars subsidized your nightlife, while venture capital (VC) money flowing into Uber, Seamless, and Airbnb subsidized your transportation, food, and travel. As the economy was burning, Facebook founder Mark Zuckerberg became a billionaire at age twenty-three, just one year after becoming a millionaire. Two years later, Jesse Eisenberg portrayed Zuckerberg in a blockbuster film, *The Social Network*. The film panned Zuckerberg but also reinforced the narrative that coders were our new business royalty.

Coding was sorcery; you could have no social or leadership skills, but if you were a rockstar coder with an idea for an app,

VCs would come off the mountaintop of Sand Hill Road to bestow you with millions. In 2005, pure technology startups reaped $20 billion in investment. By 2020, they reaped $140 billion. Sure, non-technical arts school grads like me could still find jobs in tech, but the real stars were the engineers.

As ChatGPT spread, it seemed as if AI would be the final blow, turning the slippery career path of humanity majors into a mudslide, and cementing the code economy for good. In reality, though, AI's greatest potential for disruption lay elsewhere.

While ChatGPT's writing skills dazzled early adopters, its surprising coding prowess was almost as impressive. Coding was the perfect use case for generative AI. Programming languages are simple. Thanks to a partnership with GitHub, OpenAI had a large corpus of high-quality code to train its model. With AI-generated code, you can judge whether it's objectively high quality by running automated tests to ensure it works.

For the first few months after ChatGPT came out, many people in the engineering community were skeptical. But then came March 14, 2023.

That day, the AI research lab Anthropic, founded by a band of scorned OpenAI employees, released its ChatGPT rival, Claude. Conspicuously, on the same day, OpenAI released GPT-4, its highly anticipated upgrade to ChatGPT. Both models proved much more adept at coding than the original ChatGPT. GPT-4 solved coding problems in the popular coding language Python two-thirds of the time, while Claude got 56 percent of the problems right. GPT-4's leap was so unnerving that thousands of artificial intelligence experts, entrepreneurs, and researchers signed an open letter calling for a pause on AI development. The AI giants promptly ignored them.

The AI coding arms race

Instead, AI's fast-developing coding prowess sparked an arms race to build powerful AI coding tools. Over the next several months, Meta, Microsoft, Amazon, and Google all introduced upgraded AI coding tools, targeting both individual developers and the enterprise market. The most significant leap came from Anthropic. In July 2023, Anthropic released Claude 2, which expanded Claude's "context window" to 75,000 words, meaning it could read and understand an entire code repository and execute more complex tasks like code review and multi-file refactoring.

In June 2024, OpenAI and Claude widened the lead even more with Claude 3.5 Sonnet and ChatGPT-4o. Both scored in the top quartile of competitive human coders. (For some reason, every single AI model sounds like it was named by a blackout-drunk robot.) Then, in September 2024, the big bomb dropped. OpenAI released the first publicly available "reasoning" model, ChatGPT-o3-preview (catchy!). Reasoning models represented a massive leap in AI's ability to tackle coding and STEM tasks by giving it the ability to slow down and "reason" through a problem. Instead of just predicting an answer based on training data, AI could now work through a coding problem step by step, checking its assumptions, reviewing files, and refining its approach. The result was impressive: o3 scored in the eighty-ninth percentile of competitive human coders. Similarly, it scored highly on math and STEM benchmarks and reliably completed data analysis and financial modeling projects. Google, Anthropic, and Meta quickly followed with their own reasoning models, which also performed well on these benchmarks. So did DeepSeek, a Chinese large language model (LLM) that captured global attention by beating ChatGPT-4 on many benchmarks while being developed for a fraction of the cost. Specialized AI coding tools like Cursor and Lovable entered the arena, earning billion-dollar valuations.

When ChatGPT first emerged, anchoring bias led people to assume that generative AI posed the biggest threat to writers and creatives. But what if highly technical jobs like coding and data analysis were actually the most at risk?

AI writing vs. AI coding

While AI models have made giant leaps in technical areas like coding, math, and data analysis, their writing and storytelling capabilities have advanced more slowly. As we'll explore in greater detail in the final section of this book, part of that is due to how they're trained. AI models are trained on all available text on the web, and much of that text is poorly written. And when human workers fine-tune AI models, they're instructed to rate verbose, jargon-y answers with high marks.

This is why AI writing hasn't made the same leap as AI coding. Good code is much easier to objectively define than writing, and with coding, AI can simulate tests of its code until it produces something that works when deployed. The training data for AI code, while not perfect, is also considered much higher quality. With writing, AI systems are sabotaged by a flawed training process that makes it sound like an insufferable junior McKinsey analyst from Connecticut named Brett.

AI coding has also proven much more culturally acceptable than AI writing. Dozens of studies of AI-generated content have come to the same conclusion: When people think a piece of content was generated by AI, they rate it poorly regardless of its quality. For example, in late 2024, researchers at the University of Florida gave test subjects two versions of the same story. One version was written by a human, the other was written by generative AI. Sometimes, they correctly labeled the AI-written story as AI-generated. Other times, they labeled the human-written story as AI-generated. Whenever a story was labeled as AI, people rated it poorly, regardless of whether AI actually wrote it or not. Similarly, researchers at the University of Vienna found that when people believe that an author has used AI to generate content, their perception of the author plummets.

Over the past few years, we've seen this play out dozens of times. In July of 2025, a group of Redditors discovered that a new classic rock band called The Velvet Sundown, which had started flooding Spotify playlists, was secretly AI. Users were furious at Spotify and vowed to cancel their subscriptions because the streaming service had no policy regarding the labeling or monetization of AI-generated content. They also saw it as a direct affront to human musicians who were losing streams to an AI-created band. The next month, J.Crew came under fire after a Substack newsletter, *Blackbird Spyplane*, published an investigation revealing that J.Crew was using AI-generated models in a 1980s nostalgia campaign. Followers flooded the brand's Instagram page, expressing their disappointment and disgust that the company would publish AI-generated photos without disclosing it.

It's telling that the entire category of AI-generated content has earned the epithet of "AI slop," while AI-generated coding has a much more positive nickname—"vibe-coding."[1]

The data also indicates that the use of AI tools has been shifting. In early 2025, Anthropic became the first AI model to reveal a detailed breakdown of how people were using their model. Computer programming and software development were the largest use cases by far, accounting for over 37 percent of all usage, nearly four times greater than writing tasks. When ChatGPT published its 2025 usage report, it revealed that the

---

1 It's worth noting that in the engineering community "vibe-coding" is considered as only one subset of AI coding. Whereas vibe-coding is usually associated with spinning out quick apps and side projects using natural language, AI coding involves using AI coding tools—like Claude, ChatGPT, or specialty coding tools like Cursor and Lovable—in the day-to-day engineering workflow, outsourcing coding tasks to AI.

percentage of writing tasks on the platform had decreased by 33 percent, from 36 percent the previous year to 24 percent.

Most telling, though, is the direction that AI giants are taking their products. After releasing reasoning models that dramatically improved their coding capabilities, the CEOs of Silicon Valley's AI giants began speculating that AI could do much of the work of software engineers, the most expensive line item on most companies' budgets.

In March 2025, Anthropic CEO Dario Amodei told the crowd at a Council of Foreign Relations event, "I think we will be there in three to six months, where AI is writing 90 percent of the code. And then, in twelve months, we may be in a world where AI is writing essentially all of the code."

Shortly after, Zuckerberg predicted on a podcast that AI would be writing all of Meta's code by the end of 2026, claiming, "It writes higher-quality code than the average person on the team already."

OpenAI CEO Sam Altman said that AI's coding skills would soon be "just as good as those of an experienced software engineer."

Amazon CEO Andy Jassy went further, predicting that AI would take on all technical tasks, telling CNBC in June 2025 that AI would take over coding, research, analytics, security, website localization, and spreadsheets.

Were these CEOs just talking their own book? Without a doubt. As I write this, Amodei's prediction has not come true. Nowhere near 90 percent of code is being written by AI, and many software engineers will tell you that AI is still nowhere close to getting the job done on their own. But it's trending up.

According to one extensive meta-analysis, 30 percent of all Python code was written by AI as of December 2024. Startup CEOs have reported a similar trend. In March 2025, Y Combinator CEO Gary Tan revealed that AI was producing "95 percent of the code" inside some of the accelerator's startups. In September 2025, Brian Armstrong, cofounder CEO of cryptocurrency platform Coinbase, reported that over 40 percent of the code at the company was being written by AI, with the goal of rapidly increasing that figure.

AI's coding capabilities have progressed rapidly, and it's the use case where AI labs are focusing the most. Daniel Balsam is the cofounder and Chief Technology Officer at Goodfire, a prominent AI research lab in Silicon Valley that uses interpretability software to perform "brain surgery" on large language models and make them safer and more effective. (Disclosure: I'm a small seed investor in Goodfire, and Balsam is my brother-in-law.)

He told me that we've now reached a stage where the producers of large language models need to make trade-offs on what they want their models to get smarter at due to limitations in power, microchip supply, and cost.

"That's forcing companies to make certain distribution trade-offs," he explained. "Anthropic is all-in on code. And Claude 4 is not a particularly better chat model. In fact, it might be a worse chat model than the Claude 3 series, but it automates non-trivial parts of software engineering."

Balsam buys the predictions of the AI CEOs that AI agents will soon be doing the vast majority of coding. But a couple of things need to happen first.

The first is the ability to correct generative AI in real-time. "Imagine the smart human, and you just place them in a new job and give them some half-assed sheet of paper written by one of the engineers trying to describe to them all the jobs they're going to do. Most humans will suck at that job for a considerable amount of time before they start being good," Balsam said. The issue with AI is that it's not able to truly learn and adapt to the needs of one company. "What's missing from AI now is the ability to be corrected, but that's a pretty solvable technical problem."

Next, he believes that, much like with the mobile internet, the way we develop applications needs to be adapted to make them friendlier to coding agents, a shift he sees as inevitable.

"When websites came out, no websites worked on mobile," he explained. "You could have looked at that moment and been like, 'Oh, the mobile internet is screwed. The web is all about rich information complexity. There's no way to fit it on a tiny screen.' People just had to learn to change the way they developed such that it was a priority. I think automation with agents will be the same."

Balsam has already undergone that process with his team. "We've changed the way we've developed considerably. It's speeding up our own internal research. By refactoring your own code base to be friendlier to agents, you can actually get pretty far."

He predicts that, in two years, AI will be able to write code that works 90 percent of the time, and that will lead to significantly less demand for workers with technical coding skills. You'll still need some people who have the domain expertise to understand the code base and fix bugs, but those will be a small amount of roles, shifting which skills he prioritizes. "I'd much rather hire people with really good research or product instincts," he said.

There are clear signs of a real-world shift. Computer programmer jobs have plummeted to their lowest level since the 1980s, according to the Bureau of Labor Statistics, falling 27.5 percent since ChatGPT came out. At the start of 2025, Salesforce CEO Marc Benioff announced he was putting a freeze on hiring engineers because the company had seen a 30 percent increase in productivity from AI. According to a report from the Reserve Federal Bank of New York, computer engineering graduates aged twenty-two to twenty-seven have one of the highest unemployment rates at 7.5 percent; by comparison, art history grads are at 3 percent. For over a decade, Silicon Valley firms ran massive marketing campaigns targeted at schools and schoolchildren, promising them that if they learned to code, a six-figure job would be waiting for them. As *New York Times* reporter Natasha Singer said on *The Daily*: "This represents a stunning breakdown in the promise Silicon Valley made to American school kids."

Balsam agrees that AI is progressing faster at coding than writing, and that's likely to continue for logical reasons. "There's a lot more money if you can automate code than creative writing."

Tech companies aren't just targeting coding. Anthropic and OpenAI are spending billions to train AI agents in technical business applications like Salesforce and Excel. AI has found its killer use case, and it was all the technical skills we'd been told were future-proof.

Welcome to the storytelling economy

Some economists and researchers anticipated AI's impact on technical jobs. Beginning in 2023, economists and researchers working with LinkedIn began tracking where humans were most vulnerable to AI job loss and where the greatest opportunities would be. They estimated that AI would replace 96 percent of a software engineer's current skills. "Technical and data skills that have been highly sought after for decades appear to be among the most exposed to advances in artificial intelligence," they wrote in a shared byline in the *New York Times*.

What did these researchers find to be the most durable skills for the next era of work? The ones we've long derided as "soft"— communication, leadership, empathy, and critical thinking.

For much of the past two decades, we've seen our value at work reflected in our ability to operate like high-performing machines, executing tasks. Across roles, our value will move from technical tasks to high-touch activities. Engineers' value will come less from writing code and more from understanding the business and how to solve customers' problems with novel technological approaches. Marketers' value will not come from writing Google Search ad copy but from building relationships with customers, unearthing their success stories, and telling them in engaging ways. Doctors will spend less time on diagnosis and administrative work, and more time practicing active listening to patients' stories to build trust and unearth information that might otherwise go unsaid. CFOs will spend less time crunching spreadsheets and more time building strategic relationships with other parts of the business. Salespeople will spend less time updating call and deal notes in Salesforce and more time forging connections with customers and prospects.

In an age where AI offers infinite ideas and output, the most valuable workers will have the taste to discern the best path and rally people toward a shared goal.

Ask yourself three magic questions about your day-to-day work:

1. **Is 25 percent or more of my day spent doing repeatable tasks that AI can do at an acceptable quality?**

2. **Is my judgment, domain expertise, and taste crucial to my company's making smart strategic decisions?**

3. **Do my relationships and influence with other people (offline or online) deliver surplus value compared to the average worker in my role?**

You should ask yourself question #1 every single month. If you answer Yes at any point, you need to proactively outsource those tasks to AI and reinvest that time in more strategic work—which I'll show you how to do in the final section of this book.

If you answered No to #2, you either need to move into a role that takes advantage of your domain expertise or aggressively acquire domain expertise in your new role. If you can't judge a sound AI output from a bad one, then AI won't work for you. You'll work for the AI, the modern equivalent of an elevator operator counting down the days until that pink slip arrives.

The most critical question is #3. If your relationships with customers, prospects, teammates, and direct reports aren't delivering surplus value, you need to invest in your storytelling skills aggressively and influence others. Moving forward, the most essential part of work lies in the soft skills that empower us to influence others.

Deep down, executives preaching the AI dogma secretly agree. The World Economic Forum's 2025 Jobs Report found an interesting dynamic—when you ask executives what skills they think will be most valuable in *the future*, they follow the conventional wisdom that AI skills trump all. But when you ask them about the skills they want *now*, the top five most in-demand skills were all soft skills: critical analytical thinking, flexibility and agility, leadership and social influence, creative thinking, and motivation and self-awareness.

AI skills placed eleventh. Computer programming was twenty-third, just below environmental stewardship and barely beating out "manual dexterity."

As covered in chapters 1 and 2, storytelling is the super skill that makes us better at all the soft skills that matter. We lead through stories. We communicate and sell through stories. We develop empathy and trust through stories and collaborate best when we feel like protagonists in the same plot. When we tell stories, the listener's brain activity mirrors that of the storyteller through a process known as neural coupling, which helps create a shared emotional state. If you want to become a desirable teammate (or mate), there's no more important skill than storytelling. Storytelling has been our most important skill for millennia—the trait that makes us human. And as waves of technological progress advance, it will become more crucial than ever.

Attention, narrative, and the storytelling economy

There's one more reason that storytelling will be the dominant skill of the next age of work, and that's the growing importance of capturing attention and controlling the narrative.

In a world dominated by feeds and endless streams of content, attention is our scarcest and most valuable resource. Attention and narrative determine which startups get funded, which companies win their categories, and increasingly, whether you get promoted or attract an offer from your dream employer.

As best-selling pop economist Kyla Scanlon wrote in her Substack, our most important economic inputs used to be things like land, labor, and capital. You used to start by developing a product or project, building its infrastructure, raising capital, and then acquiring attention. Now, it's reversed. The foundation of any project or product is now attention and narrative. Your ability to capture attention becomes a prerequisite for accomplishing anything, and your ability to tell a compelling narrative determines the flow of money, sentiment, and momentum. Stories are power. We are in a storytelling economy.

The AI race is a perfect example of this. As I write, OpenAI's ChatGPT is the most popular AI model. It has over 800 million weekly active users. Google's Gemini has 650 million monthly active users, while Anthropic's Claude has roughly 40 million. Yet, it's easy to argue that in many respects, ChatGPT is actually the inferior product of the three. Claude is considered a better coder. Gemini is far more versatile, embedded into your favorite work apps with jaw-dropping image and video generation abilities. At the very least, the performance leaderboard changes each time one of the tools releases a new model update.

So why is ChatGPT leading? Its first-mover advantage certainly helped. A bigger factor may be OpenAI's CEO, Sam Altman. As I mentioned at the end of chapter 2, Altman is a master at capturing attention and narrative. Altman's brilliance doesn't primarily lie in his product vision; from a UX (user experience) perspective, ChatGPT is a mess. Instead, it's in Altman's ability to command attention and drive a narrative in which ChatGPT isn't just desirable—it's inevitable. In 2023, following the release of ChatGPT, Altman embarked on a twenty-two-country world tour spanning six continents to preach the gospel of AI. He met with presidents, prime ministers, and regulators, alternating between promises of an AI-driven utopia and warnings of AI's perils, always in front of the cameras. At one point, he threatened the EU over proposed AI regulation and then took it back. Altman kicked off 2024 by releasing highly edited clips that made its new AI video tool, Sora, appear much more capable than it was, setting off momentary panic in creative industries. To take the hype to an eleven, Altman framed the release as a critical step toward AGI, a sign that AI could simulate the real world.

Every May, Google I/O—the tech giant's flagship event—dominates headlines. But that all changed in 2024. The day before Google I/O, Altman stole the story by releasing ChatGPT's new voice mode, which sounded eerily like Scarlett Johansson. Altman announced it by tweeting "her" on X, creating a multi-day news cycle analyzing whether the movie *Her* had come to life. To make the story feel even more real, OpenAI employees actively flirted with the tool at their launch event. And as mentioned in chapter 2, Altman outstaged Google I/O *again* a year later, buying Jony Ive's new, customer-less design company for $6.5 billion. He understood that it was a small price to pay for dominating the narrative about AI's future.

As serial entrepreneur and best-selling author Scott Galloway recently wrote, "In the business world, the flow of capital concentrates around good stories. Entrepreneurs, aka salespeople, aka storytellers, deploy a narrative that captures imaginations and capital to pull the future forward. Valuations aren't a function of balance sheets, but of the stories that give those balance sheets meaning and direction."

This new paradigm puts tremendous power in the hands of talented storytellers. Marketers and founders need to win not through ad buys, but by capturing attention better than anyone else. The "Law of Shitty Click-Throughs"—a popular marketing maxim, which says that all marketing channels decline in effectiveness over time—has flummoxed CMOs; It's near-impossible to drive positive ROI (return on investment) by following traditional best practices. That webinar series will not save you. The most successful founders and executives today gain an unfair advantage by winning outsized, free attention, usually by mastering the grammar of a specific audience and social platform. If they can't do it themselves, they hire employees who do, often paying them 200 to 300 percent the market rate for their positions, thanks to their ability to command an audience.

This dynamic impacts everyone who wants to make money. Over the past three years, AI has broken the job application process. Bots flood every opening with thousands of keyword-stuffed resumes. In turn, companies filter applications with AI, catching applicants in a Kafkaesque loop where it's nearly impossible to ever reach a real human. Real opportunity comes from commanding attention and standing out from others in your field. Telling the story of what you stand for and building a loyal following is no longer optional; it's a prerequisite to a successful career—even if you work in finance or HR.

To win the storytelling economy, you need to be a great storyteller. Narrative and attention are capital, and great storytellers can print it on demand. And through the rest of this book, I'll show you how.

Part II:
UNLOCK

Practicing an art, no matter how well or badly, is a
way to make your soul grow, for heaven's sake.
Sing in the shower. Dance to the radio. Tell stories.
Write a poem to a friend, even a lousy poem.
Do it as well as you possibly can. You will get an
enormous reward. You will have created something.

— Kurt Vonnegut

Chapter 4

PRINCIPLE 1:
Build a Storytelling Habit

When I was sixteen, I fell in love with an eighty-year-old man who lived in Midtown Manhattan. His name was Kurt.

It was my sophomore year of high school, and I was an unremarkable student. My teachers wouldn't have even known who I was if it weren't for The Incident. During my freshman year, a naive administrator had asked my punk band to play at a school assembly. We ambled in front of the entire student body in thrift-store blazers and women's jeans to play a sloppy, screamo rendition of "The Blitzkrieg Bop" by the Ramones and proceeded to trash the stage. I couldn't sing for shit, but that was okay—my real talent was performing. As my bandmates thrashed around, kicking over lecterns and leftover props from the school play, I attempted to scale the auditorium's curtains. I got halfway up before losing my grip and crashing to the stage. I wriggled on the floor, wailing into the microphone like a wounded bobcat. Once the faculty made sure I wasn't having a seizure, they went back to ignoring me.

That was the kind of kid I was—awkward yet attention-seeking, destined to eventually settle into a sad life managing my mom's animal hospital in Northern New Jersey. But then, in tenth-grade English, I got an assignment that changed my life.

Ms. K, my stern young English teacher, asked us each to write a bonus chapter for Kurt Vonnegut's *Cat's Cradle*. On principle, the only homework I did was for English class. I loved the book and spent hours studying Vonnegut's style and tone. When Ms. K called me to her desk, I thought I was in trouble—there were a few *damns* sprinkled into my story, and several butt jokes. Instead, she asked me to read the story in front of the class. My hands shook; my eyes went blurry. My crush, Christa, was sitting right in front of me. What if I randomly got a boner? That was always a risk in those days. But then I started reading. Before long, the class was laughing hysterically—and it wasn't because I'd left my fly open! It was because of my story.

The room shimmered. It felt like I'd awakened a dormant superpower. As a young child, stories were my sanctuary. I was raised by packs of dogs in my mom's animal hospital as she worked eighty-hour weeks. I spent hours wandering the kennels and crafting love-triangle dramas about our regulars: Sally loved Mr. Cashew, but Mr. Cashew was in love with Spot, and it was a mess.

My storytelling superpowers had faded in middle school as my self-esteem burst like the tech bubble. But now, it was back. And I had this eighty-year-old man named Kurt, who lived just fifteen miles away from me across the Hudson River, to thank for it. I had a new dream: to be a writer and storyteller. I read twenty-seven Kurt Vonnegut books that summer, hoping to absorb his secrets.

Once I'd devoured Vonnegut's books, I searched for his advice on how to be a writer. Luckily, I'd recently convinced my mom to get high-speed cable internet, still a novelty in the mid-2000s. The fact that I'd just spent the entire summer obsessively reading fiction gave her confidence that I'd use it for something other than porn. I googled Vonnegut like he was my ex's new boyfriend, searching for every bit of information I could find. Eventually, I found an excerpt of a letter that Vonnegut had sent to his wife in 1965, detailing his writing routine:

> I awake at 5:30, work until 8:00, eat breakfast at home, work until 10:00, walk a few blocks into town, do errands, go to the nearby municipal swimming pool, which I have all to myself, and swim for half an hour, return home at 11:45, read the mail, eat lunch at noon. In the afternoon I do schoolwork, either teach or prepare. When I get home from school at about 5:30, I numb my twanging intellect with several belts of Scotch and water ($5.00/fifth at the State Liquor store, the only liquor store in town. There are loads of bars, though.), cook supper, read and listen to jazz (lots of good music on the radio here), slip off to sleep at ten. I do pushups and sit-ups all the time, and feel as though I am getting lean and sinewy, but maybe not.

This was it. A playbook. By my calculations, Vonnegut only wrote for about three hours each day. Given my policy of only doing English homework, I could accomplish that. So I did two things. First, I set an intention. If I wanted to be a novelist like Vonnegut, I had to write a novel. Then I made a Vonnegut-esque routine. I spent my free periods and lunch in the computer lab writing. At home, I set aside another 90 minutes to write before bed. I didn't have scotch, but I did have Red Bull. I announced my intention to write a book to my friends, and they broke out in hysterical laughter. A few chuckles would have been fine, but they were literally rolling on the cafeteria floor. "It took you three months to write the lyrics to a two-minute screamo song, and they were terrible," the guitarist in my band said. "How are you going to write an entire book?"

A few weeks later, he approached me. "Are you pissed that we made fun of your book?" he asked. "You haven't been hanging out with us at lunch."

I smiled. "Nothing like that."

The truth was that against all odds, I was sticking with the schedule, spending my lunch periods typing away in the computer lab. As the pages in my Microsoft Word doc grew, I fell in love with the feeling of building a story from scratch.

Four months later, I'd done it. I'd penned the most cringeworthy novel ever written. It revolved around a short, curly-haired Jewish boy from New Jersey named Jake (Ha! No one would know this character is actually me!) who woos his popular-girl crush during a spring break trip to Cancun. Romantic bliss ensues on the sunny beaches of Mexico. Back at school, he loses the girl thanks to the vicious politics of popularity, but with a big romantic gesture, he wins her back, and they live happily ever after.

In real life, part of this story *did* actually happen. In my junior year, I ran into my popular girl crush in Cancun at a bar adjacent to the Hard Rock Cafe and proceeded to down eight tequila shots with her and her parents. My crush then flirted with the bouncer of a three-story mega club until he let us into the wild foam party inside, but there was no wooing. After one song, she went off with Zac Efron's doppelganger, a college guy with an unbuttoned shirt and cartoon abs that taunted me. As I looked on, forlorn, a trio of shot girls spotted me as an easy mark and pumped three shots of sickeningly sweet coconut vodka down my throat and demanded $60. For some reason, I'd given my crush my wallet to hold on to, so I dove into the waist-high foam in the middle of the dance floor and spent the next thirty minutes crawling through the beer-stained suds as three pissed-off shot girls hunted me. I walked five miles back to the hotel, still a virgin and possibly with a staph infection. As we'll see in Principle 3, "From Bad to Worse" is a timeless story arc, but it works better for existential fiction than the rom-com I was going for.

I didn't intend to show my novel to anyone, but my friends found a file I'd forgotten to delete in the computer lab and proceeded to quote from it like Shakespeare. You'd think this would have broken my spirit, but strangely, it gave me confidence. I'd written a book, so I could call myself a writer. I continued writing every day, experimenting with new forms. The following semester, I became the news editor of the high school paper and started writing a humor column. Watching the popular girls I pined for pick the paper out of their school mailboxes and laugh at my stories gave me an addictive rush.

My long love affair with storytelling had begun. I was a short, awkward Jewish kid with an untamed jewfro who dressed like a toddler who'd broken into a thrift store, but the more I wrote, the better I could talk, and suddenly, I could tell stories and make people laugh. Although my academic transcript was bleak, I captivated college interviewers with the tale of how I overcame a tumultuous childhood to become a teenage novelist. I even spun trashing the school stage into a parable about the power of artistic expression. Despite graduating in the bottom half of my class, I got accepted early decision by Sarah Lawrence College, one of the top writing schools in the country. Once there, I continued my daily habit—writing essays and short stories and penning so many humor columns and news stories for the college newspaper that they were forced to make me editor-in-chief. I even scored a paying gig as a freelance essayist for Nerve.com.

Years later, when my writing habit had led to a reasonably successful career, I realized that at sixteen, I'd unassumingly adopted a powerful tactic for behavioral change. As James Clear writes in *Atomic Habits*, "True behavior change is identity change." If you want to change your behavior, you must change your identity. And that's where your journey begins.

In Part II of this book, we're transitioning from the Why of storytelling to the How. We now understand *why* storytelling will be the super skill of the AI Age, so it's time to explore how to become a better storyteller through fifteen principles and three key stages. As I previewed in the introduction of this book, the first is **Unlock**. We are storytelling animals with innate storytelling instincts, but before we can apply them successfully, we need to unlock them. If our storytelling skills were a house, think of the principles in this part of the book as your foundation; they keep you centered, resilient against the storms of change—new channels, tactics, and technology.

For humans, storytelling is instinctual. But for us to unlock its full potential, it needs to become a habit.

How to turn storytelling into a habit

Every week, I talk to people who want to become a thought leader on LinkedIn, launch a Substack newsletter, market their company through TikTok, or write a book, and can't seem to do it. Life gets in the way, and it's easy to prioritize just about everything else. It feels like a failure of willpower or a personal defect. *I just don't have it. The storytelling muse strikes others, but not me.* But as most of the world's greatest storytellers will tell you, creative inspiration rarely strikes. If Hemingway or Austen or Vonnegut only wrote when they were stirred by the writing gods, they would have barely finished one novel. If you've struggled to consistently create content and tell stories—whether that's starting a newsletter, posting on LinkedIn, or writing a novel or screenplay—it isn't because there's something wrong with you. You just aren't giving yourself the infrastructure to succeed.

Once I reached adulthood, I started reading pop behavioral science books—as required by law for all millennial knowledge workers who work in tech. The most influential of those was Clear's *Atomic Habits*, where he reveals that the science of forming good habits has three layers:

- Outcome: What you want to achieve
- Process: The system you implement
- Identity: The person you want to be and your worldview

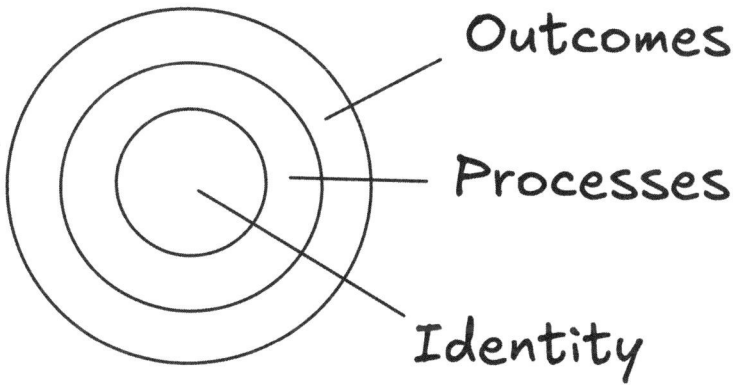

Most people start with the outcome or goal—"I want to write a best-selling book"—but get discouraged when it doesn't come to fruition. That's because you should really start with an *identity*.

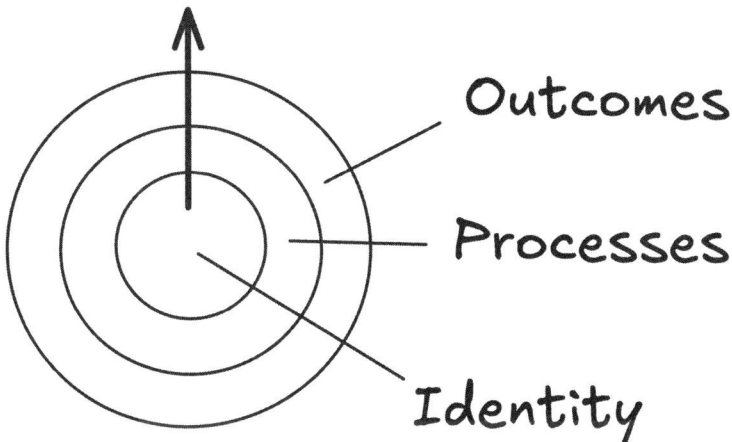

The logic is simple. If you identify as a specific type of person—"I'm a writer" or "I'm a founder who influences and leads through stories"—you'll be intrinsically motivated to establish the behaviors associated with that identity. It's a sneaky little trick we can play on our brains. For instance, when I was writing this book, I established the very specific identity of "I'm the writer of a book who shows up and produces at least 1,000 words every day." This forced me to establish the daily habits that would allow me to get a finished manuscript to my publisher by September.

Maybe you want to be an engineer who shares insights on AI every week on Substack. Maybe you want to be the kind of manager who builds rapport with your team through stories every week. Maybe you want to be a founder who single-handedly drives growth by becoming a popular podcaster and LinkedIn influencer. Behavioral science shows that once you establish that identity, you're much more likely to perform the behaviors associated with it. And the payoff of performing those behaviors is huge; practice leads to gains, and if you just get 1 percent better every week, your storytelling skills will grow exponentially over the course of a year.

The four laws of behavior change

Next comes "Process"—the system you set up for yourself to maintain your habits. Most great storytellers develop a system to keep them on track. Vonnegut wrote immediately after waking up and right after breakfast. Maya Angelou had a similar routine, with a wonderful twist. In every town she ever lived in, she'd rent a hotel room and instruct the hotel to take everything off the walls. The only objects she allowed were a Roget's Thesaurus and a Bible. She'd leave home by 6 a.m. and arrive at the hotel room by 6:30 at the latest. She'd write on legal pads while lying across the bed, encrusting her elbows with calluses. At 11 a.m., she'd drink a glass of sherry, and sometime between 12:30 and 1:30, she'd go home. Seven-time *New York Times* best-selling author

Daniel Pink shows up at his office every morning at 8:30 without his phone and writes until he reaches at least 500 words. "If I waited until I was inspired to write, I would never write a word," he explained in a recent YouTube video. During his more productive periods, Kerouac would light a candle at midnight and start writing; when he finished at dawn, he'd blow it out. (So *dramatic.*)

In 2016, Nuseir Yassin, aka Nas Daily, quit his job at Venmo to travel the world, and committed to producing a one-minute video that he'd post on Facebook every day for 1,000 days, sticking to a strict routine. "By 11 a.m., I must have an idea. By 2 p.m., a script. By 5 p.m., shoot it. By 11 p.m., edit it," he told *Creator Science* host Jay Clouse. By 2018, he had over 10 million subscribers on Facebook.

Study the contours of the routines of the world's most successful storytellers and creators, and they map to Clear's Four Laws of Behavior Change:

Make it obvious (Cue)

For many storytellers, the cue is waking up, but it can also be environmental. For Maya Angelou, the cue was when she stepped into her hotel room; for Kerouac, it was when he lit a candle at midnight. They make it unmistakably evident that it's time to get to work. When I first started writing in high school, the cue was when the bell rang for my free period or lunch. No matter what, I was off to the computer lab. Today, an afternoon calendar reminder tells me it's time to start writing (like Kerouac, I am not a morning person).

Make it attractive (Craving)

Tie the behavior to something you enjoy. For Vonnegut, it was breakfast. For Angelou, it was a glass of sherry. For Kerouac, it was a terrifyingly large amount of amphetamines! The only time I let myself eat chips is when I'm writing; the occasional glass of Prosecco might also make its way in there. Find what that is for you—with moderation. Let's all remember that Kerouac died puking on the toilet at the age of forty-seven.

Make it easy (Response)

You'll want to eliminate as much friction as possible to stay on track. Pink leaves his phone in another room and bans himself from checking email until he hits 500 words. Similarly, Angelou removed every distraction from her hotel room, down to the pictures on the wall. Nas Daily would follow a pre-planned, twenty-four-hour template that removed choice paralysis and clear deadlines. He attributes this to "Parkinson's Law," which says that work will expand to whatever time you give it to complete. By giving himself three hours to complete a script, he makes it easy to hit that mark. Vonnegut integrated clear stop signals. At 8 a.m., he stopped for breakfast; at 10 a.m., he'd go into town.

Make it satisfying (Reward)

Our brains run on rewards. The wonderful—and addictive—thing about telling stories online is that there's often an immediate reward. The dopamine hit that comes when likes, comments, and replies to your posts and newsletter pour in. I remember the first time my writing went viral. The summer after I graduated from high school, I traveled to upstate New York for New York Giants training camp, which is Coachella for football nerds. Every day, I wrote reports on my favorite team's position battles and submitted them to popular Giants' blogs. They spread quickly, earning hundreds of thousands of views and thousands of comments. *This must be what cocaine feels like*, I thought. The reward was so powerful that I extended my stay another week, cranking out daily, 2,000-word reports from our 100-degree hotel room. I've been hooked on writing online ever since.

Of course, not every post gets a big response, and not every storytelling practice involves posting online every day. Vonnegut's reward was his evening ritual—the belts of scotch and jazz on the radio as he basked in completing his daily work. For Angelou, it was the feeling of the dozen pages of writing she held in her hand, which she'd edit down in the evening. While working on this book, I record my word count in a notebook each day—a methadone dose to replace the high of online engagement. I'll also often share my progress with writer friends: oxytocin gets released when we feel a sense of accomplishment and share it with others. Find the reward that satisfies your brain, and you'll be much more likely to pick up your storytelling habit again each day.

Once you establish your identity and process, the outcome comes naturally. Like someone who identifies as a non-smoker, runner, or reader and builds the habits to back up that identity, you'll work relentlessly to maintain that habit and identity. In turn, the positive outcomes will naturally come.

Identifying your storytelling practice

It's okay if you don't already have a storytelling practice in mind, but as you progress through the rest of this book, I encourage you to think about what it might be.

Your storytelling practice could take on any medium—writing, video, podcasting, or public speaking. It can be as simple as posting on LinkedIn twice per week or opening with a story in one big presentation each quarter. It can be starting a Substack newsletter or a podcast, or creating a short-form scripted series on TikTok. It can be doing standup, writing a book, or telling a story every time you lead your team meeting.

The goal isn't just followers, leads, or promotions; it's practicing your most powerful skill. According to a study from the *Journal of Communication*, we spend up to 80 percent of our workday communicating, and we spend the majority of that time telling stories of some kind. Imagine what would happen if you were 50 percent better at telling stories. Imagine how much more effective you'd be.

So what should your storytelling practice be? Here are some key questions to consider:

What's the identity you want to inhabit?

Choosing your storytelling practice starts with the same step as developing your habits. Who do you want to be? Do you want to be an executive who captivates and influences the board in their presentations? A salesperson who woos prospects with authentic customer stories? A founder who's a leading voice in your industry? A professional creator with your own niche media brand? Start with that identity.

What are you passionate about?

If you're writing, talking, or making videos about things that you're truly interested in, you're much more likely to stick with it. Storytelling became a habit for me because I wrote about the things I loved the most—myself and football. Today, that list has expanded to: myself, technology, and storytelling. I'm a weirdo, but in all likelihood, you are too. Find your passion and let your freak flag fly. The most important thing is building those storytelling muscles.

What storytelling mediums do you love the most?

You're most likely to thrive at telling stories in the mediums that you love.

- If you love TED Talks, consider public speaking.
- If you love newsletters, start a Substack.
- If you love standup, take a crack at an open mic.
- If you love podcasts, grab a $100 podcasting beginner's kit and start interviewing interesting people.

• If you're addicted to TikTok . . . you should probably figure out a way to moderate how much time you spend on the app. But you should also experiment with telling stories via vertical video.

The great thing about storytelling is that it's *fun*. Make it a large part of your job, and you've unlocked the world's greatest lifehack. But it's most effective if you enjoy the medium.

The truth: You likely won't know if you enjoy a medium until you try it. I was terrified of public speaking until I felt the rush of a captivated audience. Every week, I meet people who never thought they could make social videos until they tried it. Explore.

What frequency of storytelling will you commit to?

A habit requires frequency. What frequency will you commit to? Will you write a LinkedIn post twice per week? Publish a video every day? Write a biweekly newsletter? Tell a story at every team meeting?

What's your cue, craving, response, and reward?

How will you leverage Clear's Four Laws of Behavioral Change? How will you make it obvious that it's time to work (cue)? How will you make it attractive, tying the behavior to something you love (craving)? How will you make it easy (response)? How will you make it satisfying (reward)?

To get started, set aside an hour to write down your answers to these five questions. As you read the foundational storytelling principles to come, think about how you might get started, and then make the leap. As Vonnegut once wrote: "We have to continuously be jumping off cliffs and then developing our wings on the way down."

Chapter 5

PRINCIPLE 2:
Master the Elements

The last time I watched an episode of *NCIS*, I was secretly undercover. My mission? Studying people's brains.

It was early 2020, and I sat in a conference room at the downtown Manhattan headquarters of Neuro-Insight, one of the world's leading neuromarketing firms. All around me, everyday New Yorkers were being fitted with caps to study their neural activity. On the TV in front of us, an episode of *NCIS* was cued to play.

As the lights dimmed, it was a "record scratch" moment. Yep, that's me—an arts school grad who almost failed high school chemistry, casually commissioning a neuroscience experiment. How the hell did I get here?

While people thought they were there to watch *NCIS*, the main event was actually the commercial breaks, during which we'd slip in political ad campaigns for the leading Democratic presidential candidates.

The goal? To peek inside voters' brains and see what messages and storytelling techniques literally changed their minds.

Using the neurosensor caps, we would measure Neuro-Insight's four key neural engagement metrics: engagement, emotional intensity, approach, and long-term memory encoding.

Most often, the difference between success and failure lies in our ability to tell a persuasive story—whether we're running for office, fighting for a budget at work, crafting a new marketing campaign, trying to sign a new client, or convincing our partner to go on a beach vacation for Christmas.

Over the past decade, I've traveled the world meeting with neuroscientists and partnering on neuromarketing research to understand how our brains respond to stories. Along the way, I've learned that there is a science to effective storytelling, and it comes down to four key elements, which I've designed into a simple framework: RENT.

- **Relatability:** The audience sees itself or its own experiences in the story.
- **Ease:** Eliminating barriers to entry into the story and hooking the audience immediately.
- **Novelty:** Presenting something new to your audience, triggering the release of dopamine in their brains and encouraging them to pay attention.
- **Tension:** Establishing the gap between "what is" and "what could be"—and opening and closing that gap over and over again, creating a state of narrative transportation in the process.

If you want to start telling more engaging and persuasive stories, renting stories in your audience's mind, these four elements are the best place to start.

Relatability

In 1992, scientists at the University of Parma attached electrodes to monkeys' brains (as we all do when we're bored) and made a startling discovery. The same neurons fired when the monkeys took an action—like grabbing a banana—as when the monkeys saw a man or monkey take that same action. The scientists called these "mirror neurons."

Subsequent studies found that humans also have mirror neurons, which are activated through stories. When we hear a great story, the neural activity of the listener mirrors the neural activity of the storyteller.

For instance, if I tell you a riveting story of being chased through the forest by a tiger and capture the adrenaline-pumping terror of the chase, your brain will respond like you're being chased by a tiger too. This "emotional contagion" creates a shared emotional state between us. As we learned in chapter 2, great stories also trigger the production of oxytocin, a powerful neurochemical associated with empathy and human connection, which deepens that bond even more.

Research shows that this neurochemical response is particularly strong when we can personally relate to the story and recognize ourselves in it. Multiple brain regions activate, including those that power self-processing and emotional memory, creating a deeper connection. Relatability amplifies the emotional impact of storytelling.

For example, think of your favorite movie. Chances are, one of the main characters reminds you of yourself.

We're instinctively drawn to characters and worlds that we can relate to. This is why we love teen movies when we're in high school, and why I saw *Mean Girls* three times in theaters. It's why my mom's favorite movie of the last twenty years is *Something's Gotta Give*. If we can see ourselves in a character or story, we're much more likely to pay attention.

Basically, we're a giant planet of narcissists, and you need to play into your audience's narcissism. If you're talking to the CEO of a startup, tell a story that she can see herself in. Maybe it's about a tough executive decision you had to make amid early-stage chaos. Or perhaps you both live in New York City, and your story is about how you saved a group of clueless tourists who jumped onto the tracks to take a selfie with Pizza Rat.

The best storytellers adjust their narratives to make them relatable to their target audience and form a deep connection. In the neuroscience research I conducted of Democratic Primary voters, we saw this on full display.

When ads opened with candidates talking about the issues, voters' brains almost immediately tuned out. When they opened with their stories, engagement skyrocketed. Take the ad we tested from Elizabeth Warren, which was one of the most high-performing pieces of content we tested. It opens with Warren telling the story of growing up poor in Oklahoma, getting married at nineteen, and how she got a second chance at her dream thanks to a commuter college that only cost $50. All of the neural engagement metrics we were tracking spiked as she hits the story's happy climax, pulling voters in. (See figure below.) While few of the New Yorkers we tested had Warren's exact experience, they related to her working-class background and how she capitalized when given a second chance. Almost everyone who survives in New York has needed a second chance at some point.

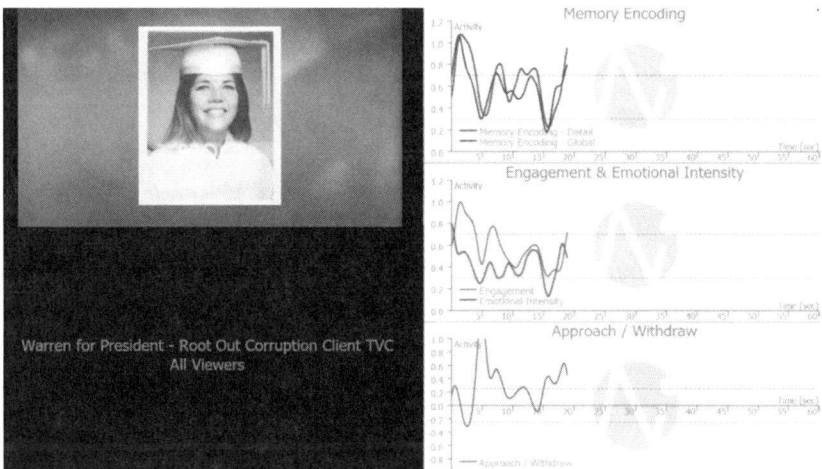

If you want more inspiration, look to General Electric (GE). In the 2010s, the company was losing the engineer recruiting war to Silicon Valley tech giants when it launched "What's the Matter With Owen?" a self-deprecating video series on YouTube. In the clips, a young engineer struggles to explain to his friends and family that he's going to GE to work on innovation initiatives, not the railroad. In one video, his dad tries to give him his granddaddy's Thor-esque hammer, not able to comprehend that he's going to crush code, not pound stakes. Engineers related to it deeply. Not only did engineering applications to GE shoot up by 800 percent, but Owen also became a minor celebrity along the way. When he visited GE's campus, the company's engineers treated him like a rock star. The series was so successful that GE turned it into a national ad campaign.

"People inside the company are just in love with the campaign," Linda Boff, GE's CMO at the time, told me. "We have brought the actor who plays Owen to some of our internal events, and really you'd think we were bringing the Beatles back together. People are so excited that here's a story about the company, but it's really a story about them. They're our Owens."

Ease

Imagine that you work at an AI-powered robotics company. Which product explanation do you think is more likely to get approved to put on the website?

> **Option A:** "This system works because of programming that makes the robot's movements more precise and less shaky."
>
> **Option B:** "This system works because of AI integration through motion scale and tremor reduction."

It's got to be option B, right? After all, we're likely selling to a sophisticated buyer. Well as it turns out, option B makes people *furious*.

That was the conclusion of a fascinating 2020 study by researchers at Ohio State University. They had one group of consumers read three paragraphs about technology that only used simple terms—like option A above. Then, they had another group read three paragraphs on the same topic, except this time, it was filled with specialized jargon, like in option B.

Even though the people who encountered the jargon were given definitions for all the terms, it annoyed the hell out of them. They didn't like what they were reading and even started arguing against it.

Conversely, the jargon-free group felt engaged and wanted to learn more.

Professor Hillary Schulman, the study's lead author, explained why: "The use of difficult, specialized words is a signal that tells people that they don't belong," she said. "You can tell them what the terms mean, but it doesn't matter. They already feel like this message isn't for them."

In other words, when you use jargon in your messaging, you're giving your audience the middle finger—and telling them you're not for them.

Most businesses are addicted to jargon. They conflate complexity with authority and think that if they use enough big words and write in a stiff, academic tone, they'll appear trustworthy and professional. In reality, they're self-sabotaging.

The first key to ease is to ruthlessly de-jargon your content. Sit down with your team to go "jargon hunting," setting aside time to go through content (website, pitch decks, sales collateral, social posts), find jargon, and rewrite it together. Implement mandatory jargon checks into your workflow. Do this for your own content and stories, too.

The second key is to obsess over the hook.

Whenever you're creating content, you're in a battle royale for your audience's attention. It's a bit of a myth that our attention spans have cratered over the past thirty years; a meta-analysis from the University of Vienna recently found that adults' ability for selective and sustained attention has actually *improved* during that time. Except now, there are so many more things competing for our attention. You need to win by making it as easy as possible for people to engage in the story you're telling. In her excellent *Link in Bio* newsletter, Rachel Karten captured a quote from Cameron Gidari, VP of Social Media and Innovation at Major League Baseball, that puts it perfectly: "People say that Gen Z has a short attention span on social media. They don't. They have a short consideration span."

Your hook launches your audience into the story you're going to tell and captures their attention from the first second. For some people, hooks have a dirty association as a newfangled social media trend, but they've been around forever. George Orwell's opening line for *1984* is possibly the greatest hook ever written: "It was a cold bright day in April, and the clocks were striking thirteen."

If your story involves a convoluted wind-up or *erudite* prose filled with words the listener might not know, you might make yourself feel smart but lose them completely. If you hook them with clear language and stakes (more on that in a minute), you'll hold their attention.

Neuro-Insight, the neuroscience firm that I partnered with on political ad research, found in a meta analysis of thousands of social videos that content that presented an early story arc and characters were much more likely to hook people and keep them engaged. We saw that in our analysis of democratic political ads as well. The Bernie Sanders ad we tested dove right into Sanders's work on issues such as raising wages, healthcare, and civil rights without any narrative, and engagement stayed extremely low. (See figure below.) In contrast, the Biden and Warren ads we tested jumped right into compelling stories that immediately spiked engagement and long-term memory across our subjects.

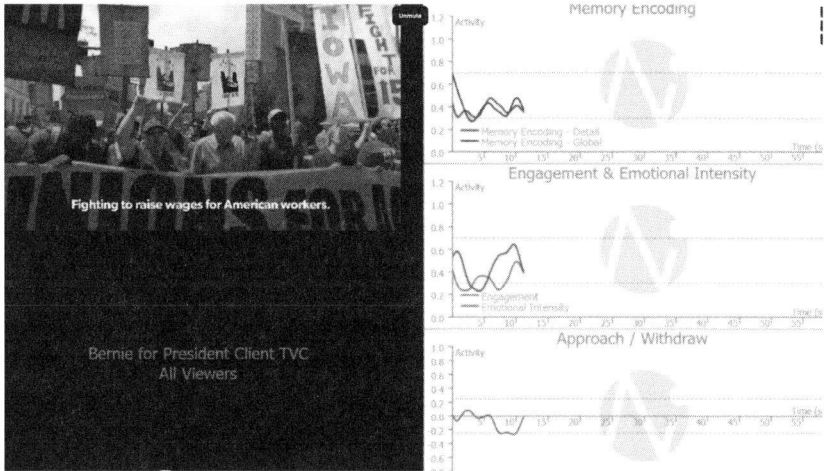

If I had been working on the Biden or Warren campaign, I would have recommended that they make their spots even more successful by using my favorite tactic for creating a story's hook: Play on the curiosity gap. Ask a question or tease something that your audience wants to find out. This is what makes the opening line of *1984* so effective: *Why is the clock striking thirteen?*

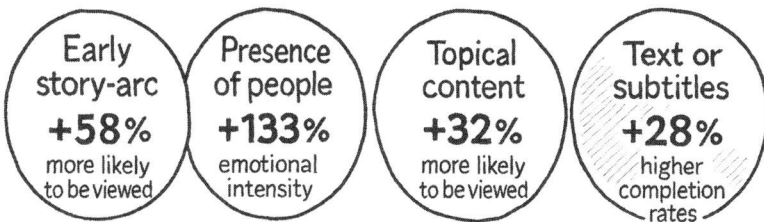

Recently, Yale Cleaners, a small, eleven-store dry-cleaning chain in Tulsa, Oklahoma, got over 35 million views and 3 million likes for an epic, seven-minute tale of saving a wedding dress. It started off with this simple curiosity gap hook: "Have we ever had a wedding dress we couldn't save?"

3. Novelty

In December 2010, a young improv comic named Michael Dubin attended his dad's Christmas party. After a few scotches, one of his dad's friends saddled up to Michael with a strange proposition: Would Michael want to help him sell 250,000 razors he'd acquired from Asia? Michael considered bowing out of the conversation to go get another drink. That was the logical thing to do. But then he had an idea. He hated going to the pharmacy and buying expensive razor blades from behind locked cabinets. All of his friends did, too. What if he just shipped them to people every month for $1?

The problem is that Dubin couldn't get the funds to support his idea. So with his life savings of $20,000, he made one of the weirdest, most novel brand videos you'll ever see.

The video is ninety seconds of mayhem: polio jokes, a clumsy bear, a machete, and a giant "money gun" spraying singles in front of the American flag. Viewers had never seen anything like it, and somehow, it touted all of the benefits of Dubin's service, which he called "Dollar Shave Club."

"Are our blades any good?" Dubin deadpans to the camera. "No, our blades are fucking great."

The video went viral, triggered a flood of dopamine in people's brains, and inspired them to want to learn more. Dollar Shave Club got 12,000 orders in the first forty-eight hours. The clip also convinced former MySpace CEO Michael Jones to sign on as Dubin's partner. The company kept creating crazy new videos for every product release, shipped "bathroom reader" magazines with every order, and started an outspoken men's magazine, *Mel*.

In July 2016, Unilever bought Dollar Shave Club for a billion dollars, in large part due to the deep relationships the brand had built with its audience through content. That's one hell of a return on a $20,000 video. The key to its success? Novelty.

It's long been known that novelty helps us learn more effectively. But we didn't know why until twenty years ago. That's when two neuroscientists named Nico Bunzeck and Emrah Düzel used fMRI technology to examine people's brains as they saw novel images. The area of the brain closely linked to memory and learning lit up.

When we experience something new, our brain delivers a hit of sweet, sweet dopamine, encouraging us to pay attention. This is why generic stories ("I graduated college, then I went to McKinsey, then I decided to take a corporate job at Coca-Cola") make us space out, while novel stories ("After graduating Oberlin, I traveled to Hungary to wrestle bears at the circus") lock us in. In other words, if you want to capture your audience's attention, show or tell them something new or unusual.

In the digital age, this often means capturing the audience's attention with a visual cue that stands out from everything else they've been watching so far. In the political ads we analyzed, the highly engaging Biden and Warren ads opened with grainy, black-and-white footage of their childhoods, and engagement peaked. The audience was seeing something new that looked unlike all the other commercials they'd been watching.

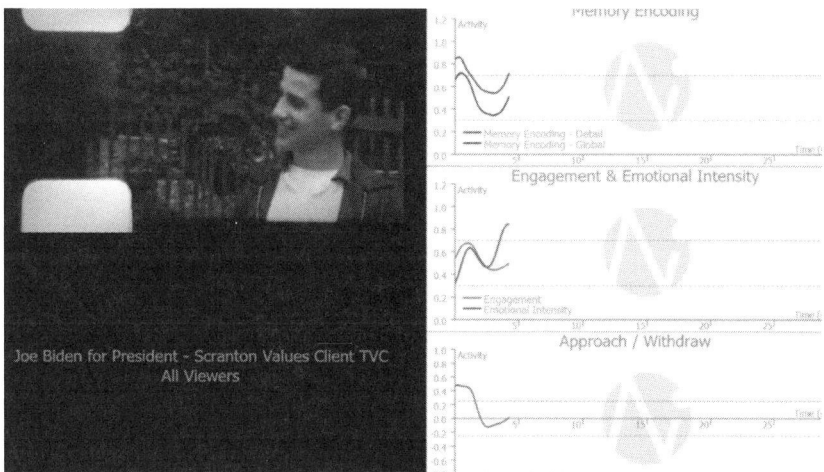

This has never been more true than today, when AI makes it trivial to flood the web with a sea of average, generic content. The stories that break through are new and unusual, vivid and provocative, screaming out in the feed.

For example, brands on TikTok and Instagram have recently been producing cinematic content that stands out because it has distinct lighting and color gradients, compelling sound design, and is shot like a film. *Link in Bio*'s Rachel Karten has done a fantastic job chronicling this trend, highlighting viral examples like *Followed*, an Instagram-native short film starring model and influencer Nara Smith for the sustainable women's clothing brand Reformation, which earned nearly two million views and over 85,000 likes in just a few weeks.

Novelty can also mean presenting a provocative and new idea. This is the entire game that Influencers-in-Chief like Sam Altman and Anthropic's Dario Amodei practice; they're constantly pushing provocative predictions for the future of tech that you haven't heard before. Right now, I'm staring at a headline that shows Sam Altman just predicted that AI will surpass human intelligence by 2030.

The next time you're writing a blog post, making a video, or preparing a presentation, ask yourself: Am I introducing something new into the world? New stories, new research, new ideas? Or is this something people can find fifty other places with a simple Google search?

4. Tension

There's a scene in the 1993 Academy Award–winning film *Homeward Bound: The Incredible Journey*,[2] when Sassy, an extremely cautious talking cat, falls into the water while trying to cross a river in the California wilderness.

She's swept up in the rapids. Shadow—the wise, old golden retriever—bolts to rescue her. He races along the riverbank, urging Sassy to keep her head above water. He finds a log, races into the water, furiously doggy paddling to save her. But it's in vain. Sassy tumbles over the waterfall, seemingly lost forever.

---

2   As awarded by the Joe Lazer Academy for movies about very good dogs and cats.

When I first saw this movie in theaters with my mom at age seven, I really had to pee. (The rushing water didn't help.) But the tension kept me glued to my seat. For the next hour and twenty-four minutes, the danger facing the animals kept me transfixed. As they wander home, they're chased by bears and confronted by a mountain lion. A thick tension hangs over every interaction.

Homeward Bound was the perfect story for me for a few reasons. It was relatable. I grew up surrounded by cats and dogs, since my mom was a veterinarian. I got absorbed in the story with incredible ease; Peter Jackson could learn a thing or two from the crisp eighty-four-minute pacing. It was novel because I'd never seen a live action movie with talking animals before. But most crucially, there was tension, which is the fourth foundational element of storytelling. It's ultimately what makes a story, well . . . a story.

Long before *Homeward Bound* changed our lives forever, Aristotle said the key to a great story was establishing the gap between what is and what could be, and then closing and opening that gap over and over again.

Think about your favorite rom-coms. They center on the tension gap between what is (a lonely, single life) and what could be (true love). For two hours, you watch that gap almost close before something goes wrong and the gap widens again—the guy says something dumb, the jerk ex-boyfriend comes into the picture, ulterior motives are revealed.

The force that keeps us on the edge of our seats is conflict. Neuroscience research has found that this dynamic is what makes us immersed and emotionally engaged in stories.

Many founders and brands that I've worked with are allergic to real tension in their stories at first. They want to tell a story in which things are always going well. Their company has always been on an easy upward trajectory. Their career has sailed smoothly. Their customers found success without a hitch. But these stories aren't just inaccurate—they're boring as hell.

Tension Gap

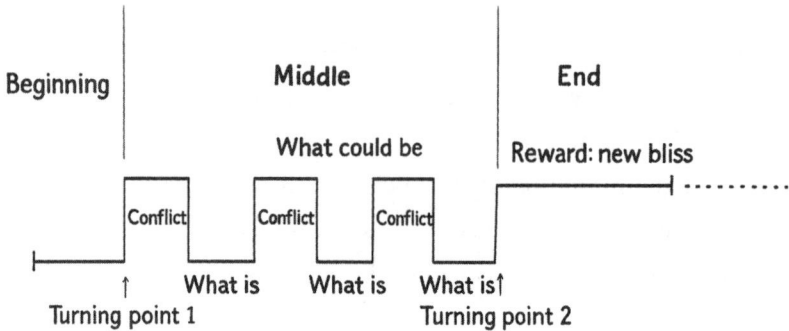

Tension allows you to win the most valuable commodity in our economy today: *attention.* Take Cluely, an AI startup founded by Columbia students Chungin "Roy" Lee and Neel Shanmugam with the motto "Cheat on everything," which Kyla Scanlon highlighted in her newsletter on the economic power of attention. Lee and Shanmugam originally built Cluely as a tool to cheat on technical interviews, which are filled with algorithmic riddles. The app is an ethical disaster, but Lee is an attention master. He posted a video of himself using the tool to cheat through an Amazon internship interview, sparking outrage, and the app took off from there. Columbia put Lee on disciplinary probation, which Lee used to garner even more attention on social media. Eventually, his inflammatory posts mocking the university got him expelled, which the media covered voraciously. He went on tech podcasts and racked up millions of views. *New York Magazine* made him the focal subject of its cover story on AI in college. Soon after, Lee and Shanmugam released a sleek product video for Cluely that went viral. It showed the twenty-one-year-old Lee on a date with an attractive thirtyish-year-old woman. Lee's glasses contain an AI interface that listens to their conversation and helps Lee lie about his age and career. But then the waiter swipes his fake ID and things go haywire.

None of the technology in Cluely's video exists, but it didn't matter. The video triggered an intense reaction—people either loved it or hated it. Cluely raised a $5.3 million pre-seed round led by Abstract and Susa Ventures, followed shortly by another $15 million in a Series A round led by a16z. Cluely had attention and a gifted storyteller as founder and CEO. They could figure out the tech later.

The best brand storytellers today embrace tension. Sam Altman positions OpenAI as the main character in a grand narrative in which science fiction has come to life and paradise or apocalypse hangs around every corner. As we'll explore in more depth later in this book, Sara Blakely became the world's youngest self-made billionaire by seizing the tension between what women need and what the fashion industry offers. At the unicorn AI startup Writer, May Habib is taking on OpenAI and Google head-on for enterprise AI supremacy by telling a story of how Silicon Valley giants are taking a wasteful approach while she's found a better way, training enterprise models for a fraction of the financial and environmental cost.

We saw this in our analysis of political ads, too. Biden's ads drove spikes across all the metrics we tested when they talked about the real problems facing real people. "Too many middle-class and working-class people aren't able to look their kids in the eye and say, 'Honey, it's going to be okay,'" Biden says over shots of him hugging worried and distraught voters. And Warren's ad drove an engagement spike when she railed against the corruption of the rich and powerful over a shot of Trump with then Senator Majority Leader Mitch McConnell.

If you want to seize people's attention, you need tension.

Over the years, I've realized that the most impactful content I've created has tackled what's wrong in my industry and addressed how to do it better. My work often details how I've personally messed up in the past and learned from mistakes.

Don't be afraid to talk about how you—and your industry—have come up short and where you need to go. Talk about what you're currently working on. Use personal anecdotes to keep people hooked. That's the key to a story that sticks in your audience's minds.

Every time you're crafting a new story—whether it's a novel, script, essay, video, podcast, or internal presentation—use these elements as a checklist:

- Are you introducing a **relatable** character that your audience can connect with?

- Are you making it as **easy** as possible for them to become engrossed in your story and give you their attention? Are you capturing their interest in the first few seconds?

- Are you presenting **novel** characters, ideas, and situations to hold their attention?

- Are you constantly ratcheting up the **tension** to keep your audience at the edge of their seat?

Literally print these elements out as a checklist. (You can download one at joelazer.com/superskill.)

Master just one of these elements, and you'll have your audience's attention. Master all four, and you'll build a deep connection, RENTing space in their minds for years to come.

Chapter 6

PRINCIPLE 3:
See the Shapes

In 1946, a young Kurt Vonnegut enrolled in the anthropology program at the University of Chicago, fresh out of World War II. He joined millions of other soldiers flooding campuses fresh off the GI Bill, but he was very unlike the others in his program.

While other anthropology students wanted to study pots and spears, Vonnegut wanted to study stories. He had been devouring popular novels, and he had a theory that you could outline our most popular stories in simple shapes on graph paper. He believed the shapes of those stories contained tremendous insights about our society.

His proposal was rejected immediately.

Why? "Because it was so simple and looked like too much fun. One must not be too playful," he recounted years later in his memoir, *Palm Sunday*.

So Vonnegut quit the program and did what many writers do when feeling stuck with bills to pay: He got a job in marketing. Vonnegut became one of the world's first content marketers at GE, telling stories of futuristic innovation.

But like so many content marketers who would come after him, he continued to write on the side—using what he learned about science and business as inspiration for his first of many brilliant satirical sci-fi novels, *Player Piano*.

Vonnegut never stopped thinking about the shapes of stories—he'd use them throughout his career while crafting his novels. Once he became famous, he'd teach them in guest lectures at colleges across the country. (You can watch one at joelazer.com/superskill.) His story graph is brilliantly simple. The X-axis runs from beginning to end. The Y-axis runs from good fortune to bad fortune.

For instance, Man in a Hole—"a story we can't get enough of," according to Vonnegut—looks like this. Someone living a normal life runs into serious trouble (the hole) and needs to get out of it:

Man in a Hole

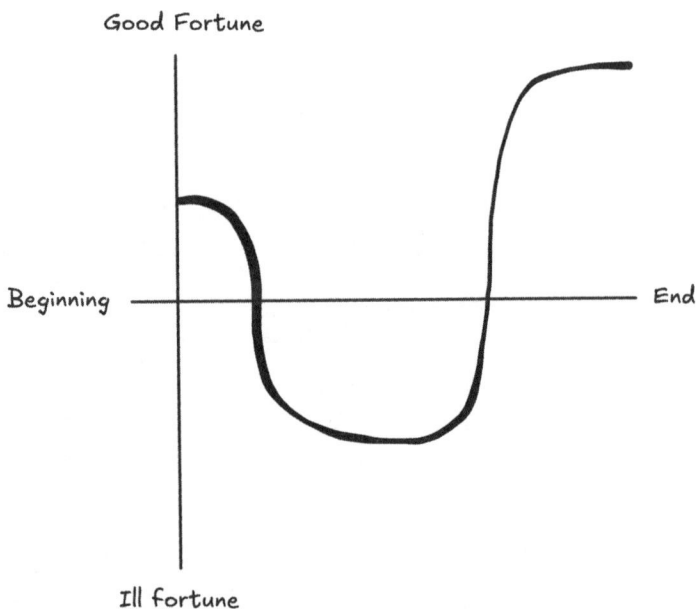

I discovered Vonnegut's shapes of stories when I was in college, and I've found it immensely helpful to visualize the arcs of the stories I'm telling. I'm not alone. Countless storytellers have diagrammed their stories—from Joseph Campbell's *Hero's Journey* to Dan Harmon's *Story Circle* to Christopher Nolan's deliriously brilliant plot map for the movie *Inception*.

In Principle 3, See the Shapes, we're going to master the simple shapes of the stories our brains can't help but love. If you want to unlock your innate storytelling superpowers, these frameworks are incredibly powerful.

Taking Shape

In 2007, a young designer fresh out of the Rhode Island School of Design named Brian Chesky arrived in San Francisco with his roommate Joe Gebbia. Before long, they found themselves unemployed with no way to pay the rent, so out of desperation they yanked Gebbia's air mattresses out of a closet and rented sleeping space on their floor to attendees of a sold-out design trade show—calling it an "air bed and breakfast."

It worked, so they thought, "Why not turn this into a business?" Chesky and Gebbia recruited a third cofounder—an engineer friend named Nathan Blecharczyk—to launch Airbedandbreakfast.com. They tried to raise seed capital, but venture capitalist after venture capitalist rejected them. *Who the hell would want to stay in strangers' houses?* Before long, they'd racked up over $40,000 in credit card debt, and only had ten to twenty bookings per day.

"You know those binders that you put baseball cards in? We put credit cards in them," Chesky told LinkedIn cofounder Reid Hoffman on his podcast *Masters of Scale*. Desperate to pay off some debt while spreading the word about the company, they created two themed breakfast cereals ahead of the 2008 Democratic National Convention: Obama O's and Cap'n McCains.

The idea took off. The cofounders sold 1,000 boxes at $40 each, enough to keep them afloat. The free publicity got them accepted into Paul Graham's Y Combinator, a prestigious accelerator for tech startups, where they shortened their name. In 2010, Airbnb finally raised a $7.2 million Series A round of funding.

A year later, the company would be worth over $1 billion. As I write this, Airbnb's market cap is $82 billion. Over the past fifteen years, Chesky has told this story again and again, making him a media darling and one of the most beloved founders in Silicon Valley.

Notice anything about this story? It follows the arc of Man in a Hole, the simplest yet most potent of Vonnegut's Shapes of Stories. If you pay attention to viral founder and business stories, many of them follow this arc—from Chesky to Alibaba founder Jack Ma to Bumble founder Whitney Wolfe Herd. It's also the arc of many of our favorite books and films: *Finding Nemo, Jane Eyre, Die Hard, Rocky,* and *The Old Man and the Sea.* We adore stories in which people get in trouble and need to find a way out.

Once upon a time, it was a matter of survival. Our brains evolved to pay attention to stories about overcoming challenges because they contained crucial survival lessons. Man-in-a-Hole stories also help us understand and process our own setbacks—we all fall into a hole at some point in our lives. There's nothing more inspiring and emotionally comforting than stories that show us how to escape trouble and get back on our feet.

Vonnegut's Shapes of Stories included eight frameworks in all, but three are the most fruitful for business storytelling: Man in a Hole and two others that are Man in a Hole with a twist—Boy Meets Girl and Cinderella. The other five are helpful if you're writing fiction or narrative nonfiction, but they're not easily applicable to business storytelling. (Explore the rest at joelazer.com/superskill.)

Man in a Hole: Airbnb

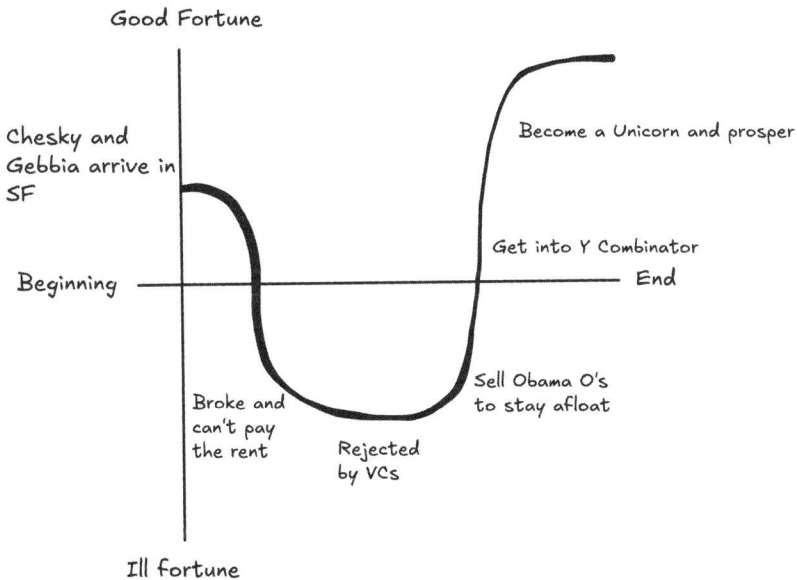

Good Fortune

Chesky and
Gebbia arrive in
SF

Become a Unicorn and prosper

Get into Y Combinator

Beginning —————————————————— End

Broke and
can't pay
the rent

Sell Obama O's
to stay afloat

Rejected
by VCs

Ill fortune

Boy meets girl

Boy Meets Girl (or boy meets boy, or girl meets girl, or they meets them) is the plot of every rom-com, and it follows a similar pattern to Man in a Hole—except instead of Fall-Rise, it follows a Rise-Fall-Rise pattern. The protagonist meets their dream partner, experiences momentary bliss, screws everything up, and then fights for redemption and wins. This plot is 95 percent of Netflix's holiday programming strategy, and it works. Did you know that two of 2024's most-streamed movies were *The Merry Gentleman* and *Hot Frosty*? That's the Boy Meets Girl shape at work.

Boy Meets Girl

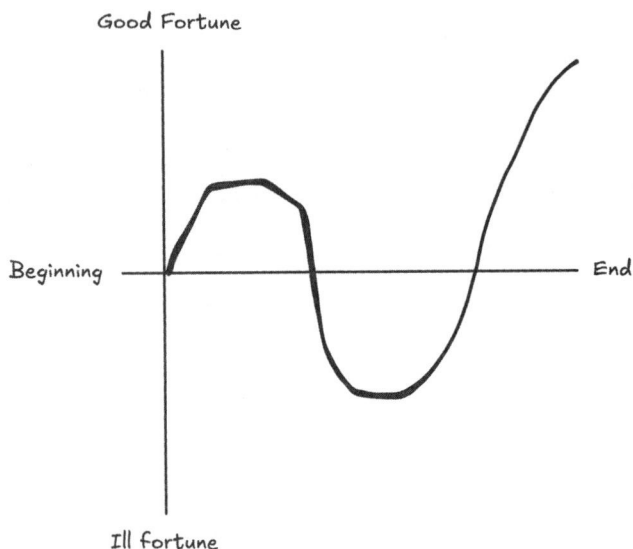

Of course, Boy Meets Girl doesn't have to map to a romantic story. It can be about achieving any sort of goal, with early success followed by setbacks along the way. Some examples:

The "Industry Challenger" Story	
Rise	You discover a counterintuitive way of doing things that challenges industry norms, and you gain traction.
Fall	You get hit with pushback from established players. It looks like you're doomed.
Rise	You push through. Your persistence pays off, and you achieve unparalleled success.
Great for	Press interviews, job interviews, LinkedIn
Example	Sara Blakely/Spanx (challenged big pantyhose and won)

The "Resilient Leader" Story	
Rise	You assemble a dream team of talented people, and things look promising.
Fall	Then the honeymoon wears off; the team doesn't click. Key projects seem doomed.
Rise	But you step in, solve communication and collaboration issues, and take your team to new heights.
Great for	Job interviews, board meetings, LinkedIn
Example	Howard Schultz/Starbucks

The "Pivot" Story	
Rise	You start by pursuing an idea, either as a founder or an ambitious go-getter within your company, and it shows promise.
Fall	But then it falters; you recognize that it's doomed to fail.
Rise	So you pivot to a new idea, find perfect product-market fit, and achieve breakthrough success.
Great for	Press interviews, investor meetings, job interviews, thought leadership
Example	Odeo/Twitter (Twitter started as Odeo, a podcasting platform)

The "Career Pivot" Story	
Rise	You start in one field and find success.
Fall	You have an epiphany that it's not your calling. You struggle as you find your way.
Rise	You find your new calling and emerge stronger.
Great for	Job interviews, Thanksgiving dinner conversation, LinkedIn
Example	Vera Wang (started as a fashion editor)

Boy Meets Girl: Career Pivot Story

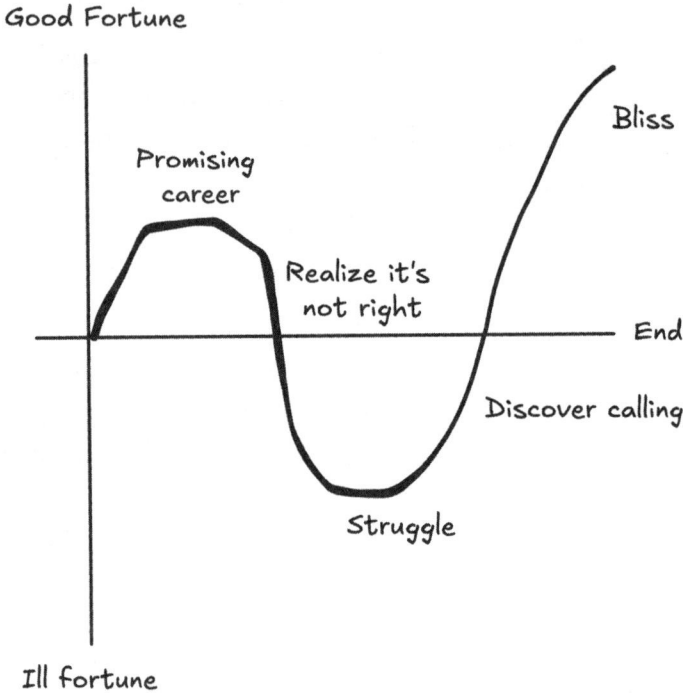

Cinderella

Then there's the most popular story in our civilization—the one where, according to Vonnegut, "Every time someone tells it, they make a million dollars"—Cinderella.

In the Cinderella arc, a character starts in deep misfortune and receives a series of gifts from a deity (e.g. fairy godmother) that propels their fortune, only for it to come crashing down (the clock strikes midnight) before they live happily ever after.

As Vonnegut recognized, this is also the shape of the most powerful tale of all time: the New Testament. It's *also* the arc of the second most powerful story of all time: *Magic Mike*.

Cinderella

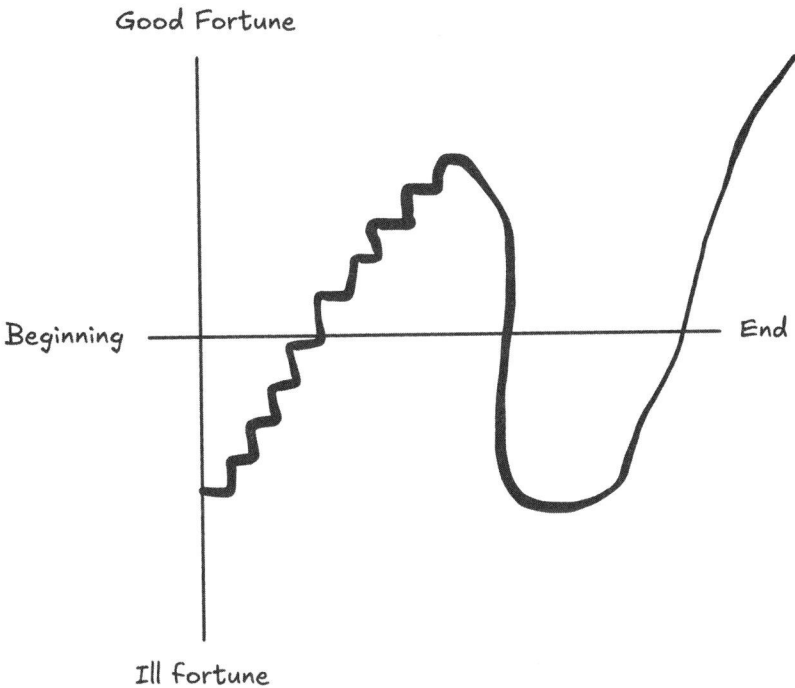

Like Man in a Hole and Boy Meets Girl, Cinderella is a powerful framework when adapted to business storytelling:

The "Rags to Riches Founder" Story	
The misfortune	Starting from poverty, no connections, or major obstacles (immigrant family, small town, etc.)
The "fairy godmother"	Key mentor, investor, or breakthrough opportunity that changes everything

The fall	Major crisis threatens to destroy everything (funding falls through, key partnership ends, market crash)
Transformation	Emerging stronger and achieving extraordinary success
Example	Jan Koum, founder of WhatsApp: began as a poor immigrant from Ukraine, built WhatsApp, almost ran out of money, sold to Facebook for $19 billion.
Great for	PR, LinkedIn, investors

"Career Transformation" Story (Non-Founder)	
The misfortune	You're stuck in a dead-end role, overlooked for promotions, with skills that are becoming obsolete.
The "fairy godmother"	Mentor who opens doors
The fall	An unexpected event threatens your progress.
Transformation	You emerge as a recognized expert/leader in your field.
Example	Bozoma Saint John: rose to become CMO of Uber before the company's controversy nearly took her down. She recovered to become the CMO of Netflix and Endeavor.
Great for	Job interviews, LinkedIn

"Brand Renaissance" Story	
The misfortune	Product seen as outdated, losing relevance, customers abandoning it
The "fairy godmother"	Rebranding opportunity, celebrity endorsement, or cultural shift

The fall	Major PR crisis or competitor threatens to kill momentum.
Transformation	Becomes the must-have item for new generation
Example	Domino's: The quality of their pizza fell off, and the brand was getting roasted on social media. They launched a new campaign acknowledging that they sucked. It worked before triggering a backlash, but when people realized the pizza really had improved, it sent the company's stock soaring.
Great for	Case studies, brand narratives, PR

The Underestimated to Industry Leader Arc	
The misfortune	Being overlooked, underestimated, or starting in a junior position due to your background
The "fairy godmother"	Receiving key opportunities, training, or recognition from influential people
The fall	Facing a major professional crisis or failure that threatens your reputation
Transformation	Emerging as a respected leader/expert in your field
Example	Oprah: born into poverty in rural Mississippi, received mentorship from media figures, got fired as an evening news co-anchor for being "too emotional," started the *Oprah Winfrey Show*, and became freaking Oprah.
Great for	Job interviews, LinkedIn, thought leadership, PR

Cinderella: Underestimated to Industry Leader Arc (Oprah)

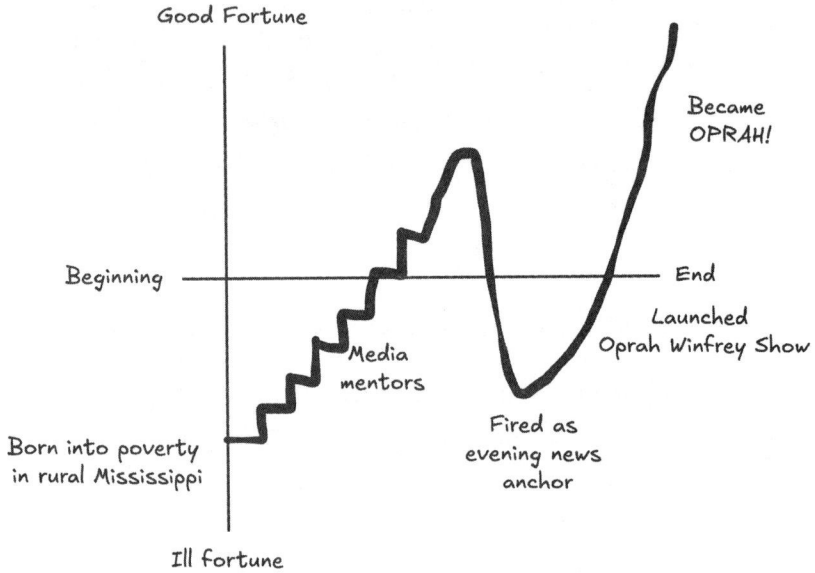

Good Fortune

Beginning ————————————— End

Born into poverty in rural Mississippi

Media mentors

Fired as evening news anchor

Became OPRAH!

Launched Oprah Winfrey Show

Ill fortune

Unlocking your storytelling superpowers with Vonnegut's shapes of stories

In one of Vonnegut's famous lectures about the Shapes of Stories, he theorized that "there's no reason these shapes couldn't be fed into computers" to figure out which stories readers would be most drawn toward. So a few years ago, a group of researchers decided to do just that—using AI machine learning to analyze nearly 2,000 popular works of fiction to see if Vonnegut's theory about stories having universal shapes was right.

Was he right? Of course he was! He's Kurt freaking Vonnegut. Not only was he right, but he also predicted a future in which our AI overlords would prove him right. (Which sounds like the plot of a very meta Vonnegut novel.)

In aggregate, the arcs of the stories analyzed by the researchers matched Vonnegut's shapes of stories almost exactly.

That teaches us a key lesson: these shapes aren't only meant to be some nerdy framework you talk about with your writer friends or print out as inspiration to paste above your writing desk like a "Live Laugh Love" poster. They're meant to be put to use. Here's how you can do it.

1. Draw the shapes of your favorite stories.

This may seem obvious, but the shapes of your favorite stories are meant to literally be drawn—ideally on a giant chalkboard while wearing a tweed jacket and smoking a pipe.

Drawing the shapes of your stories is one of the most powerful ways to unlock your creativity, even if you don't self-identify as a visual learner.

The physical act of drawing creates what neuroscientists call "multimodal encoding." Your motor cortex is controlling your hands and fingers at the same time that you're engaging the planning center of your brain—the prefrontal cortex—as you think about the shape of your stories. This gives your brain multiple neural pathways to remember and analyze the structure of the story you're telling: the motor memory of drawing, the visual memory of seeing it, or the memory of planning the story itself.

To practice, start by drawing the shapes of stories you love. Let's take one of the favorite books of millennials everywhere, *Harry Potter and the Deathly Hallows*, the seventh and final book in the Harry Potter series. The plot seems intricate, but as the researchers found when they ran it through their machine learning analysis, it's just "Man in a Hole" over and over again. The continuous conflict and resolution keep us glued to the page.

When you're binging Netflix and HBO Max this cuffing season, challenge yourself to draw the narrative arcs of the stories you love the most. You'll start to recognize patterns. I find myself drawn to "Cinderella" narratives—the series of magical gifts creates a happy momentum that propels the story forward, and then you're crushed as it all comes crashing down. Studying stories this way will help make your own narrative choices more instinctual, much in the same way that training for a sport develops your hand-eye coordination and fast-twitch muscles.

2. Work backward from the emotional journey you want your audience to go on.

Do you want your audience to experience hope? Joy? Resilience? Catharsis? Horror? Different shapes of stories map to different emotions.

For instance, I've been writing a TV comedy about a group of misfits who have to take over a business in a very dangerous part of the universe. We want the audience to feel a sense of resilience and hope but also anxious for the fate of our heroes along the way. That means we'll lean on the Man in a Hole and Cinderella structures. From Bad to Worse would be way too dark.

Want to create a sense of tension and joy? Choose **Man in a Hole.**

Inspiration and resilience? Tell a **Boy Meets Girl** story.

Triumph and vindication? Might I recommend **Cinderella?**

Existential dread? From **Bad to Worse,** baby.

3. Map characters' arcs against each other.

I usually write short stories and essays, but lately I've been working on longer works of fiction for the first time since college. (Look at me, evolving in my thirties!) If you are too—or working on a more intricate piece of brand storytelling, like a documentary—I've found that drawing different characters' arcs against each other keeps me on track. Parallel shapes can show connection—for example, in *Game of Thrones*, the Stark kids all go through similar Man in a Hole arcs. Intersecting points where characters meet each other while rising and falling are great moments for confrontation. Think Walt and Jesse in *Breaking Bad* or Gatsby and Tom in *The Great Gatsby*.

4. Check your pace.

Like most people, I overwrite first drafts, and the culprit is usually the same: I linger on plateaus for too long, basking in the awesome and awful. Mapping each scene to the shape of the story helps me figure out when I need to make cuts and get things moving. For example, when I was writing *Resignation*, the TV show I co-created, I'd continually overextend comedic scenes starring my favorite character, Jordi. They were fun to write but didn't really progress the plot. Mapping my scenes against Vonnegut's shapes helped me identify when I wasn't moving the plot along. The same thing was true when I wrote some of the longer stories in this book, like the tales of Sara Blakely (chapter 13) and Holly Herndon (chapter 18). When I suspect I'm lingering, it's incredibly helpful to draw it out.

5. To get everyone on the same page, get them on the same shape.

If you're writing with other people—either for a TV show or business book or, God help you, some sort of "brand story" pitch deck with twelve different cooks in a kitchen—drawing these arcs is a great way to get everyone on the same page. Over the years, I've used this tactic repeatedly when crafting brand narratives for clients, and it acts like an easy button for eliminating pushback. We start with the shape of the story we want to tell and then map the story against it.

Once you start looking for the Shapes of Stories, you'll see them everywhere—in your favorite shows, on Broadway, at happy hour in your best friend's story about their awful date. You'll realize there really are universal stories that unite all of us, and you'll unlock your storytelling superpowers. So it goes.

Chapter 7

PRINCIPLE 4:
Become an Active Listener

Brandon Stanton's journey to becoming one of the world's most famous storytellers began in the unlikeliest of places: a Chicago bond trading desk.

Stanton never planned on being a bond trader. In college, he majored in history. He also loved politics—in 2007 and early 2008, he canvassed for Barack Obama's campaign across the country. He grew so convinced that Obama would beat Hilary Clinton for the Democratic nomination that he took out a $5,000 student loan to bet on Obama's victory. When he told this story to a friend who was a bond trader in Chicago, the friend offered to get him a job. A willingness to take risks, the friend said, was the one trait that separated successful traders from mediocre ones.

Stanton was the type of person who gets *obsessed* with his hobbies. He majored in history because he devoured historical biographies, reading them every day. He didn't just canvas once; he went all in. So naturally, he became obsessed with bond trading, and his risky style paid off. It was like a high-stakes game of poker every night. In his first year out of college, he made six figures, more money than he'd ever imagined.

But the Great Recession disrupted the markets, rendering Stanton's risk-heavy approach a loser. He grew terrified of losing his job; bond trading had become his entire life. He realized he needed something that would give him a sense of purpose and identity outside of the markets, so after a brutal day at work, he made an impulse purchase: a Canon EOS 7D camera. Stanton spent his weekends traveling all over Chicago, photographing graffiti, landscapes, and candid photos of people.

A few weeks later, Stanton busted out for the last time and lost his job. His great fear had come true. So he took a walk and asked himself, "What do I want to do?" For two years, he had been so focused on mastering bond trading that he'd barely thought about anything else. He made a vow: he'd make just enough money to allow himself to spend his time doing something that nourished him. And that was photography.

A few days later, Stanton moved to New York City with a bold plan. He'd photograph 10,000 New Yorkers and plot them on a map, creating a photographic census. Sure, he'd never *been* to New York and only knew two people there, but it was one of the most diverse cities in the world. What better place for this kind of art project? He started a blog to document his work and called it *Humans of New York*.

His friends and family thought he was insane.

The $620 in unemployment he received every two weeks was just enough money to rent a small room in Brooklyn and survive, as long as he only ate peanut butter and jelly sandwiches and eggs. He committed to working nonstop and raced around the city, taking pictures of 30–40 people each day, determined to hit his goal of 10,000 portraits as soon as possible.

After six months and thousands of pictures, Stanton's blog

was floundering. He'd spent Christmas Eve alone in a diner, wondering what he was doing with his life. To gain traction on the blog, he'd started a Facebook page, but his posts usually only got a few likes.

Then came the Green Lady.

She was dressed all in green—green shoes, socks, pants, gloves, jacket, muffler—even her hair was green. It was as if her stylist was Kermit the Frog. Stanton took a picture of her and hated it; the composition was all wrong. He was close to scrapping it when he remembered an exchange they'd had.

"So do you do a different color every day?" he asked.

"No, I used to go through different stages. But then I found that I was happiest when I was green, so I've been green for fifteen years," she responded.

Stanton put that quote above the picture and posted. It got sixty-seven likes—by far the most he'd received. "It was a eureka moment," he later told newsletter *The Profile*. "I realized that people were much more interested in learning about these people than they were in seeing these people."

Stanton changed strategy. Instead of racing around New York photographing people, he started listening to their stories, often chatting with his subjects for over ninety minutes. He began incorporating short profiles about each subject alongside their photo on his blog and Facebook. People loved it. In 2011, he took a walk in Central Park with a friend and excitedly announced that he was gaining ten new followers a day on Facebook. At this rate, he'd be at 10,000 followers in three years!

Stanton's projection was way off. Three years later, he'd have *10 million* followers and sit atop the *New York Times* best-seller list for nonfiction.

Stanton's career turned on a critical moment—one where he stopped rushing and started listening. So often, we think of storytelling as a performance—seizing the stage, grabbing attention, and putting yourself front and center. But the world's greatest storytellers know something else. If you want to be a great storyteller, you need to be a great listener. Active listening is one of the most critical skills in your storytelling arsenal. It not only allows you to mine the raw material you need to tell great stories and craft rich characters; it *also* helps you build stronger bonds with everyone in your life.

The power of active listening

In 2014, researchers in Japan set out to answer a simple question: What happens in someone's brain when they feel heard?

To find out, they invited each participant (twenty-two in all) into an fMRI machine, which would track the activity in their brain. As the subject laid inside the machine, they told stories about emotional experiences to a counselor who sat just outside the machine. But there was a twist—sometimes the counselor responded to the participant's stories with active listening. They were engaged and expressed empathy with their experiences. Other times, the counselor was passive and indifferent.

What the researchers discovered was striking. When participants talked to a counselor who practiced active listening, the part of the brain associated with reward and pleasure, the ventral striatum, lit up. Being listened to felt incredible. It triggered the same parts of the brain that activate when you're having sex, doing drugs, or eating a delicious cake. But that wasn't all. Other parts of the brain associated with emotional regulation and empathy—the right anterior insula and the inferior frontal gyrus—lit up as well, suggesting that participants were also reprocessing past experiences more positively.

The participants opened up more and rated the active listening counselors much higher. They liked them. They trusted them. And they were eager to collaborate with them on future tasks.

Active listening has two powerful effects. First, it makes us better storytellers—bestowing us with the insight, inspiration, and characters we need to craft a story that resonates with readers.

Second, active listening strengthens relationships with the people around us. We are storytelling animals, and our brains light up when others listen to our stories. It's the easiest way to build affinity and trust with your colleagues, bosses, direct reports, customers, and prospects. By actively listening, you trigger the pleasure sensors in their brains and win their trust. Even if you never write a word, practicing active listening will strengthen your bonds with your bosses and colleagues, giving you a key advantage in your career.

How to become a better active listener

For years, I've been fascinated by how to become a better listener. I've interviewed close to 1,000 people in my career, and I'm always in awe of how world-class interviewers like Oprah, *Fresh Air*'s Terry Gross, and Stanton make it seem so easy. What magical powers do they have that get people to tell their stories? I've listened to hours and hours of successful interviewers explaining their process and dug into the science of active listening. Along the way, I've developed five keys to active story-listening that will build stronger bonds and invite people to share their stories with you:

Synchronization
Trust
Opening questions
Reflection
Yielding space

1. Synchronization

In chapter 2, we explored how the neural activity of the storyteller and listener literally syncs through mirror neurons when we tell a great story. If I tell you the story of a harrowing travel experience when my cruise ship was taken over by pirates, your brain will see the pirates and mirror that experience. It's a powerful bonding experience that you can trigger not only by being a good storyteller, but also by being a good *listener.*

Being a good listener starts with demonstrating that you're in sync. That means using body language and facial expressions that mirror the speaker's emotional state and responding in subtle, natural ways.

As Stanton began interviewing his subjects for *Humans of New York,* he realized that his superpower was his ability to approach people in a relaxed way that put them at ease. "Over time, I learned it has nothing to do with the words I was saying. It has everything to do with the energy I was giving off," he told photographer Eric Kim. He always approaches people from the front with his arms in a wide, relaxed stance. And when he goes to ask someone if he can take their picture, he crouches down, making himself as small and non-threatening as possible.

Over her storied career, Oprah has interviewed over 37,000 people. In an interview at the 2013 Forbes Summit, she revealed that everyone she interviews—from Barack Obama to Tom Cruise to Beyoncé—asks the same question: "Was that okay?"

"What I learned in all of those thousands of interviews is that there is a common denominator in all of our human experience," she said. "Everybody wants to know, did you hear me, and did what I say matter?"

Oprah has learned that the key to a great interview is making her subjects comfortable, and more than anyone, she's mastered the art of doing so. She uses "facial language" to sync with her subjects: steady eye contact, empathetic expressions, and physically leaning in to let her subjects know that she's listening and connected to their story. There's an entire grammar in her cheeks, eyes, and brow that makes the interviewee feel secure, and the audience feel like they're part of an intimate moment. Ninety percent of human communication is nonverbal, and Oprah speaks this language better than anyone else.

Whenever you're sitting down with someone that you want to invite to share your story, focus intently on your body language. Are your arms open rather than crossed? Are you relaxed? And as they begin to tell their story, are you leaning in, making eye contact, and following along with every word? Active listening starts with showing you're in sync.

2. Trust

Therapeutic research shows that if you want people to open up and share their stories, you need to create an environment of trust and "psychological safety"—the belief that they can speak without risk of punishment or humiliation.

Stanton accomplishes this in three ways: First, he pulls out his phone and shows his subjects *Humans of New York* to demonstrate that this isn't some weird street prank, and that he'll represent them positively. Before the interview, he tells people that some of the questions will be hard, and that they don't need to answer anything they don't want to. He also tells them that if they share anything sensitive, they can opt to have their hands or feet photographed instead of their face so they remain anonymous. If they decide afterward that they don't want him to post their story, he'll honor their request.

Most great interviewers have a similar ritual to build trust with interviewees. At the 2022 Tribeca Film Festival, Oprah revealed the question she's asked every guest backstage since 1989: "Please tell me what your intention is." She then shares her own intention for the interview to create a sense of trust and alignment.

Fresh Air's Terry Gross immediately eliminates concerns that she's going to catch her guests in a "gotcha" moment. Before every interview, she tells her guests, "Let me know if I asked you anything too personal and we'll move on to something else because I don't want to push you beyond what you're comfortable saying."

Ira Glass, host of *This American Life*, establishes trust by telling a quick story about himself to encourage others to share their story. "I try to create a comfortable climate," he told *The New York Review of Books*. "You tell a story about yourself where you're being a human being. That permits them to be a human being back. It helps to get things more real."

Creating an environment of trust and psychological safety not only helps you get people to share their stories. If you're a manager, it can also improve the performance of your team. In her landmark 1999 study, Harvard Business School professor Amy Edmondson found that creating an environment of psychological safety boosts team learning, performance, and willingness to report critical errors.

If you want to invite someone to share their story, ask yourself: "What concerns do they have? What can I say to make them feel safe and like I care?" It's a powerful approach whether you're interviewing someone for a podcast or a YouTube show, getting job candidates to open up, or trying to build stronger relationships with your team.

If you're a manager, let them know that anything they say will stay between you, and share your own story to invite reciprocation. If you're mentoring someone, you could tell them about a time you screwed up early in your career, emphasizing that mistakes are an inevitable part of learning. If you're trying to build rapport with a prospect, it can be as simple as asking them why they decided to take the call. And if you're interviewing someone for a show you're hosting or a story you're writing, take a page from Oprah—ask what their intention for the interview is and then share your own.

3. Opening questions

What makes *Humans of New York* so engaging is Stanton's ability to get people to share the most intimate moments of their lives. He usually begins an interview with one of three questions:

1. What's the greatest struggle in your life right now?
2. What do you feel most guilty about?
3. How has your life turned out differently than you expected it to?

Since Stanton has already built a sense of connection and trust, people open up right away, revealing their struggles with money, love, health, and even their identity.

The key is to start with an open-ended question that invites a story rather than a yes/no answer. Research on ethnographic interviewing shows that the most effective questions focus on *feelings*, not facts.

Change up your opening questions based on who you're interviewing and what you know about them. For instance, Stanton traveled to Jordan and Turkey in 2017 to document the lives of Syrian refugees who had been cleared for entry to America. Instead of his usual questions, he went straight to the story he knew that people needed to tell: "Tell me about the day you left Syria."

"They would start speaking in Arabic, and they would stop, and then tears would start coming down their face," he told ABC News. Their stories led to an incredible series, "The Syrian-Americans," that raised empathy for Syrian refugees.

4. Reflection

In 1957, renowned psychologist Carl Rogers coined the term "active listening," introducing one of the most powerful tactics for demonstrating empathy: reflecting and paraphrasing the speaker's words and emotions back to them.

For example, if someone says, "I just feel so overwhelmed lately," you can reflect back by saying, "It sounds like you're carrying a lot right now and it's starting to weigh you down," demonstrating empathy and inviting them to share more.

Oprah is a master at this. Her reflection technique pairs emotional validation with strategic reframing, taking what guests say and reflecting it in slightly different language that invites deeper exploration. Take her 2021 interview with Meghan Markle and Prince Harry after they were stripped of their royal protections. She opens by inviting Meghan to share her story—her early work, independence, and advocacy for women's rights, prompting Markle to open up. "That's the sad irony of the last four years," she said. "I've advocated for so long for women to use their voice . . . and then I was silent."

"Were you silent? Or were you silenced?" Oprah responded.

In just seven words, Oprah shows that she's listening to Markle intently, inviting her to finally share the turbulent story of her time with the royal family. The interview that would be watched by over 60 million people.

Later in the interview, Markle, who's half-Black, mentioned that the royal family had expressed concern about her baby's skin color, and Oprah reflected the question to her, inviting her to reveal more: "There's a conversation with you about how dark your baby is going to be?"

Terry Gross's method is to focus on a specific word that the subject said, and reflect it back to them, asking them to go deeper. "I'll take a key word that somebody has said, or phrase, and I'll say, 'You said this, what do you mean by that?' Because it's a way of getting deeper into what they just said. Often the way of getting deeper is to go back to what somebody said and basically say, take it to the next step," she explained during a

2020 National Press Club Journalism Institute event.

For *Humans of New York*, Stanton put a twist on this practice by challenging subjects, pointing out inconsistencies. As he told *The Profile*: "Challenging somebody is a form of respect because it shows that you're listening so closely that you're noticing inconsistencies in their story." Other than his go-to openers, Stanton never comes with any other preset questions. His interviewing style is reflective, inviting people to go deeper and share more of their story.

If you want people to let you in and share with their story with you, consciously practice reflecting their words back to them. You'll be surprised by how much they share.

5. Yielding space

In a 2018 interview with author and podcaster Tim Ferriss, Stanton reflected on what has made *Humans of New York* such a sensation, with over 30 million followers across social channels, a TV show, and millions of books sold. He attributed it to his ability to yield space to his interview subjects, creating a bubble where the rest of the world melts away.

"*Humans of New York* works because the people on the street that I meet are thankful to have someone really listen to them," he explained. "This magic happens where they're willing to let me into a space in their mind or their souls that they don't let people into. . . . The way you get into that deep space is presence. It's 1,000 percent being there. You're not looking at a list of questions."

The other part of yielding space is silence. Therapeutic research reveals that yielding space by being fully present without judgment creates the psychological safety needed for someone to be vulnerable and tell their story. Stanton tries to feel for these moments when he should be silent. "You can feel when the person is being truthful, no matter what language they're speaking," he wrote in his 2020 book, *Humans*. "Because truth is often spoken haltingly. With pauses. Like it's being dug up, one spoonful at a time, from somewhere deep. Truth feels heavy. It has gravity."

Yield space for those pauses, and incredible stories will flow. Like Stanton, you'll unlock countless new stories to tell and build lasting bonds with bosses, teammates, customers, and every industry leader you interview.

Chapter 8

PRINCIPLE 5:
Find Your Muse

When best-selling author Daniel Pink gets writer's block, he has a secret weapon, and it's not AI.

It's a tiny red chair.

The tiny red chair sits on his desk at all times. "When I'm stuck, I think, 'Okay, imagine there's somebody sitting in that chair, and they're reading something I've written. What's that experience like? And am I wasting their time?'" he told me.

You feel this singular focus reflected in Pink's work. When I read his books about the science of working and living smarter, I'm often struck with the feeling that he wrote them just for me.

Pink's approach isn't unique; it's the same trick used by many of the greatest storytellers of all time. Stephen King wrote for one person: his wife, Tabitha. "If you know the tastes of your ideal reader at least half as much as I know the tastes of mine, it will not be difficult for you to imagine what he will like, and what not," King wrote in his memoir, *On Writing*. C.S. Lewis wrote *The Lion, the Witch and the Wardrobe* for his goddaughter, Lucy. Kurt Vonnegut always wrote for one person too—his sister. "Please write for one person," he advised young writers. "Open the window and make love to the world, so to speak, and your story will get pneumonia."

When you write for everyone, you write for no one, and your story is left out in the cold. If you want to unlock your storytelling superpowers and resonate deeply with your audience, you need to write for one person. You need a muse.

Conjuring the muse

I didn't fully know what a muse was until a few years ago, when I hit a creative wall and finally read Steven Pressfield's *The War of Art*, a creative bible recommended by nearly every accomplished storyteller I know.

The War of Art is a brilliant manual for winning your inner creative battles and doing great work, and in those battles, the muse is your greatest ally. As Pressfield explains, muses come from Greek mythology. They were the nine daughters of Zeus and Mnemosyne, and the term "muse" translates to "memory." Their entire job was to inspire artists (each muse was responsible for a different type of art). Even 2,800 years ago, the ancient Greeks understood that creating for someone specific inspires creativity. It's the secret force that fuels our storytelling superpowers. As Pressfield writes:

> When we sit down each day and do our work, power concentrates around us. The Muse takes note of our dedication. She approves. We have earned favor in her sight. When we sit down and work, we become like a magnetized rod that attracts iron filings. Ideas come. Insights accrete.

In the first four Principles of this book, we've focused on unlocking our storytelling superpowers through technique:

building storytelling habits, mastering the elements of stories, seeing their shapes, and becoming an active listener. Now, it's time to get inspired.

The science behind the muse

A muse turns storytelling into an act of empathy. You're thinking of someone who epitomizes your audience and asking: *What can I create to help them? Teach them something new? Entertain them? How can I help them see the world in a new way and experience wonder?*

As a fascinating recent study shows, empathy is the key to unlocking our creativity.

In late 2024, a team of researchers from Southwest University in China and the University of Vienna set out to understand the link between empathy and creativity. Specifically, they focused on "cognitive empathy"—where, like Daniel Pink and his little red chair, you're trying to imagine another person's point of view. The researchers found that people who demonstrate cognitive empathy were much more likely to engage in creative acts, like writing, producing videos, and sculpting.

But that's not all. The researchers also found that empathetic people were more creatively productive, and they accomplished more. "People who identify as more empathic tend to be more creative but also tend to produce," one of the study's co-authors, Matthew Pelowski, told *Greater Good*. "Perhaps having some of these cognitive empathic abilities gives you the tools to really be a productive, creative person."

Neuroscience backs this up. Empathy is strongly linked with oxytocin production, which boosts dopamine in the brain. And, oh boy, does the brain feel creative on dopamine—the feel-good neurotransmitter we spend our lives chasing, along with its sidekick, serotonin. Boosting dopamine is the greatest creativity hack researchers have discovered so far.

This is why, when you conjure the muse, you literally feel it in the brain. Something lights up inside of you—and around you. There are five tactics you can use to unlock your muse:

1. Go to events with your target audience and hear their stories.

Recently, I introduced the concept of finding your muse to the CEO of a fast-growth startup I work with. "Oh, I think we already have this," he said, pulling up a buyer persona slide his marketing team had made. The slide was titled "Marketing Mary," accompanied by a stock photo of a disturbingly cheerful blonde woman, her smile stretched so wide it looked like she might be on the verge of a psychotic break. The slide told me that Mary was:

- Thirty years old
- A senior digital marketing manager at a Fortune 500 company
- Driving a Chevy Equinox (not sure why that was relevant, but okay)
- Reading marketing publications like *Search Engine Land* and the Ahrefs Blog
- Struggling to keep up with the latest digital marketing trends

Here's what I told the CEO: You can't find your muse in a PowerPoint deck. Yes, this buyer persona slide is somewhat useful—you'll now be able to stalk her with LinkedIn ads more effectively! But it won't actually help you develop empathy or unlock your creativity. Maybe ChatGPT secretly develops empathy from that, but humans do not. They find it somewhere else: in stories. The best place to find your muse is by talking and listening to your audience as much as possible and hearing *their* story.

To find your muse, you need to spend time with your target audience and ignite your active listening.

I was reminded of this when I recently started ramping up my public speaking and conducting interviews for this book. I started spending much more time with my core audience of marketers, entrepreneurs, and creatives—either talking to them on the record or drinking with them off the record at happy hour. (That's where you get to hear the *really* good stuff.)

As I listened to their stories, challenges, and aspirations, my sense of my muse brightened. One conversation, in particular, solidified my muse for this book. Right before I gave a talk at a conference, I met a young creative. She'd studied journalism in college, and for the past five years, she'd worked in marketing at a Fortune 1000 company. She liked the job but felt terrified about what AI meant for her future. She loved telling stories, and worried that even if she kept her job, she'd spend the rest of her career outsourcing her creativity to a machine. When I told her about the concept for this book, her face lit up. "Yes! This is exactly what I need," she said. "When will it be out?"

Every day, as I sit down to write, I ask myself the same question Pink does, "What experience will she have reading this chapter? Am I wasting her time?"

My muse evolves depending on the type of writing I'm doing. When I write personal humor essays, my muse is my wife, Nicole. What would make her laugh? What stories and details would capture her attention, hold her gaze, spark a twinkle of delight in her deep blue eyes? What would make her feel something new?

If your muse is your spouse, spending time with that person is pretty easy. If it's a professional audience, it requires a little more effort. Go to industry events—even if a new episode of *Survivor* is out and you really don't want to change out of sweatpants. If there are no industry events in your area, join virtual communities and jump into the Zoom discussion.

2. Conduct muse interviews.

In addition to attending events, tap into your inner Oprah and interview people who fit your ideal audience. People *love* to be interviewed. DM them on LinkedIn or Instagram and ask if you can talk to them for a story you're writing. Even when I was an unknown twenty-three-year-old journalist, I was shocked by how most people said yes. Even marketing god Seth Godin gave me an hour of his time!

If you want to reach CMOs, interview CMOs. If you want to reach founders, interview founders. An easy approach is to say that you're writing about the challenges and opportunities that people in their roles are facing. Then, use Principle 4's **STORY** active listening techniques:

- **Synchronize** with them through a relaxed and open approach.
- Build **trust** by explaining what you hope to get out of the story and reassuring them that you'll represent them positively.
- Ask strong **opening questions** to invite their stories. Some of my favorites in a business setting:
  - Did you always want to be in your role when you were grow-ing up? (Invites people to open up about their childhood.)
  - What seemingly tiny decision ended up reshaping your life?
  - What's your greatest struggle right now?
  - If I gave you $5 million in cash in a giant money bag and the only rule was that you had to work on one project every day for the next year, what would it be?
- **Reflect** their responses back to them to demonstrate under-standing and connection.
- **Yield space,** particularly when they're telling stories about their challenges and aspirations. Be present but let them fill the silence.

Listen closely to their stories until their dreams and fears feel like your own, and a muse will start to form. It might be an amalgamation of people; it may be one person who stands out. Trust the process. You'll know when you find it.

3. Write a letter to a friend.

During the summer after my sophomore year of college, I got my first big writing opportunity. I was interning at *Nerve*—a popular online sex and pop-culture magazine in New York City. After I'd impressed our managing editor by writing erotic horoscopes and punching up sponsored fashion guides, he accepted my pitch for a 2,000-word humor essay about how I'd lied about being a virgin when I got to college.

It was a huge deal. My literary heroes—Chuck Palahniuk, Jonathan Ames, Joyce Carol Oates—had written for *Nerve*. (So did Norman Mailer, who *was* my literary hero before I learned about his prolific misogyny.) Plus, they offered to pay me $250 on top of my $50 daily internship stipend. I did the math. That was 500 cans of PBR!

The only problem: I was frozen. What was the right tone? Who was this essay for? I was a schlubby twenty-one-year-old Jewish kid from Jersey. How could I live up to the standard of Chuck freaking Palahniuk? I emailed one of my creative writing professors, and she reminded me of a writing exercise we'd practiced that year, first developed by novelist Anne Lamott.

The "letter to a friend" technique is simple. You start your assignment—whether it's a short story, an essay, a LinkedIn post, or a speech—by writing it as a letter addressed to one specific person. For this essay, I chose my college girlfriend, Hadley. After all, I was coming clean to her in the essay after two years.

It worked. I found my voice. The essay flowed. By the end, I realized that all the essays and stories I'd written in college had been for her all along.

Once you have a potential muse in your mind, invoke them using the "letter to a friend" technique:

- **Choose your recipient.** Select the person you want to write for. It could be a direct report you're mentoring, a customer you're close with, a sibling, friend, or romantic partner.

- **Start the letter with "Dear _____."**

- **State your intention.** Start the letter with "I want to tell you the story about X" or "I want to explain Y to you."

- **Set a timer and write for thirty minutes without stopping.** Don't worry about whether what you're writing is good or not, and if possible, write by hand.

Now take a step back. Did it feel right? Did your prose flow more easily? Did you feel the presence of the muse with you, at least a little bit? If not, repeat the exercise the next day with a different muse in mind.

4. Make a promise.

When I spoke to Daniel Pink about his writing process, he grabbed the tiny red chair off his desk that represents his audience and wagged it at me. "When it's usually a more frustrating situation, I will grab this chair, look at it and say, 'Okay, you're writing this. There's someone sitting there. What promise are you making?'"

For Pink, making and upholding the promise to your reader is everything. It's a rule he learned early in his career when he turned in a draft of a long magazine story to his editor. But he knew something was off. "What's the promise to the reader?" his editor asked. It transformed his perspective on writing.

As you invoke your muse, ask, "What promise am I making?" Are you promising to entertain them? Make them see the world in a new way? Teach them something new? Write it down. As you edit, ask yourself, "Did I fulfill the promise?"

Do this enough, and your muse will solidify, unlocking new storytelling superpowers. You'll create for that one specific person but end up reaching thousands. You'll start to notice a spark of inspiration that wasn't there before. And before you know it, you won't have to find your muse. They'll be there already.

Chapter 9

PRINCIPLE 6:
Develop Taste

When Ira Glass was nineteen, he was working in the shock trauma unit of a medical center. His parents were thrilled—it would look *amazing* on his med school application. But Glass had other plans. He wanted to be a storyteller. An acquaintance tipped him off to an unpaid internship for National Public Radio (NPR) doing promos, and he took it. By the end of the summer, he had a choice: He could continue on the med school track or stay at NPR, working as a production assistant. To his parents' horror, he chose NPR.

Today, Glass is one of the most famous and celebrated radio personalities on Earth. He's won almost every major radio storytelling award. His hit show, *This American Life*, revolutionized audio storytelling and launched the careers of writers like David Sedaris. But famously, none of this came easily for Glass. He languished as a low-level assistant at NPR for nearly two decades before he got his big break. And in an interview with Current TV in 2009, he explained why:

Nobody tells people who are beginners—and I really wish somebody had told this to me—is that all of us who do creative work . . . we get into it because we have good taste. But it's like there's a gap, that for the first couple years that you're making stuff, what you're making isn't so good, OK? It's not that great. It's really not that great. It's trying to be good, it has ambition to be good, but it's not quite that good. But your taste—the thing that got you into the game—your taste is still killer, and your taste is good enough that you can tell that what you're making is kind of a disappointment to you, you know what I mean?

A lot of people never get past that phase. A lot of people at that point, they quit. And the thing I would just like say to you with all my heart is that most everybody I know who does interesting creative work, they went through a phase of years where they had really good taste and they could tell what they were making wasn't as good as they wanted it to be—they knew it fell short, it didn't have the special thing that we wanted it to have.

And the thing I would say to you is everybody goes through that. And for you to go through it, if you're going through it right now, if you're just getting out of that phase—you gotta know it's totally normal.

For the past fifteen years, this quote has gone viral every few months, typically framed as a testament to good old-fashioned American perseverance. A tale of the power of hustle; keep doing the work and, eventually, you'll get better and break through. That's all true, but I think there's an even more important lesson here: Taste is a prerequisite to great creative work.

If you want to unlock your storytelling superpowers, you have to know what you like and what good storytelling looks like to you. At first, you'll find this taste-talent gap frustrating, but it will also serve as a North Star. You'll see clearly what you want to achieve in your work. The taste-talent gap will illuminate the path you need to be on, with every story you tell moving you a step closer to your destination.

I still remember when I first noticed the gap. I was twenty-one, studying abroad in London, the city that made "Mind the Gap" famous. No longer a teenager, I finally knew what I liked: punchy modernist writing; the New and Gonzo journalism of Joan Didion, Gay Talese, and Hunter S. Thompson; and the hilarious first-person essays that had taken over the internet— Bill Simmons, Sloane Crosley, Elizabeth Spiers, David Sedaris. Back in New York, I'd been editor-in-chief of my college newspaper, but I never loved writing in an objective, journalistic style. I wanted to make people laugh and feel something.

Sedaris, in particular, haunted me. I was finally getting some breaks as a writer. My first feature essay for *Nerve*—which I wrote using the "Letter to a Friend" approach covered in the previous chapter—had been a semi-viral hit, earning hundreds of thousands of views and thousands of comments. My editor greenlighted a second essay for another $250—a godsend, given how fast I was burning through my savings on pints of Stella. (A true upgrade from the PBR I was drinking back in the States.) But I was distinctly aware of the gap between Sedaris, who had become my new writing idol, and me.

Sedaris had been stuck cleaning houses for rich New Yorkers well into his thirties when Ira Glass stumbled upon him reading "The Santaland Diaries," a brilliantly funny essay about his time spent working as an elf inside Macy's Santaland. Glass invited Sedaris to read it on NPR's *Morning Edition* in 1992. Sedaris became a breakout star and published five best-selling essay collections over the next fifteen years. I read them again and again. He turns the smallest event into a hilarious story that makes you think about the world differently. It was greatness I could see but not reach. His essays veered into unexpected alleys yet always brought you back home, every paragraph punctuated by a gut-busting metaphor that left me giggling like a schoolgirl atop a double-decker bus.

That's where I spent a lot of my time that semester in London. After class, I'd ride around the top of a double-decker bus, alternating between rereading Sedaris's essays and scribbling in my Moleskine notebook, desperately trying to close the gap between his writing and mine. If I saw a sign for a pint that was £2 or less, I'd hop off and write in the pub. I'd love to say that one day everything clicked and the gap snapped closed, but in reality, it was a slow, creaking process. I submitted that essay and then another. When I got back to New York, one of my old bosses at *Nerve* was starting a new digital news site called *The Faster Times* and asked me to come onboard. I was still in college, but three days a week, I'd take the train for eighty-five minutes to Brooklyn to work out of our makeshift offices in a coffee shop designed to mimic a Scandinavian ski lodge. The ceilings were high, the tables were wide, and no one seemed to mind that we nursed one coffee for six hours. There, I wrote relentlessly—sometimes as many as eight stories per week, never less than three. Each week, each month, each year, I felt the gap between my taste and my talent close. It's still there, but it no longer haunts me. I've grown to love it. It tells me what to strive for.

Why taste is becoming harder to develop

Taste is becoming increasingly rare in the age of algorithms.

Once upon a time—2011, to be exact—you had to seek out what you liked. Books, songs, articles, videos. For help, we turned to curators, but the curators you chose were also a reflection of your taste. The taste of someone who read *The New Yorker* was usually different than someone who read *Maxim*; the taste of someone who read *New York Magazine* was different than someone who read *The National Review.*

But then Facebook introduced a machine-learning algorithm to determine what you saw in its News Feed. Suddenly, what we saw wasn't just determined by who we followed, in simple chronological order. Instead, it was determined by what the algorithm thought we were most likely to engage with, factoring thousands of signals into its rankings. Suddenly, we no longer had to seek out media and decide what we liked; it simply came to us. The only choices we made were who we followed, but even that was just one data point in the algorithmic slot machine. Over the next few years, every major social media platform followed suit. These algorithms didn't capture what we truly *liked*, just what we lingered over for a second too long. Before, taste had been a decision—a reflection of our identity and who we wanted to be in the world. Suddenly, that agency was gone. The algorithms were supposed to be a mirror, but really, they were a projection of who the algorithm thought we were. Were we watching or reading something because we really enjoyed it or because the algorithms were telling us that it was something that someone with our data should enjoy?

Over the next few years, every major social media platform followed suit. The biggest paradigm shift, however, came from TikTok.

In late 2018, TikTok caught fire in the United States thanks to a simple innovation: An algorithm that didn't care who you were following. It just cared about what you liked.

TikTok's addictive algorithm and "For You" page made it the fastest-growing social media app of all time, and over the past few years every major social media platform has been copying it. They're showing you less content from people you're connected with in favor of content the algorithm thinks you'll like—primarily TikTok-style vertical video. As a result, even LinkedIn added a Reels tab, frantically pushing hustle porn to the professional masses.

The knock-on effect of these algorithms is that we no longer have to make any conscious decision about what we like or enjoy. The algorithm simply infers it based on how long we spend with each piece of content and how much time people similar to us spend with it. This dynamic is everywhere. Listening to music? Spotify's algorithm tells you what to listen to next. Watching TV? Netflix and YouTube have predetermined what you'll watch next. Buying something? Amazon knows what you'd like to purchase. It's hard to know whether we like things anymore or if we just *think* we like them because the algorithm tells us we do. It's like gazing into a fun-house mirror. Is this me? Or is it just the algorithm's distorted projection of who I am? Am I watching this because I like it or because it's something the algorithm thinks I should enjoy? Before, taste had been a decision, a reflection of our identity and who we wanted to be in the world. Suddenly, that agency was gone.

We've been sold this as a matter of convenience. But taste isn't an inconvenience—far from it.

These algorithms—one form of AI—are fusing with generative AI to forge a Dark *WALL-E* reality: AI algorithms feeding generative AI slop straight into our occipital lobes. There are three big ramifications of this:

1. First, it's becoming harder to develop taste. When the algorithms are always telling us what to consume, we lose the ability to decide for ourselves.

2. As a result, taste is becoming rarer. Fewer people are developing it.

3. And finally, people really don't like their algorithm-dominated lives. We know that a life dominated by

algorithms isn't healthy for us. An entire digital detox wellness industry has popped up to wean us off the feed. Fed-up parents are forcing legislatures to ban phones in school. Even teenagers secretly agree—in a 2024 Harris poll, nearly half of teens say that they wish TikTok and X never existed.

The upshot: If you can develop taste, it will become your secret weapon.

Taste in the AI age

As AI usage grows, taste will grow in importance due to two realities: First, research shows that when we know a piece of content is made purely by AI, it gives us the ick (as we covered in chapter 3). As the cost of creating mediocre content approaches zero and slop floods our feeds, people will seek out people with the taste to curate which content is worthy of their attention, as well as those whose own content stands out as a refuge amidst a hurricane of slop. The second reality is that—somewhat ironically—the emergence of generative AI as a core technology necessitates taste. Since AI is adept at giving us infinite ideas and producing formulaic content assets (landing pages, press releases, nurture emails, etc.), an increasingly important skill will be knowing which ideas are good and which content is up to standard. As we'll explore in the final section of this book, you also need good taste to instruct AI well. AI is like an intern with an incredible work ethic and little taste. If you want to get anything truly useful out of these tools, you need to be able to articulate exactly what you want and give detailed feedback.

How to develop taste

By this point in reading this book, you've probably noticed that I'm obsessed with making content memetic—easy to understand, remember, repeat, and spread—a concept that we'll explore more next chapter. So I am here with another memetic acronym to help you remember how to develop taste and use it to become a stronger storyteller: TASTE.

- Take back the wheel
- Attune your taste
- Study the masters
- Try and fail
- Embrace the gap

Take back the wheel

Dr. Eric Solomon grew up dirt poor in Northern California, the son of a weed dealer, before earning a full ride to Reed College. After four years in that liberal arts utopia, he took an unusual turn and headed to Northeastern University to get his PhD in artificial intelligence and machine learning. It was 1999. "Genie in a Bottle" by Christina Aguilera topped the Billboard charts, and the AI field was still fledgling.

I met Eric twenty-four years later, in 2023, when he became an advisor for A.Team, the AI startup where I led marketing. Eric's AI research had taken him on a wild ride; like the Forrest Gump of AI, he always found himself at major moments in tech history, working inside Silicon Valley giants as they developed the algorithms that would dominate our lives. Except while Gump was a bystander, Eric was a high-powered executive at YouTube, Spotify, Google, and Instagram. Then one day, he woke up and left it all behind. He and his colleagues knew our algorithmic-driven feeds were inflicting incredible damage on us, but no one seemed to care. So he left big tech to start Human OS, his consultancy to help business leaders and brands discover and communicate their purpose in an algorithm-driven world.

Eric quickly became one of my favorite people to debate AI and the future of work with—we nearly wrote this book together. And he introduced me to a powerful concept for regaining your agency and sense of taste in an algorithm-driven world: Take back the wheel.

Constantly ask yourself: Am I deciding what I like and consume, or am I ceding control to the algorithms?

As Eric explained in his fantastic 2025 TEDx Talk, taking back the wheel starts with simply noticing. Are you picking up your phone and flipping open a feed every time you brush your teeth because you *want* to? Because it satisfies you and gives you meaning? Or are you just doing it because you're programmed to by this addictive technology? Study yourself anthropologically: think of yourself as an alien observing a human for the first time. Then, simply make a choice to watch, read, or listen to something each day that's outside of what the algorithm recommended for you. Start small—pick one thing during your morning coffee and another after work. Then build from there.

Attune your taste

As I write this, David Sedaris's diary sits on my bookshelf. You might think it's because I'm so obsessed with him that I broke into his New York City apartment and stole it. I would! But in truth, anyone can buy it.

Sedaris has been keeping a daily diary for forty-eight years; it's such a critical part of his creative process that it's been published as two gigantic volumes and devoured by superfans like me. Sedaris carries a notebook everywhere he goes, and early in his career he made a habit of going to as many readings of other writers as possible, making notes of what resonated with him and the audience, attuning his ear to why certain stories succeeded.

Attuning your taste is a conscious act. It requires actively listening to the stories of others, noticing the elements and shapes of the stories they tell. Quentin Tarantino was a high school dropout. "When people ask me if I went to film school, I tell them, 'No, I went to films.'" In his twenties, he spent five years working at Video Archives, a California video rental shop, and spent every day devouring movies alongside his co-worker Roger Avary. They spent all day introducing each other to new genres, from 1970s samurai flicks to obscure French New Wave, discussing what they liked and what worked. Together, they wrote *Pulp Fiction*, which would win the Oscar for Best Original Screenplay and turn Tarantino into a star for his genre-blending style and trademark taste.

For Ira Glass, attuning his taste began during his NPR internship when he assisted Joe Frank, an early innovator in narrative audio storytelling, blending memoir, absurdist fiction, and sound design. "I remember sitting in one of NPR's old first-floor studios on M Street in Washington, listening to Joe as he recorded a monologue, feeling all caught up in everything he was saying, wondering what would happen next in the story, transported in a way I'd never felt before listening to the radio," he wrote on the *This American Life* blog in 2013. "I wondered how he did it. I wanted to do it myself. Of course, I'd listened to lots of radio before that, but I'd never heard anyone tell a story on the air that was actually truly can't-turn-away-think-about-it-for-days-after compelling."

For the next fifteen years, Glass honed his taste while producing shows at NPR, developing an instinctual ear for the engaging, literary style that would allow him to spot hidden gems like Sedaris, and turn *This American Life* into one of the most popular radio shows in the world, even though it doesn't feature celebrities. It's just ordinary people telling their extraordinary stories.

When you attune your taste, you're not just studying storytellers; you're studying yourself. Attunement means paying attention to your own reactions, to the physical sensation and joy that a great story or work of art makes you feel. Ask: *Why do I love this? What moments or qualities draw me in?* Just as important is noticing what you don't like. What turns you off? Just like chefs must attune their taste buds to the dishes and flavors they love most, you need to attune your taste buds to the stories and styles that resonate most deeply with you.

Attunement is easier when you don't do it all alone. Storytelling is a social practice, and it's much more fun to attune your storytelling sensibilities with other people, discussing the elements of storytelling that made something resonate with you. Sedaris went to every reading he could find. Glass surrounded himself with mentors and colleagues at NPR. Tarantino spent every day discussing film with his co-worker Avary. Every great storytelling movement has been positively influenced by community—from the modernists gathered in Paris cafes in the 1920s to the Beat poets of the 1950s to the first-person blogging revolution of the 2000s, which took root both in media capitals like New York City but also in digital communities, forums, and comment sections. Community feels harder than ever to find in the digital age, where people across generations go out less, throw fewer parties, and have fewer friends. But it's still there if you look for it—join a book club or film club; sign up for a weekly writing workshop. Can you do this with AI too? Sure, it can be a useful tool for sussing out what you like best, but there's a particular magic that comes from attuning with other humans.[3]

Study the masters

When Benjamin Franklin was a teenager, he was a mediocre writer, but he knew what he loved: *The Spectator*, a British culture and politics magazine. He studied the magazine's essays

---

3   Head to joelazer.com/superskill for more on where to find these—as well as virtual and in-person storytelling events I'll be hosting personally.

obsessively and designed a system for learning their secrets. He'd take notes on each sentence, leaving himself hints. Then, a few days later, he'd attempt to reconstruct the piece from memory—noting where he fell short. Over time, he made the exercise increasingly difficult. Sometimes he'd jumble the hints. Other times, he'd turn the essay into a poem. Steadily, he improved, mastering both the flow and narrative structure of his idols. Before long, he found that he'd even managed to make some improvements. As he wrote in his autobiography:

> By comparing my work afterwards with the original, I discovered many faults and amended them; but I sometimes had the pleasure of fancying that, in certain particulars of small import, I had been lucky enough to improve upon the method or the language, and this encouraged me to think I might possibly in time become a tolerable English writer.

"A tolerable English writer." You could say that. Franklin would go on to become the most influential writer and publisher of his day and a Founding Father of America.

Franklin's method is one we can all learn from. (Although we don't have to take it quite to the extreme he did—that man was built different.) Once you start to attune your taste and recognize and note the storytellers and artists you like, study the hell out of them and try to mimic their work. Ira Glass's taste for narrative journalism that told the stories of ordinary people started with his initial work at NPR with Joe Frank. As Glass went to work for Keith Talbot, the NPR producer tasked with finding new ways to do a radio documentary, his education deepened. Glass studied the work of Studs Terkel, the legendary, Pulitzer Prize–winning writer and broadcaster, who told the stories of celebrities and ordinary people alike on his radio show in the 1950s and '60s. Glass admired and studied Joan Didion too.

Didion pioneered the New Journalism movement of the 1960s and '70s, which melded journalism with literary nonfiction, bringing the author's subjective experience into the story. Over the first decade of his career, Glass strove to mimic the work of these giants, failing at first but then succeeding wildly with *This American Life*.

You can see Didion's fingerprints all over *This American Life*—from the scene-by-scene construction of stories, to the first-person narration, to the deeply immersive reporting, like 2013's Peabody Award–winning two-part episode "Harper High School." *This American Life* embedded three reporters at a Chicago high school for five months, where twenty-nine recent or current students had been shot in the past year. The episode drove more than $250,000 in donations from listeners and even prompted a visit from First Lady Michelle Obama.

David Sedaris wasn't a big reader growing up; he wanted to be a visual artist but had no talent for drawing, no matter how hard he tried. When he got to college, he tried his hand at experimental theater before dropping out. Afterward he lived in a small town in Oregon in a trailer with no friends, so he went to the public library and got a library card. He started by reading all the books he was supposed to read in high school, starting with *Babbit* by Sinclair Lewis. When he found a book he liked, he'd see who blurbed their book, and then read their books. Which led him to Raymond Carver.

Carver made Sedaris think that he too could be a writer. Sedaris felt like he knew the people Carver chronicled. They resembled the ordinary people in Sedaris's own life. He wrote in simple sentences, and Sedaris thought, I can do that.

As I've said, I learned to write by obsessively imitating Sedaris. As it turns out, Sedaris did the same thing with Carver. When Sedaris returned to college years later, he wrote a short story called *The Atlas*. His professor awarded a small grant to turn Sedaris's story into a small, thirty-page, small press book—mistakenly thinking Sedaris's story was a brilliant parody of Raymond Carver.

There are enough examples like this to fill an entire library: Ernest Hemingway fastidiously studied Mark Twain; Toni Morrison studied Jane Austen and Leo Tolstoy; Taylor Swift studied Joni Mitchell and Tim McGraw (so much so that her 2006 debut single was named after him). Steve Jobs—the greatest business storyteller of all time—drew inspiration from Bob Dylan, Pablo Picasso, and Socrates, telling *Newsweek* that he "would trade all my technology for an afternoon with Socrates."

Once you discover the storytellers and thinkers you love, study their work. Mimic it. It won't just hone your taste. It's also a hell of a lot of fun.

Try and fail

The only way to truly pressure-test and refine your taste is to go out and start telling stories. Perhaps you'll be one of the lucky few prodigies who find instant success; more likely, you are going to fail. And that is exactly what you should be doing.

Despite what LinkedIn influencers say, there's no shortcut to storytelling success. Sedaris wrote every day for fifteen years before his first book was published. Even when he won that small grant for his short story in college, it was only because his professor thought he was deliberately parodying Carver. In reality, Sedaris was just trying to do his best at writing a short story.

In the late 1980s, Tarantino spent three years making a movie called *My Best Friend's Birthday* that went nowhere, but the process refined his taste and sense of storytelling. "I was very disappointed when I realized it wasn't any good. But it was my film school—and I actually got away really cheap. When it was all over, I knew how to make a movie," he said at ComicCon in

2006. He went on to make *Reservoir Dogs* and *Pulp Fiction* in the years that followed.

And as Glass explained, doing the work is the only way to close the taste-talent gap:

> Do a huge volume of work. Put yourself on a deadline so that every week or every month, you know you're gonna finish one story. 'Cause it's only by actually going through a volume of work that you're actually going to catch up and close that gap, and the work you're making will be as good as your ambitions. In my case, I took longer to figure out how to do this than anybody I've ever met. It takes a while. It's gonna take you a while. It's normal to take a while, and you just have to fight your way through that.

This is one of the hardest aspects of storytelling to accept in an instant gratification world, where we're faced with nonstop peer pressure in our feeds from chest-puffing grifters touting their success. Failure is inevitable, and it's the most important part of the learning process. Don't let it dissuade you from maintaining your storytelling practice.

Whenever I'm feeling stuck, or discouraged by a newsletter or column that didn't resonate the way I hoped, I think of this quote by *Fahrenheit 451* author Ray Bradbury: "Write a short story every week. It's not possible to write 52 bad short stories in a row."

Embrace the gap

The simple truth is that the taste-talent gap never goes away, and I've come to think of it as a living thing, always there with me, pushing me forward.

For starters, your tastes change as you grow older; I loved the problematic frat bro tales of Tucker Max when I was in high school, but I haven't picked up his books in twenty years. I didn't touch a single pop business or narrative nonfiction book in college, but they're a big part of my diet today. And since ChatGPT, I find myself reading hard sci-fi[4] almost constantly. I love it, and it opens my mind to the possibilities of what's to come. I find myself constantly in awe of the work of the storytellers I love—from Sedaris to *Succession* showrunner Jesse Armstrong to (*braces for backlash*) Lena Dunham, whose show *Girls* captures the millennial experience with a deft touch that leaves me seething with envy through every rewatch. It's funny: writing this chapter made me realize that my taste is a little bit insane. Ira Glass, David Sedaris, Quentin Tarantino, Lena Dunham, Ben Franklin—what a crazy blunt rotation. And it's not something that any of the algorithms have ever come close to capturing. They might break if they tried.

My own taste-talent gap isn't as big as it used to be because I now know who I am and what I can accomplish, but it's still there, like an old friend. As storytellers, it pushes us to get a little bit better each day, allowing us to tell the kind of authentic, human stories that stand out in a sea of AI slop and algorithmic clickbait. It serves as a North Star to guide us—one we'll need as we unleash our storytelling superpowers and put them into action.

---

4   Science fiction that's scientifically accurate and draws on the hard sciences.

Part III:

UNLEASH

"The most powerful person in the world is the storyteller. The storyteller sets the vision, values, and agenda for an entire generation."

— Steve Jobs

Chapter 10

PRINCIPLE 7:
Identify Your Big Idea

On September 23, 1997, Steve Jobs took the stage in front of Apple's leadership. He wore his signature black turtleneck paired with short gray shorts and sandals. His thinning hair was messy, and he clutched a cup of coffee. He told the crowd he'd been up till 3 a.m. working on a big idea.

Everything was at stake. In an act of desperation, Apple CEO Gil Amelio had bought Jobs's computing company NeXT for $400 million, bringing back the exiled founder after twelve years away from Apple. Six weeks earlier, Jobs quickly staged a boardroom coup and seized the role of interim CEO, taking over a company on the brink of collapse, with only a few months of cash left in the bank. The clock was ticking. *Time* reported that there was "a literal deathwatch on Apple." Its market share had plummeted to less than 4 percent. Employees were skittish. When asked what he'd do with Apple if he were Jobs, rival CEO Michael Dell quipped, "I'd shut it all down and give the money back to shareholders."

Jobs needed to do something bold to turn the company around. You couldn't blame the employees gathered in front of him for wondering where it all went wrong. After all, they'd followed industry best practices, diversifying their product line across printers, handhelds, and myriad desktop and laptop models. Mimicking Microsoft's successful strategy of broad distribution, Apple had licensed its operating system to third-party manufacturers of "Mac clones."

Industry observers expected Jobs to accelerate the development of advanced products to appeal to business users and combat Apple's reputation as a "toy" for creatives and kids. Instead, he did the opposite.

Standing in front of Apple's leadership team, Jobs announced that they were slashing most of the company's initiatives. A few weeks earlier, when the product team briefed him on the company's long list of product initiatives, Jobs shouted, "Stop! This is crazy," and went up to a whiteboard and drew a 2x2 grid. On the top, he wrote Consumer and Pro. On the side were Desktop and Portable. Apple would simplify its product line to one product for each quadrant.

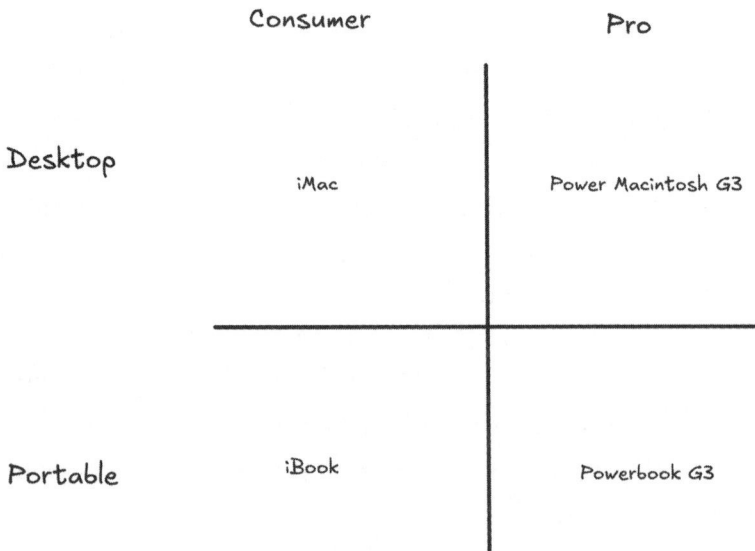

	Consumer	Pro
Desktop	iMac	Power Macintosh G3
Portable	iBook	Powerbook G3

"We're really thinking differently about the things we have to build," he told the assembled leaders. "I came out of a meeting with people who just got their projects canceled, and they were three feet off the ground because they finally understood where the heck we were going."

While most industry observers expected Apple to lay low and rebuild, Jobs announced they were launching their first big brand campaign in years, even though they weren't launching a new product. He'd brought in the agency responsible for Apple's iconic "1984" ad, Chiat/Day, and they weren't going to talk about features or technical specs.

"What we're about is not making boxes to get their jobs done, although we do that well," he said. "We do that better than anyone, in some cases. But Apple is about something more than that. Apple at its core—its core value—is that people with passion can change the world for the better."

The theme of the new campaign and TV ad? "Think Different," honoring "the people who think different and move this world forward." It read like a poem, narrated by Richard Dreyfuss, over black-and-white footage of legendary creative thinkers like Albert Einstein, Bob Dylan, John Lennon, Pablo Picasso. "Here's to the crazy ones," it began. "The misfits, the rebels, the troublemakers, the round pegs in square holes. The ones who see things differently. They're not fond of the rules."

Instead of running away from Apple's reputation as a toy for creatives, Jobs leaned into it. Instead of talking about features and specs, he emphasized Apple's values. When the ad aired, Apple's stock rose despite having no new products. Within twelve months, its stock price would triple—buoyed by the Emmy Award–winning spot, Jobs's financial turnaround of the company, and the bold introduction of the iMac in August 1998. Apple was back.

The power of a big idea

Few people know this, but Jobs secretly feared that the "Think Different" campaign would lead the press to skewer him as an egomaniac who'd gone off the rails. But he had the courage to trust his gut, buck the best practices advice, and come out swinging with a big idea.

If you want to be a great business storyteller and win people's attention and loyalty, you need a big idea—the bold, refreshing perspective you bring to the world. It's how you differentiate yourself to people inside your company and outside of it in the market. It's how you escape the hamster wheel of empty-calorie viral content and resonate deeply with their audience, sticking in their minds. It's inspired by your muse, informed by your taste, and born from your passion and conviction. A big idea is provocative and cuts against the grain, contrasting the best practices and conventional wisdom in your industry.

Jobs's big idea was that the way back for Apple wasn't to sell specs; it was to sell a worldview, framing Apple as the tool for creative nonconformists who move the world forward. He told a story that made people feel more creative just by placing their hands on an Apple product. That story remains at the heart of the Apple brand today. While they've introduced other brand campaigns since—like "I'm a Mac"—"Think Different" remains the tagline most associated with the brand today. Like all truly great big ideas, "Think Different" was built to last.

A big idea isn't only for legendary founders like Jobs or business writers like me. Today almost *everyone* needs a big idea, whether you're a writer, founder, or an operations manager. Work is changing rapidly. The era of the "company man" is dead. Across nearly all industries, the average tenure of employees has plummeted; in Big Tech, it's less than three years. An increasing number of workers are giving up full-time employment altogether to go freelance or "fractional," the post-pandemic term for executives selling pieces of their time to the highest bidder.

In this new age of work, most knowledge workers are free agents. Communicating what you stand for and building a loyal following is no longer optional; it's how you give yourself true career security, even if you work in finance or HR. In a world where job-hopping and fractional work are the most reliable ways to maximize your earnings, you need to consistently market yourself as a trusted voice in your field.

The big idea of my last book, *The Storytelling Edge*, was that great storytelling—not hyper-optimized performance marketing—was the most effective way to grow your business and transform your relationships with customers. It cut against the conventional wisdom of the marketing industry. It was an idea that resonated deeply with the founders, marketers, and creatives I wanted to reach. It had staying power, helping me grow Contently into one of the world's leading content technology companies and attract nearly 200,000 subscribers to my newsletter. My big idea in this book is that storytelling, not AI, will be the most important skill of the next age of work, and I plan to talk about that idea for years to come.

That's why Part III of this book—"Unleash"—starts here. We've learned how to unlock our innate storytelling superpowers, and now it's time to unleash them, using our storytelling skills to build a more successful and satisfying career.

Big ideas are finite. There are only so many great big ideas in your industry, and you want to lay claim to yours before someone else does. They're also powerful; AI can remix existing ideas in interesting ways, but it lacks the perspective and taste to truly develop something new. Your big idea is the foundation of your personal platform. It informs all the stories you tell. And it empowers you to stand out in a world of half-baked ideas and AI "workslop."

How to identify your big idea

Most content falls short for a simple reason: It's commoditized. Over the past decade, I've helped hundreds of founders and brands develop their content strategy, and I hear a few things repeatedly:

- "We want to start a podcast and interview leaders in our industry."
- "We want to create content like [X Competitor]—our agency created this spreadsheet of their most popular content, and we're using it to create our content calendar."
- "We had ChatGPT analyze top-performing LinkedIn posts so we can go viral."

A podcast in which you interview people in your industry is commoditized. Everyone has this idea, and there are already hundreds of versions of this podcast decaying in the dark corners of Spotify. Copycat content strategies are commoditized; anyone can do it, especially in the AI age. And commoditized content is destined to fail. If something works for your competitor, it's unlikely to work for you because you're not delivering any unique value to your target audience. Sure, you may be able to occasionally rack up likes by posting a meme or regurgitating the latest AI hype, but the impact will be superficial. If you want people to remember you, you need a big idea that resonates with people.

Big ideas don't come instantly, but there's a simple five-step process to develop and refine them:

1. **Passion (obsession):** What do you nerd out over at work?
2. **Lens (belief):** What truth in the world do you see that others miss?
3. **Promise (change):** What happens if we adopt your lens?
4. **Story (distillation):** The narrative that communicates your lens and promise.

5. **Tagline (hook)**: The pithy turn of phrase that makes your big idea sticky.

1. Passion

What really gets you going? What's the topic that you're excited to talk about at happy hour, even if it leads to eye rolls from friends?

For *Atomic Habits* author James Clear, whose work we explored in Principle 1, the topic was habits.[5] Clear is *obsessed* with habits, and that obsession led him to sell over 25 million copies of his book and spend over five years on the *New York Times* best-seller list.

Clear's obsession started as a teenager. During his sophomore year of high school, he suffered a horrific baseball injury when a teammate accidentally hit him in the face with a bat. His brain swelled. He stopped breathing, and doctors rushed to put him into a medically induced coma. Clear recovered—albeit with one eye bulging out of its socket for weeks—but his once-promising baseball career was in ruins. Before the injury, Clear had been a rising star; the following year, he couldn't even make varsity due to his slow recovery. During his senior year, he made varsity but barely played.

Once he got to Davidson College, Clear decided to fastidiously build excellent health and exercise habits so he could make the baseball team. It worked. By his senior season, he'd been selected to the ESPN Academic All-American Team. Clear loved his new habits so much that he started writing about them on his blog twice per week. For months, his audience grew slowly, but Clear kept at it, and before long, his newsletter took off—just three years later, his audience surpassed 200,000 subscribers, earning him his first book deal.

---

5 This is the type of incisive analysis you came here for.

To develop a big idea about something, you need to obsess over it—thinking, reading, writing, and talking about it constantly. Clear was able to develop his big idea—that the key to establishing lasting habits is to build an identity-based system, not chase goals—because he spent years thinking, reading, and writing about how to make good behaviors stick. Steve Jobs was able to co-create and evangelize "Think Different" because he was so passionate about personal computing and Apple's core value that "people with passion can change the world for the better." I developed my big idea for my last book because I'm bizarrely passionate about content marketing and the science of storytelling; I developed the big idea for this book because I'm obsessed with generative AI and how it will change the future of work. Passion alone won't gift you a big idea that resonates with people, but it's where you need to start.

Jay Acunzo is a keynote speaker, author, and speaking coach who helps entrepreneurs and business leaders develop their big ideas and IP. He told me that there are two ways to approach a big idea: outside in or inside out.

Most people take an outside-in approach. They say whatever they think people want them to say, chasing whatever gets the most likes. He advises his clients to start inside out, focusing on what they're most passionate about and uniquely qualified to say.

"When you're outside in, you end up looking and sounding like everybody else," he told me. "You commodify yourself, and so you have to race faster. Shout louder. Spend more."

So what is that topic for you? Typically, it will fall into one of a few categories:

- Your industry
- Your role
- A technology (where my work management software freaks at?)

- A professional skill (like leadership, storytelling, habits, creativity, or productivity)

Often, the best topics are an intersection of two or more of these categories. This book is about storytelling and AI. Clear wrote about habits through the lens of behavioral science. Sheryl Sandberg's *Lean In* focuses on leadership in technology. Seth Godin's books focus on creativity in marketing. The best big ideas come inside out, so focus on what gets you fired up.

2. Lens

What do you see that others miss? What assumptions do people in your field make that you know are wrong? This is your unique lens.

Your lens should be provocative and contrarian. If you want to capture your audience's attention, you need to surprise them and challenge their existing assumptions. You want them to stop and think, "Wait, why *do* I do that?" or "Wait, why *does* everyone say to do it that way?" You're establishing tension between the way things are and the way they could be.

Clear challenged the common assumption that the key to developing successful habits was to set goals; our graveyard of New Year's resolutions wasn't due to our willpower but our approach. Jobs challenged the best practices of the tech industry, focusing on values, not technical specs. The "Think Different" campaign was so striking because it depicted Apple computers as the tool of counter-culture rebellion, reminding people what they loved so much about the brand during the mid-1980s, when the "1984" Super Bowl commercial stunned audiences across the globe. I've made my career challenging the orthodoxy of the marketing industry, questioning best practices that overinflate the value of performance marketing and cheap SEO content, and undervalue the impact of storytelling and thought leadership.

It's earned me some snarky comments from self-titled "growth hackers" and a growing audience of thoughtful marketers and creators.

Once something becomes conventional wisdom, people are incredibly hesitant to challenge it. We're only a few years removed from many smart people in tech believing that digital cartoons of a "bored ape" were the future of currency and worth millions of dollars. Most marketers still believe in putting a form in front of every half-decent piece of content they create, even though they drive 90 percent of prospective buyers away. Most sales teams continue to hire twenty-three-year-olds to spam potential buyers with "outbound emails" even as conversion rates plummet. Startup founders and HR teams continue to hire for culture fit, even though research definitively shows that you need cognitive diversity and intellectual friction to spark innovation.

Your great opportunity is to challenge that conventional wisdom, something fewer people may do in the age of AI, since LLMs recycle established orthodoxy by default and can erode critical thinking. What are people in your industry getting wrong, and what price are they paying as a result? You need to capture their attention. Grab them with a relatable problem and novel lens. Keep them hooked by establishing tension and stakes. Make them think about their industry in a new way.

3. Promise

Next, what promise are you making to your audience? What will they accomplish if they adopt your lens?

Apple is built on a genius promise: If you use a Mac, you'll become more creative. In *Atomic Habits,* Clear promises that if you adopt his system, you'll build better habits and make tiny improvements that compound into remarkable results. The promise of my last book, *The Storytelling Edge*, is that if you invest in great content and storytelling, you'll grow your business faster than your competitors and develop lasting relationships with your customers. The promise of this book is that if you invest in your storytelling skills, you'll gain a huge advantage over people who follow conventional wisdom and only learn how to use AI. Examine every famous author with a big idea, and their work follows the lens-promise pattern:

Steven Pressfield (author of *The War of Art*)

- **Lens:** Resistance is the enemy of creative work.
- **Promise:** If you show up like a pro every day and fight through resistance, you'll break through your creative blocks and accomplish great things.

Cal Newport (author of *Slow Productivity*)

- **Lens:** Great accomplishments are made by people who optimize for accomplishments across three-to-five-year year time spans, not thirty-minute blocks.
- **Promise:** If you only focus on one or two projects at a time and create room for uninterrupted focus work, you'll accomplish much more in the long run.

Sheryl Sandberg (author of *Lean In*)

- **Lens:** Structural barriers matter, and so do the everyday choices women make in rooms of power.
- **Promise:** If you "sit at the table"—actively asserting your ideas with confidence—you'll increase your influence and expand what's possible for other women.

Angela Duckworth (author of *Grit*)

- **Lens:** Grit—the combination of passion and perseverance toward long-term goals—is more important than talent.

- **Promise:** If you cultivate grit, your skills will compound and you'll see results.

Business content is pretty simple: if you can help someone do their job better and get promoted, they'll love you forever. So what do you see that others don't? And what promise can you make (and keep) about what people will accomplish if they follow your advice?

4. Story

Most people focus on the pithy phrase that encapsulates a big idea. For Apple and Jobs, it was "Think Different." For Clear, "Tiny Changes, Remarkable Results." For Sandberg, "Lean In." But all of these thinkers start somewhere first: with a story.

The story is the delivery system for your big idea. It's how you get someone to buy into it. With the "Think Different" campaign, Apple told that story through a beautiful spot celebrating innovators throughout history. Clear opens *Atomic Habits* with the gripping tale of how he almost died from being hit in the face with a baseball bat, and how his transformative recovery taught him the magnificent power of compounding habits. In *Grit*, Angela Duckworth opens with the story of the grueling West Point Beast Barracks, which are designed to push cadets to their mental and physical limits, revealing how grit was a better predictor of cadet success than SAT scores or athletic ability. I began this book with the story of how my son was born at the same time as ChatGPT, sending me on a journey that ended with the discovery of my big idea: that storytelling will be the superpower of the AI Age. The best big idea stories follow our four elements of great storytelling explored in Principle 2 (RENT):

- **Relatability:** They're about a character your audience can relate to. Big idea books like *Atomic Habits* and *Grit* are designed to appeal to high achievers, and they almost always open with stories of high achievers. If your big idea is about how CFOs should operate differently, open with the story about a CFO.

- **Ease:** There's a strong hook and it's easy to understand. The lens is stated simply, and so is the promise.

- **Novelty:** The lens and story are original and unexpected. You're not just ripping off something that 1,000 other people in your field are saying on LinkedIn.

- **Tension:** There's a gap between what is and what could be for your audience. If they follow the advice you're giving, they'll succeed. If they don't, there's a potential cost.

5. Tagline

Once you find a story that communicates your promise and resonates with people, then it's time to focus on the pithy tagline or turn of phrase that your audience will repeat to others. Everyone wants to start here because it's the sexy part. It's what we see on book covers and billboards. But a tagline alone is hollow; without a story to seed it, it won't resonate.

You're likely going to need to test multiple lenses, promises, and stories before you find the one that sticks. You need to think about these steps as a feedback loop. Test them on different platforms. I'll often explore a new idea or framework as a LinkedIn post to gauge people's reaction. This is usually the roughest version of the idea; it's no big deal to me if a LinkedIn post flops, and the comments give me useful feedback. Then I'll turn it into a newsletter. If that newsletter gets a strong reaction, I'll turn it into a keynote speech at a conference. If *that* hits, then it's worth considering turning it into a book. And if *that* really hits, then I'll consider making it my first tattoo.

Big Idea Testing Stages

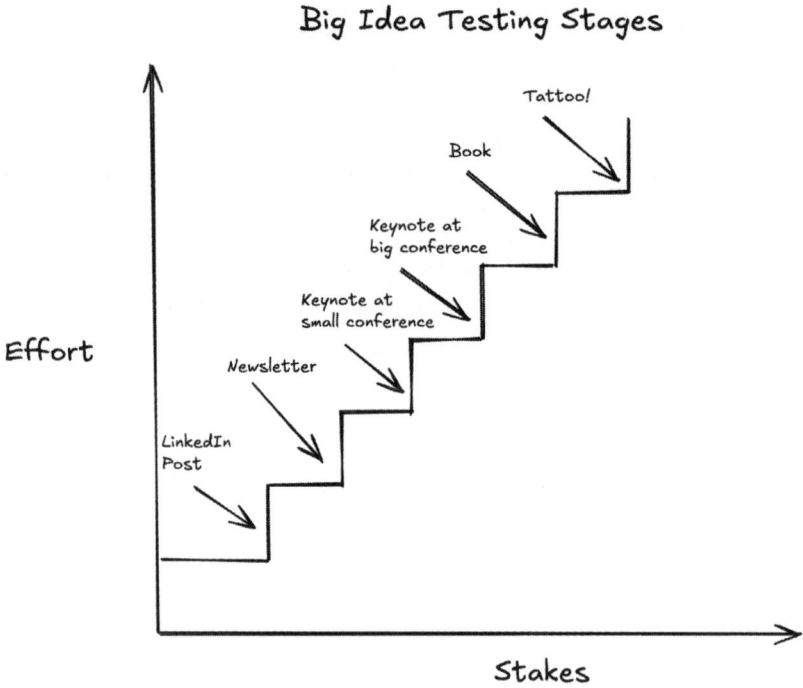

How do you know an idea is resonating with your audience? Acunzo, the speaking coach, has a six-point scoring system that I love:

No response (0 points): No response. Literal crickets.

Disagreement (1 point): The people who do respond in comments and email replies don't agree. You may just have the wrong audience, but there also may be something to learn.

General questions (2 points): People are showing interest and asking you to expand on your idea.

Passionate agreement (3 points): It hits! People love it. But they're not relating it back to their own life or a situation they're in.

Building on your ideas (4 points): People are "yes and"-ing you and crafting a thoughtful response.

Personal questions (5 points): People are asking you how you would apply your ideas to their situation. (This is my favorite type of email to get.)

Reflecting back on their own story (6 points): People relate to your idea so much that they tie it to a story of something that's going on in their life.

If you hit the disagreement and general questions stage, don't give up. This is useful feedback you can use to refine your ideas and try new angles and hooks. If you get to passionate agreement, you've hit on something big, but you may be able to go deeper. Once people start building on your ideas and relating it to their own lives, you have something powerful.

If you hit a wall, that's okay. There are more ideas in the sea. Go back to your passions and repeat the cycle.

Big Idea Feedback Cycle

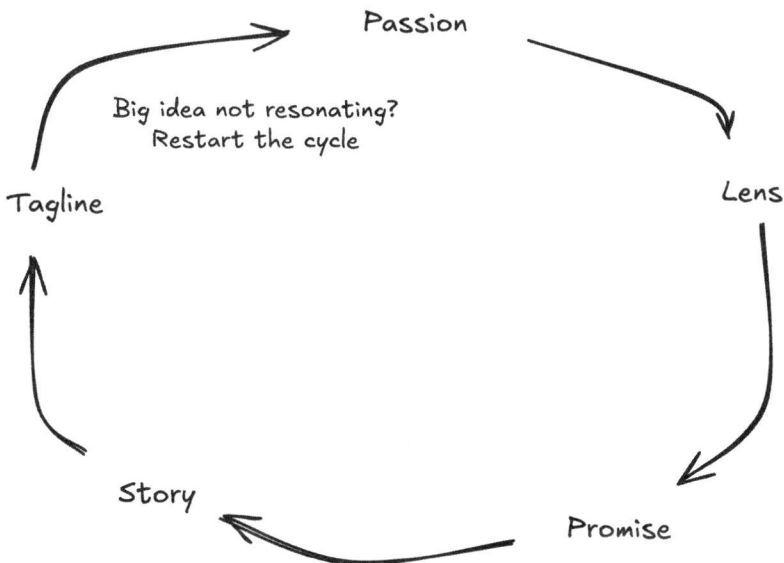

Make no mistake: Developing a big idea means being bold. Revealing your lens takes guts because it means pointing out what many leaders in your industry get wrong. But often, the most dangerous thing you can do is play it safe. As Jobs once told his team, "It's better to be a pirate than join the Navy." Your big idea is your black flag. The sign that you're not just following the fleet.

Chapter 11

PRINCIPLE 8:
Be Vulnerable

Lil' Kev the Bastard was doing everything he thought a successful comedian should do.

After graduating high school, he started performing at
Philadelphia's Laff House, imitating his favorite physical comedians—Chris Tucker and J.B. Smoove. His shows were painfully
inconsistent. Sometimes he got laughs; other times he bombed.
One time, a heckler threw a half-eaten chicken wing at his face.

"I was trying to be everybody," he told the *New York Times*
in a 2012 interview. "I didn't know what to do."

That's when a veteran comedian named Keith Robinson
approached him. Robinson had seen Lil' Kev's act several times,
but still didn't know much about him. "You need to draw your
comedy from you, so it sounds uniquely yours," Robinson
advised.

It was a turning point. Robinson became his mentor, and Lil'
Kev the Bastard began tapping into his own story and struggle,
like growing up with a father addicted to cocaine who did crazy

shit like steal a police dog. "I knew it was a police dog because he had canine on his vest. I saw it. At least take the vest off the dog, Dad. The dog is still on goddamn duty. He didn't even let the dog finish the job."

Lil' Kev the Bastard also ditched the stage name and started going by the name on his driver's license: Kevin Hart.

Before long, Hart's standup earned the attention of Judd Apatow, who cast him in the 2001 cult classic TV series *Undeclared*. Over the next three years, he landed roles in *Paper Soldiers*, *Scary Movie 3*, *Soul Plane*, and *In the Mix*. In 2009, he scored his first comedy special, *I'm a Grown Little Man*, but he really broke out with his 2011 comedy special *Laugh at My Pain*. It was independently produced yet broke into the box office Top 10, shocking industry analysts and earning almost $8 million. As the title suggests, Hart went deep. Hart told stories of his dad disrupting spelling bees, nearly letting him drown, and getting kicked out of the house by his mom. He turned dark memories into comedic gold. Afterward, he told the *Times* that his key to success was being candid about everything happening in his life, "Because of what I do, it has to be an open book. But that book is still being written."

The vulnerability loop

Hart rocketed to fame by leveraging one of the most powerful psychological principles in storytelling: the vulnerability loop.

Harvard professor of organizational behavior Jeffrey Polzer has spent his career studying team dynamics, and in the late 2000s, he discovered something surprising: Trust and connection develop in a counterintuitive way. Most people assume that once we trust someone, then we can open up to them. But Polzer's research showed the opposite. Trust is the byproduct of vulnerability.

Polzer coined this dynamic the "vulnerability loop."

1. Person A takes a small risk by sharing something vulnerable; they admit a mistake, express uncertainty, or tell a personal story about themselves.

2. Person B detects this signal and is compelled to reciprocate.

3. Person B reciprocates by signaling their vulnerability.

4. Person A detects this signal, and a new dynamic has been established.

5. Person A and Person B feel closer and trust each other more.

The Vulnerability Loop

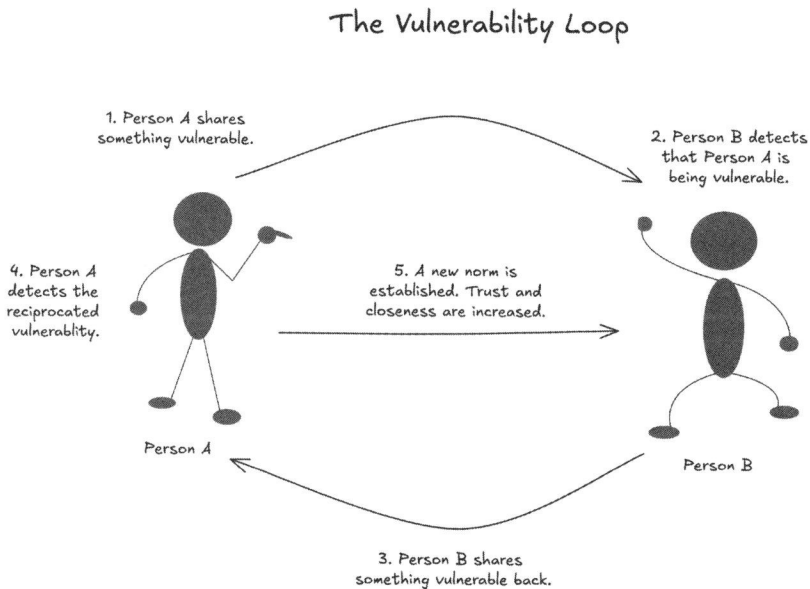

1. Person A shares something vulnerable.

2. Person B detects that Person A is being vulnerable.

4. Person A detects the reciprocated vulnerablity.

5. A new norm is established. Trust and closeness are increased.

Person A

Person B

3. Person B shares something vulnerable back.

As Daniel Coyle wrote in his best-selling book *The Culture Code*, "Vulnerability doesn't come after trust. It creates trust." And stories are the greatest delivery mechanism for vulnerability. When we share our mistakes, struggles, and uncertainties, listeners empathize, seeing themselves in our experience. Their oxytocin levels spike, and they become more generous and likely to reciprocate. When you tell a vulnerable story, you activate the neural coupling between you and the listener, creating a shared vulnerable state. When your audience laughs and nods with empathy, drops an encouraging comment, or shares a story of their own in kind, the loop closes, bringing you closer together.

For comedians like Hart, reciprocation comes in the form of the audience's response; they're engaged, laughing, and nodding, accepting Hart's stories of struggle. They come up to him afterward, expressing appreciation and offering vulnerable stories of their own.

This dynamic explains why, as we learned in chapter 1, storytellers are the most desirable mates and teammates in the tribe: People feel close to them. If you want to build deeper bonds with your team at work, there's no substitute for a great story.

In business, vulnerable storytelling is rare. Go on LinkedIn, and it feels like being stuck at a dinner party from hell. The table is filled with people who won't stop telling self-aggrandizing stories: awards they've won, deals they've closed, famous people they've met. Their stories aren't *stories*, exactly. They're a list of accomplishments that leave you sitting there, wondering if you could plausibly sneak out from the second-story bathroom window without breaking your ankle.

The most relatable stories don't hide our pain and flaws. They zoom in on the little mistakes that make us human, revealing how they made us grow. Without stumbles, success stories are insufferable.

In the AI age, truly human, vulnerable stories are increasingly rare. Two technological forces are pushing us away from them. The first is social media, which compels us to present a false, glossy version of our lives. The second is generative AI, which not only flattens our prose but is also inherently incapable of telling the kind of stories that connect with other people. When we fully outsource content creation to AI tools, we're also forgoing the chance to mine our personal experience and share something real. We're outsourcing all the little choices— word by word, detail by detail—that make storytelling and art meaningful. Truly human stories are AI proof. Even if AI gets ten times better at writing, it will never have the lived experience to connect with an audience. It won't know the trauma, joy, love, hate, and wonder that bind us.

AI can write, but it can never be a storyteller.

In this section of the book, we're learning how to unleash our storytelling superpowers in different contexts: in communicating our big idea (Principle 7), in leadership (Principle 9), and in marketing and sales (Principle 10). If we want those stories to break through, we need to learn how to embrace vulnerability. Anyone can talk about their accomplishments, but the stories we remember are the ones that reveal our humanity.

How to make your stories more vulnerable

On a sunny, unseasonably warm morning in October 2015, I was racing around the Bowery Hotel in Manhattan, putting the finishing touches on the most important event of my career.

Contently had just been named one of the Top 100 fastest-growing companies in the country. Below a blue blazer, sweat stained the armpits of my pink V-neck Contently T-shirt. We'd soon welcome 200 of the top CMOs, CEOs, and content leaders in the country for our annual Contently Summit, and everything had to go perfectly. We were at bar mitzvah levels of collective anxiety. No one had even seen the slides for our founder Shane's opening keynote, and ninety minutes before doors opened, he was still back in his apartment finishing it. In typical Contently fashion, we also threw in a curveball: We'd invited The Moth, New York City's famed oral storytelling group, to conduct a storytelling workshop. After all, our mission was to help brands tell great stories. Our homepage was just the words "Tell Great Stories" superimposed over a picture of Edgar Allan Poe wearing sunglasses, followed by two call-to-action buttons. (Marketers: you'd be *shocked* by how well this converted.)

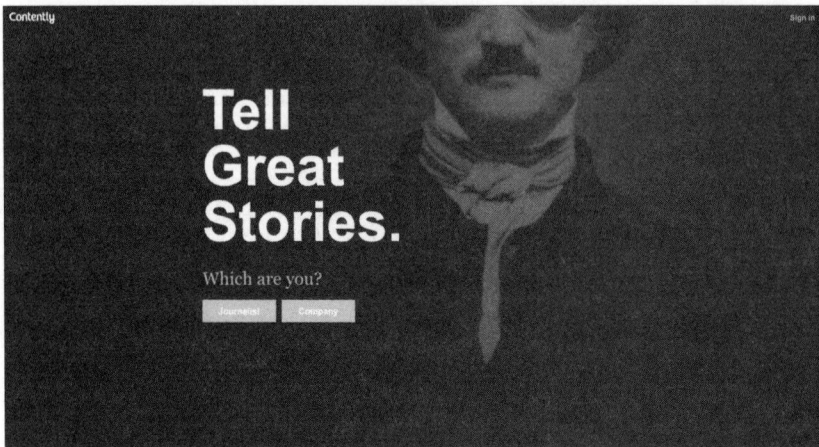

As the event started, things began to click into place. Shane, as usual, pulled off a brilliant last-minute keynote. I followed him, moderating a panel on content strategy in which I managed to keep my sweat stains hidden. Then it came time for The Moth.

The Moth's storytelling coaches took the stage and asked us to tweet an answer to a simple question with the hashtag #ContentlySummit.[6] "What's a time you tried to be something or someone you aren't?" I was riding high, the endorphins of a successful event pumping through my brain. So I dashed off a tweet: "When I lied about being a virgin and had to come clean #ContentlySummit."

I sat back in my seat. *That'll help encourage people to get in on the fun.* The Moth storytelling coaches flipped through the tweets on their phone, laughing. "Okay, this is the one," they said.

Minutes later, I was standing on stage holding a mic while they coached me through telling this story live. I'd forgotten my jacket. I prayed the sweat stains had dried because I could feel a small waterfall pooling on my forehead. Think about what led you to the particular moment you tweeted about, they told me. Why does it stand out to you?

---

6 Yes, hashtags were still a thing back then.

The mic shaking lightly in my hand, I launched into the story: I'd been permanently stuck in the friend zone in high school and, inspired by the movie *American Pie*, had been determined to lose my virginity before graduation, only to have a mild panic attack the one time things got close. Upon getting into college, I decided to reinvent myself as a hard-drinking writer and seasoned lover, and that's when I met my college girlfriend Hadley. The moment the words "seasoned lover" came out of my mouth, a little voice in my head screamed, *Get the hell off this stage before you get fired!* But then I looked at the crowd, and they were laughing and smiling, their eyes locked on me. They looked like they were having more fun than anyone I'd ever seen at a marketing conference. So I continued, regaling them with the various excuses I made to avoid revealing myself as a fraud. By the end, I was comfortably telling the CMO of Morgan Stanley how, actually, I *was not that bad* when I finally had sex for the first time. After I delivered the surprise ending where I came clean to the world in an essay for *Nerve*, the crowd erupted in ovation.

Walking off the stage, I was simultaneously elated and terrified. Had I really just told a story about losing my virginity to all our customers and prospects? And my co-workers? At the happy hour that followed, CMOs of our dream customers surrounded me, sharing stories of their college escapades. My boss just shook his head and laughed. It ended up being the highest ROI event we ever threw.

Look for the ouch

Afterward, I was struck by how The Moth's coaches had coaxed this story out of me in just a few minutes, although it helped that I'd written it down years earlier. Since being founded in 1997 by novelist George Dawes Green, The Moth has built one of New York's most famous storytelling institutions by helping everyday people tell incredible, vulnerable, deeply human stories that forge deep connections with their audience. The Moth believes that great stories aren't just wild party anecdotes, like the time you broke your ankle jumping off the roof into a swimming pool after prom, or opportunities to brag, like the time you won a Peabody and met Ezra Klein. They have stakes. They make people deeply worried and invested in you. And most important, they transform you. Before a Moth StorySlam, the coaches spend dozens of hours coaching people on how to craft their story, and they have a golden rule: Look for the ouch.

As the organization explains in its excellent guide, *How to Tell a Story*, the most authentic and memorable stories come from mining your personal experiences and finding the moments that changed you. Their favorite prompts ask you to think about a time when you:

- Did something you never thought you'd do
- Tried to be something or someone you aren't
- Made a tough choice for the right (or wrong) reason
- Changed your relationships with someone—for better or worse
- Had a secret revealed—by you or someone else

Now, I wouldn't advise that you necessarily follow my lead and tell a story about losing your virginity in front of your clients. The story has to fit the setting, and the New York tech scene in 2015 had a unique, adult summer camp kind of vibe. But mining your personal experiences will make your stories at work so much more powerful.

Take Brené Brown. In 2010, Brown was invited to give a talk at TEDxHouston. As a professor and researcher at the University of Houston, she was a veteran at giving talks on vulnerability. But this was TED. She wanted her talk to pop. So she decided to do something she'd spent most of her life avoiding.

She decided to be vulnerable.

Brown told the story of how she'd spent her early academic years in social work. For her entire career, she was surrounded by people whose motto was "Life's messy, love it," while her way of thinking was more "Life's messy, clean it up, organize it, put it into a bento box." She was the type of person who liked to be in control. To have everything in order.

Her experience in social work had taught her that the key to a positive human experience was connection. People who felt connected were happy; those who felt disconnected were unhappy. And as she started her big research project, she realized that there was a potent impediment to connection: shame.

Underpinning that shame was an excruciating sense of vulnerability—socially-disconnected people feared they weren't worthy of connection. This excited Brown. She *hated* feeling vulnerable. So what if you could control, or even eliminate, shame by controlling vulnerability? She vowed to science the shit out of vulnerability and understand how it works, outsmart it, and "beat it back with my measuring stick." If she was successful, she'd have found a solution for shame, and a path to greater human happiness.

Then she told the story of what happened next.[7]

She became obsessed with controlling vulnerability and shame. One year of research turned into six—"thousands of stories, hundreds of long interviews, focus groups." People were even sending her diary entries. She developed a theory on shame and published a book, but then realized that something wasn't sitting right. Deep down, she wasn't convinced by her own work.

So she went back to her research and reexamined the subjects who had a sense of worthiness and connection, contrasting them with those who did not. Then she realized something devastating: The key was vulnerability, but not in the way that she thought.

---

7 You can watch the full video of her talk at joelazer.com/superskill.

The people who felt a strong sense of love, belonging, and connection *embraced* vulnerability. "They believed that what made them vulnerable made them beautiful," she explained.

Vulnerability, the feeling she had loathed and avoided in her own life, was actually the key to happiness. This realization felt like a personal "betrayal." She had set out to control and predict vulnerability, and "had turned up the answer that the only way to live is with vulnerability and to stop controlling and predicting." Her worldview was shattered.

"This led to a little breakdown," she confessed. It was so upsetting that she spent a year in therapy and stopped her research. It was "a year-long street fight. It was a slugfest. Vulnerability pushed, I pushed back. I lost the fight, but probably won my life back."

After a year, Brown returned to her research. She realized she wasn't alone. That we all struggle with vulnerability. That you can't numb it because letting go of the fear of vulnerability and the desire for control is the best path to joy.

"Courage, the original definition of courage, when it first came into the English language—it's from the Latin word *cor*, meaning heart—and the original definition was to tell the story of who you are with your whole heart," she told the audience. "And so these folks had, very simply, the courage to be imperfect. They had the compassion to be kind to themselves first and then to others, because, as it turns out, we can't practice compassion with other people if we can't treat ourselves kindly."

The median TEDx talk gets fewer than 5,000 views. Brown's talk has been watched over 90 million times on YouTube and the TED site. TED ranks it as the second most popular talk of all time, only behind Simon Sinek's "Start With Why." Her career took off after the speech. She's now written five *New York Times*' #1 best-selling books. She became so famous that, in 2019, she even got a Netflix special.

Usually, when we give presentations about research or data, they're painfully dry. Brown shows us that with the right approach, a story about research can go viral if you make it human.

The key? She went into her talk with two intentions. First, she wanted to be vulnerable. "My experiment was: Let me just try being vulnerable while talking about vulnerability," Brown recalled on the *On Being* podcast. "Let me see what that's like." Second, as she began her talk, she introduced herself to the audience as a storyteller-researcher. "I am a storyteller. I'm a qualitative researcher. I collect stories; that's what I do . . . stories are just data with a soul."

Brown's story hooks the audience, and her vulnerability establishes trust and connection. She communicates her big idea by masterfully using all four elements of storytelling (RENT):

- **Relatability**: At the start of the talk, she tells a hilarious story about how people assume she's boring when they hear she's a researcher and immediately connects with the crowd. Throughout, she shares her discomfort with vulnerability, a feeling that everyone has experienced at some point in their lives.

- **Ease**: After her opening joke, she delivers a killer hook that teases the lens and promise of her big idea: "I want to talk to you and tell some stories about a piece of my research that fundamentally expanded my perception and really, actually changed the way I live and love and work and parent. And this is where my story starts." Who *doesn't* want to get better at living, loving, working, and parenting? I'm in.

- **Novelty**: Brown plays on the curiosity gap, constantly teasing the next breakthrough she'd discover as part of her research. She lets her audience know that they're about to discover something new and important, signaling that it's time to pay attention.

- **Tension:** Brown foreshadows that her quest to "beat back vulnerability with a stick" won't go well, establishing a constant state of tension. And when she experiences her breakdown, the tension gap widens. The audience yearns to know how she'll recover.

Brown's story also follows Vonnegut's classic Boy Meets Girl arc. (Which, again, can be used for much more than heteronormative rom-coms!) She experiences some initial success in her research, but then has a total breakdown. After a year of therapy, she climbs out of the hole—becoming fully transformed as she faces her greatest fear by being completely vulnerable on the TEDx stage.

Boy Meets Girl Arc: Brené Brown Ted Talk

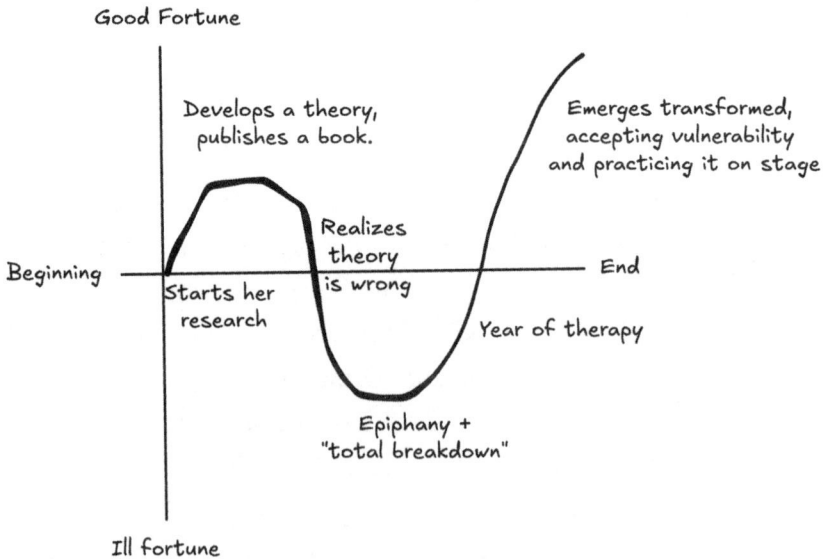

Good Fortune

Develops a theory, publishes a book.

Emerges transformed, accepting vulnerability and practicing it on stage

Beginning

Starts her research

Realizes theory is wrong

End

Year of therapy

Epiphany + "total breakdown"

Ill fortune

Vulnerability and voice

One of the fantastic effects of embracing vulnerability is that it allows you to locate that elusive entity content strategists talk about constantly but rarely capture: your voice.

This is the magic of The Moth's process. When you strip away the bullshit and reveal your true self, it's hard not to find your voice. When you find humor in the most vulnerable moments in your life, the most human version of you shines through. It's the kind of thing AI can never do.

Watch Brown's talk, and you immediately root for her because of her unique voice. When most people detail the background of their careers, you tune out. When Brown does it, she uses self-deprecation to pull you in. You get an immediate sense of who she is and want to learn more.

The same goes for Kevin Hart; watch his standup, and his voice shines through most in those vulnerable stories of his childhood. When Hart tells the hilarious story of his dad arriving coked-up to a spelling bee, that's a joke only he could do. And it's unmistakingly *him*.

If you want to find your voice, embrace vulnerability—and make fun of yourself a little bit along the way.

Vulnerability at work

When practicing vulnerability in your business storytelling, you need to use all of the tools you've developed.

You need to leverage the four elements of great storytelling to hook your audience, and the shapes of stories to craft a compelling tale. You also need to call on your muse. Doing so is relatively simple if you're crafting a story for an audience of one, like a direct report or boss with whom you want to build trust. Your muse is the person you're trying to connect with. But it's tricker when, like Brown, you're telling a vulnerable story to a larger audience, either on stage or in your newsletter or on TikTok or LinkedIn. Don't think of the crowd. Think of the one person you create for. What would you like to share with them? What stories would help them trust your perspective and intentions?

Finally, you need to unleash your taste. Study the storytellers you love the most. How are they most vulnerable? From the time I published my first essays in *Nerve* for the world to see, I always took inspiration from Sedaris. I was awed by his ability to turn the biggest embarrassments and failures of his life into hilarious and poignant stories. "The most embarrassing thing that you can mention is usually the one most people can relate to," Sedaris told *Time*, "and if something embarrassing happened to you, chances are it happened to a lot of other people."

Chapter 12

PRINCIPLE 9:
Lead Through Stories

On April 7, 2025, Fiverr CEO Micha Kaufman fired off an email to the company's 5,000+ employees worldwide.

"So here is the unpleasant truth," he wrote. "AI is coming for your jobs. Heck, it's coming for my job too. This is a wake-up call. It does not matter if you are a programmer, designer, product manager, data scientist, lawyer, customer support rep, sales person, or finance person—AI is coming for you."

Kaufman proudly posted the memo on LinkedIn and Twitter, going semi-viral. In the process, he sparked a trend: Suddenly, CEOs from Duolingo, Zapier, Box, and others went to LinkedIn and X to share the urgent, doomsday AI memos that they, too, had sent to their employees.

These memos were great for LinkedIn engagement. But as a leadership strategy? They were the perfect case study in what *not* to do.

The CEOs were using what my friend Shane Snow, best-selling author of *Dream Teams*, calls the "Get onboard or get off the ship" approach to change. The issue? Most employees will choose to get the hell off.

Today, most companies are in a crisis of culture and belief. Across industries, job tenures are shorter than ever, falling by 15 percent over the past decade for almost every age and demographic group. In many big tech companies, the average employee lasts less than two years. According to Gallup's State of the Global Workforce report, the percentage of engaged employees in the United States and Canada dropped to just 31 percent in 2024, with 50 percent saying that they're actively looking to leave. A separate Gallup study found that just 40 percent of employees agree with the statement, "The mission or purpose of my company makes me feel like my job is important," and just two in ten feel connected to their company's culture.

The consequences of unengaged and disconnected employees are dire: lower engagement, greater absenteeism, and lower quality of work. But if you can get your team to buy into a shared mission and story, the upside is massive. A Korn Ferry study found that companies that focused employees on the organization's purpose and mission had an annual growth rate three times higher than the average company in their sector.

So how do you do that? As Snow advises, you need to create a shared history among your team and make them feel like they're part of the same tribe, working toward a common goal. And a surly coach who changed his stripes can show us how to do just that.

Jerome's last run

On December 4, 2005, the Pittsburgh Steelers trudged off their home field demoralized. This one hurt. They'd lost 38–31 to the archrival Cincinnati Bengals, their third straight loss. As the Steelers entered the tunnel to the locker room, they watched Bengals players shining their shoes with the Steelers' famed Terrible Towels, which fans typically waved and whipped in celebration. But there was nothing to celebrate here.

The Steelers had begun the season as Super Bowl favorites behind a stifling defense, long-serving coach Bill Cowher, breakout star quarterback "Big Ben" Roethlisberger, and a pounding rushing attack led by running back Jerome "the Bus" Bettis. But now, the season was slipping away.

As the players entered the team meeting room the next day, a whiteboard stood at the front where Cowher tracked the team's goals, stats, and progress throughout the season. It was a hallmark of Cowher's analytical approach, something he'd done for ten years. Cowher grabbed an eraser and wiped the board clean. The players were shocked. In its place, he wrote one word: Chicago.

"Chicago. This is it," Cowher said. Alongside team leaders like Ben Roethlisberger, Cowher began to rally the team with a story. Each game would be one stop on an epic journey to drive "the Bus" home.

Jerome "The Bus" Bettis was a Steelers legend—a bowling ball with a beer belly and ballerina feet destined for the Hall of Fame. At thirty-three, Bettis had lasted years longer than most running backs, who usually exit the league before their thirtieth birthday thanks to the brutal pounding they took rushing the ball. After the New England Patriots had defeated the Steelers in the AFC Championship Game the previous season, Bettis had planned to retire, but Roethlisberger implored him to come back. "Give me one more chance, I promise I'll get you to the Super Bowl."

Poetically, that year's Super Bowl was in Bettis's hometown of Detroit. So Cowher and Roethlisberger developed a fresh story to rally the team and keep everyone focused on each game in front of them. Their mission was to give Bettis his fairy-tale ending, hoisting the Lombardi championship trophy in his hometown. To do that, they needed to win eight straight games—the last four games of the regular season to make the playoffs, and then four more games in the playoffs. They'd focus on one battle at a time. Their journey started in Chicago.

In Chicago, the Steelers looked like a different team. They faced the NFC North-leading Chicago Bears, led by one of the greatest defenses of all-time. Bettis had taken a supporting role earlier that year to rising-star running back Willie Parker, but in the snow Cowher put the "snow tires" on Bettis and he plowed over the Bears for over 100 second-half rushing yards to secure a 21–9 victory.

The team began to believe. "That's all we talked about, taking it home for Jerome," Parker, Bettis's backfield mate, recalled. "Ben [Roethlisberger] used to reiterate it in the huddle. We would talk about it in practices. That put the team on one goal. We had blinders on. We were going to send him out right. No matter what it took, we were going to get the job done for Jerome. Everyone bought into that."

The players were also surprised by the change in Cowher. In his fourteenth season as the Steelers coach, he was nicknamed "The Chin" for his abrasive, no-nonsense approach, epitomized by his jutting jaw clenched in fierce tension. He'd reached the AFC championship game five times, losing all but one of them. He still hadn't won a Super Bowl. Despite Cowher's overall success, some fans in Pittsburgh were calling for his job, convinced he could never win the big one. Players joked about how he recycled the same two or three stories over and over. He was typically more fixated on his metric-filled whiteboard. But the meticulous control freak surprised everyone by wiping that whiteboard clean and embracing a fairy-tale narrative to motivate his team. He'd also decided to let go in another way: He gave full control of the offense to offensive coordinator Ken Whisenhunt, letting him call whatever plays he wanted.

It worked. Determined to bring Bettis home, the Steelers made the playoffs by winning their last three games by the combined score of 94–24. They earned the final playoff spot, the cursed six-seed. No six-seed had ever made the Super Bowl, as it required winning three straight games on the road. The Steelers were undaunted; they had a mission to bring Bettis home.

In the first round, they got revenge, pummeling the Bengal rivals 31–17. After the game, Roethlisberger handed Bettis the game ball. "We're one step closer."

The following game, they traveled to Indianapolis to play the Colts, led by future Hall of Fame quarterback Peyton Manning. The Steelers entered the arena as massive underdogs. Manning and the Colts had been unstoppable that season. They'd won thirteen straight games to start the season before resting their starters for the final month.

The Steelers shocked the world, taking a 21–3 lead, but late in the game, Manning charged back, cutting the lead to a field goal. Nursing that three-point lead late in the game, Bettis fumbled just as he was rumbling in for a game-clinching touchdown. The Colts' Nick Harper scooped the ball and began racing the other way. If he scored, the Steelers season was over. The only person between him and the end zone was Roethlisberger. All he could think was that he couldn't let Jerome go out that way. It pushed the lumbering 6'5" quarterback just a little bit harder; he spun around and snagged Harper's ankle, yanking him to the ground. The Steelers defense held, forcing a missed field goal. After the game, Roethlisberger handed Bettis the game ball yet again. "We're one step closer!" he repeated.

Suddenly, the Steelers were on the brink of making history as they traveled to play the Broncos in Denver for the AFC Championship Game. The stakes were high for Cowher. He couldn't lose a fifth AFC Championship game. He'd go down as a choke artist. So he had a decision to make. He could give his usual no-nonsense pep talk. Or he could cede the floor to Bettis. Over the previous weeks, he'd barely had to reinforce the story of the journey the team was on together to bring Bettis home. They were telling it to each other constantly. Cowher followed his gut.

The room grew quiet. Bettis stepped forward and delivered an impassioned speech, imploring them to finish their journey. "Just get me to Detroit! Just get me to Detroit!"

Steelers players were choked up and fired up. The Broncos never had a prayer. As the clock ticked down on a Steelers blow-out victory, Cowher embraced Bettis, declaring, "You're going home!" Steelers players then surrounded their beloved teammate, chanting, "We're taking him home!"

When the team arrived for their flight to Detroit to play the NFC Champion Seattle Seahawks, Cowher arranged with team leader Joey Porter for the entire team to wear Bettis's No. 6 Notre Dame college jersey as a tribute. As they lined up in the tunnel to be introduced before the game, Porter turned to Bettis and said, "JB, lead us out there." Bettis entered the arena, letting out a primal scream. The team followed.

Midway through the fourth quarter, the Steelers clung to a 14–10 lead near midfield. Roethlisberger tossed the ball to running back Willie Parker, who flipped it back to wide receiver Antwaan Randle El for a reverse. Then Randle El pulled up and launched the ball toward the end zone, into the arms of wide receiver Hines Ward for a forty-three-yard touchdown. Players were shocked that Cowher had let Whisenhunt run a trick play in the biggest game of his career. "He always said, 'If you need to trick 'em, you can't beat him!" Bettis later recalled. But on the journey to Detroit, Coach Cowher had changed. The Steelers held on to win 21–10. As the Steelers accepted the Lombardi Trophy on stage after the game, Bettis tearfully announced his retirement, declaring, "The Bus's last ride is here in Detroit."

Cowher and Bettis led the Steelers to an unprecedented Super Bowl victory because they knew something all great leaders know: If you want to rally a team to take on a monumental task and beat the odds, you need to tell a story of their journey together.

There's something magical about telling this kind of story. Rah-rah inspirational stories have the power to motivate, but the real power comes when an entire team or society internalizes the narrative, telling it to each other. This narrative technique has been one of humanity's greatest leadership tactics for millennia, from early hunter-gatherer tribes to top sports franchises and Fortune 500 companies today.

As we explored in chapter 1, the leaders of early hunter-gatherer tribes used similar storytelling tactics to form cohesive tribes, regulate behavior, and inspire people to work together. It's what allowed us to survive the Ice Age while the Neanderthals went extinct. As we learned in Principle 2, a shared story literally synchronizes our minds through neural coupling. When this happens, researchers have found that we're more focused and learn and communicate better, a crucial trait for a team like the Pittsburgh Steelers, which needed to learn and execute complex game plans as one synchronized unit. Not surprisingly, researchers have also found that teams whose brains are in sync outperform the average team on problem-solving tasks.

If you want to inspire your team and get them to collaborate better, craft a narrative of the journey you're going on together. Inspire them to internalize it, telling it to each other, even when you're not in the room. And luckily, there's a simple framework to help us do that, which comes from another one of Steve Jobs's creations: Pixar.

Find your spine

In 1997, Rebecca Stockley had possibly the coolest job in the world: "Improvisation Consultant" at Pixar. One day, she took an improv class with teacher Kenn Adams, who introduced his students to a simple structure he'd created to simplify the storytelling process. He called it the Story Spine.

Beginning
1. Once upon a time . . . (the setting or shared world)
2. Every day . . . (the routine)

Event
3. But one day . . . (break to the routine or status quo)

Consequences

4. Because of that . . . (consequences)

Climax

5. Until finally . . . (climax / big reveal)

End

6. And ever since then . . . (transformation)

7. And the moral of the story is . . . (lesson / new reality)

Stockley fell in love with Adams's Story Spine and began teaching it to the studio's writers and directors at an improv class she hosted at the company headquarters. Before long, the Story Spine became the backbone of Pixar's approach to storytelling, empowering the studio to build on the smash success of its debut film, *Toy Story*. Its next eight movies?

- *A Bug's Life*
- *Toy Story 2*
- *Finding Nemo*
- *The Incredibles*
- *Cars*
- *Ratatouille*
- *WALL-E*
- *Up*

As the father of a toddler, let me assure you: All of these movies are *excellent*.

Pixar's Story Spine is a more detailed variation of Vonnegut's "Man in a Hole" arc, and I've found it immensely useful in telling leadership stories. That's because it's more prescriptive than "Man in a Hole," with seven detailed steps that usher a team into a shared journey, showing how you'll overcome adversity together and transform for the better.

At Contently, I used Pixar's Story Spine when I was asked to lead a large team whose manager had just been fired. The team was fractured and fighting, and I needed to remind them of their shared history and create excitement for the future. During the height of COVID, I used Story Spine to help our CEO tell the story of how we'd get through a devastating time for our business. At A.Team, I used it to sell my team on a strategic pivot after our biggest customer segment—startups—collapsed amid the 2022 VC-funding apocalypse. If you think back to Principle 7, it's what Jobs did at Apple too. Before he unveiled his big idea to the world with the "Think Different" campaign, he inspired his employees with the story about where Apple began—where they were going next.

The Leadership Story Spine

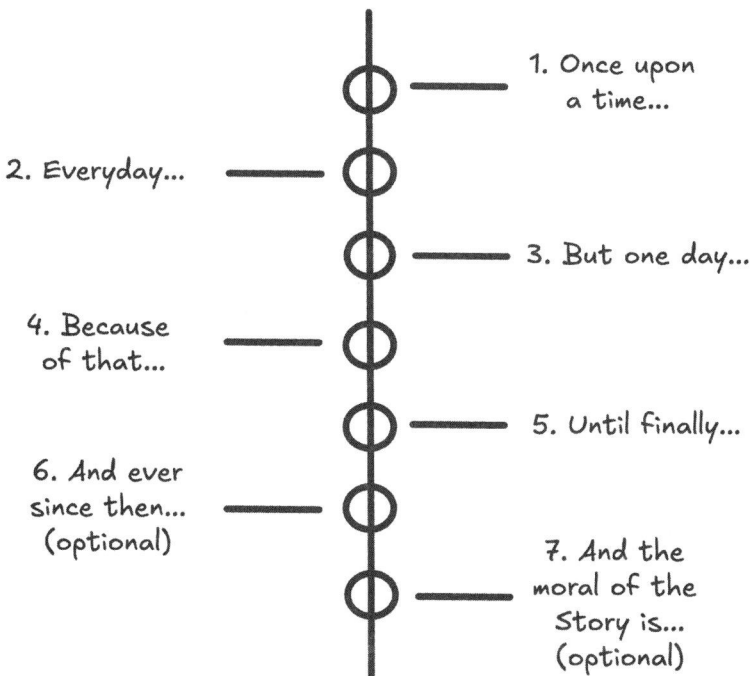

1. Once upon a time...

2. Everyday...

3. But one day...

4. Because of that...

5. Until finally...

6. And ever since then... (optional)

7. And the moral of the story is... (optional)

Beginning

1. Once upon a time . . . (shared world)

2. Every day . . . (the routine or context)

Begin by reminding your team of the shared journey that you've been on so far. In Jobs's speech to Apple employees before introducing the "Think Different" campaign, he reminded them of Apple's early days and legacy as "one of the half-a-dozen best brands in the world . . . right up there with Nike, Disney, Coke, Sony." Coach Cowher would constantly remind the Steelers of their shared goal of winning a championship together. In the early days of Contently, cofounder Shane Snow would start any presentation about a big change at the company by reminding us of our founding story and mission. Telling this shared story establishes relatability. Let your team see themselves in you. Make them feel like you're all on the same team.

In the case of the CEOs telling their employees that "AI is coming for you," I would have advised them to begin with the story of how they'd evolved to the company they are today, instead of just launching into a terrifying ultimatum.

Event

3. But one day . . . (the break to the routine or status quo)

Once you establish the status quo, introduce the event that's breaking it—hooking your audience with tension.

For Cowher and the Steelers, it was the fact that their mid-season losing streak had put them in a hole, and they now needed to fight against the odds. For Apple and Jobs, it was the fact that the brand had "suffered from neglect."

If I were one of those CEOs talking to my team about AI, I would have talked about how AI is changing the industry, in a calm and non-hyperbolic way. When I began introducing AI to my team, we discussed the ways it had the potential to impact our day-to-day marketing work, and the use cases that could alleviate the "constantly overworked and overwhelmed" feeling that most startup employees have. It's mind-boggling that so many CEOs frame AI not as an opportunity but a direct threat.

For you, maybe the event is a change in the market that presents the opportunity for a strategic pivot. Instead of demanding a change in direction off the bat, present the event as a natural evolution in your shared story.

Consequences

4. Because of that . . . (consequences)

Next, show what's happening or will happen as a consequence of that event.

This is where Cowher introduced the journey to drive "The Bus" home to Detroit. They'd need to focus on one game at a time, playing it like it was their last. Because if they lost, it *would* be Bettis's last.

Jobs's message was simple: Apple needed to bring the brand back from the brink. They'd do that by hiring the agency that had made them famous, Chiat/Day, and returning to their core value: the belief that "people with passion can change the world for the better."

In your story, this is where you illuminate the path forward. What changes will you make because of the event that's changing the status quo? How will you get through this together?

In Fiverr CEO Michael Kaufman's memo, he provided seven tips for adapting to AI, but those tips put all the onus on employees without offering any help and support. "Stop waiting for the world or your place of work to hand you opportunities to learn and grow—create those opportunities for yourself," he wrote.

This part of the story needs to show the journey you're going to go on together as a team, not leave people alone on an island.

Climax

5. Until finally . . . (climax / big reveal)

Once you lay out the consequences, present the big reveal: the new reality you'll create together.

For Coach Cowher, this was the moment the Steelers would take Bettis home and raise the Lombardi Trophy. For Jobs, it was the "Think Different" campaign, which promised to restore Apple to its rebellious glory days, the pirate flag raised over the headquarters once again.

This is where you present the promise of your big idea, the transformative end state that your plan will deliver. I'd advise CEOs to portray what the best-case scenario looks like with AI: a world where we spend our days engaged in strategic thinking and original storytelling, not spreadsheets. Where we do work that makes us proud and shapes our careers. Where we develop skills together that increase our value in the job market. Motivate, don't intimidate.

End

6. And ever since then . . . (transformation)

7. And the moral is . . .

These last two steps are optional, since ending on the climax can be a pretty badass move, but they present an opportunity to reinforce your message. How will your company be transformed moving forward? For Jobs and Apple, this was a return to a values-driven company that celebrates people who think different. For Coach Cowher, it was a team that would accomplish something no one had ever done before. Paint a vivid picture of what the future will look like and the lessons you'll have learned. In the case of the CEOs talking about AI, I'd depict a transformed state in which we have a leg up on the competition, work reasonable hours, all get fat bonuses, and have become a model in our industry for AI transformation.

Like any of Vonnegut's Shapes of Stories, the Story Spine is only a foundation. You still need to layer in the four elements of storytelling to win and keep your audience's attention, find your muse to develop empathy for your audience, use your taste to strengthen your story, and make it human with strategic moments of vulnerability.

Leadership isn't just for CEOs, politicians, and football coaches—we all need to lead, whether that's leading a small project team, rallying friends together for a good cause, or pitching an innovative new idea at work. From Cowher to Jobs, the best leaders are storytellers, and that's something that will never change. No matter how far technology advances, humanity will always need people who can rally us together.

Chapter 13

PRINCIPLE 10:
Sell Through Stories

If Sara Blakely bombed this meeting with Neiman Marcus, her dream was dead. And five minutes in, the Grim Reaper was at the door.

By day, Blakely was a door-to-door fax machine salesperson, which—yes—was a real job in the late 1990s. By night, she was an inventor. For over a week, Blakely had called a new product buyer at Neiman Marcus named Diane every few hours, hoping to get a chance to showcase her new invention: a twist on pantyhose.

Finally, Diane picked up. Blakely wasted no time. "I've invented a product that's going to change the way your customers wear clothes. And I'll fly to Dallas and show you."

Usually, people had to grind it out at tradeshows for years before they'd get a meeting at Neiman Marcus, but Blakely's confident pitch hooked Diane. She told Blakely that if she flew to Dallas, she'd give her ten minutes.

Blakely hopped on a flight from her home in Atlanta wearing her lucky red backpack—a beaten-up Eastpack that her friends begged her not to bring into *Neiman freaking Marcus*. But it was her lucky backpack. She wasn't going to the most important meeting of her life without it. Inside the backpack was a proto-type of her invention and a mockup of the bright red packaging, which featured an illustration of a fashionable blonde woman who resembled Blakely and the tagline, "Don't worry—we've got your butt covered."

As Blakely hustled into Diane's office, she was nervous. These ten minutes would determine the next ten years of her life. Five minutes in, she felt it. Years of selling fax machines had given her a spidey sense for when she was losing someone's attention. And she was losing Diane.

She had to act fast.

"Diane, you know what, I know it's a little weird, will you come with me to the bathroom?" Blakely asked in her charming Southern drawl.

Diane looked at her, bewildered. Was this random woman really asking her to go to the bathroom? Maybe she should have vetted this meeting a little more closely but . . . what the hell. "Uh"—Diane hesitated—"okay."

Diane followed her to the bathroom, and Blakely explained what she was going to do. She wanted Diane to take note of how she looked in her cream pants right now. Then, after she put on her invention, she wanted Diane to note the difference.

Diane waited outside the stall as Blakely shimmied out of her pants, wondering if she was being punked. Was Ashton Kutcher hiding somewhere? This was—without a doubt—the weirdest meeting of her life. But then Blakely opened the stall and stood in front of Diane, twirling to show off her sleek new form.

Then Sara Blakely told Diane the story of the cream pants.

Two years earlier, twenty-seven-year-old Sara Blakely was lost. She'd once dreamt of becoming a lawyer but failed the LSATs twice. So she operated rides at Disney World before taking a job selling fax machines door to door. It wasn't as fun as a theme park, but it paid more. She'd always imagined herself as a protagonist in a great adventure. Now, she was so depressed she'd drive around aimlessly, thinking, "What's happening? I'm in the wrong movie."

To cheer herself up, she bought a $78 pair of cream pants to wear with open-toed shoes to a party. The pants were an extravagance given her small salary, and when she tried them on, she was crushed. Panty lines ruined the look.

She could stay home or endure another night feeling like a character stuck in the wrong cinematic universe, but then she decided to try something. She grabbed a pair of control-top pantyhose and cut off the feet so she could wear them with pants and open-toed shoes. Like magic, the panty lines were gone. She looked slim and sleek. She felt incredible. And then she had an idea.

The footless pantyhose was far from perfect; the crotch was still uncomfortable, the frayed edges rolling up to her knees. What if she invented a new kind of shapewear that could work with any outfit and was way more comfortable than anything on the market?

For days, Blakely couldn't stop thinking about her concept. She had $5,000 in life savings. If she went all in, she might just be able to get a prototype made, but it was a big risk. So she asked the universe for a sign. When she turned on the TV, Oprah appeared, discussing how she had cut the feet off her pantyhose so she could wear pants and open-toed shoes. It was a sign from the heavens. If Oprah needs this, Blakely thought, then everyone needs this.

Blakely barely knew how to sew, but she stitched together a crude prototype. For two weeks, she went to the Georgia Tech library every day to research patents, until a merciful soul in the stacks told her she could search a government website instead—a novelty in the late '90s. No one had patented her idea. When a lawyer asked for her life savings to write the patent, she decided to do it herself. Her mom illustrated the design, which featured elastic cuffs that allowed the shapewear to work with any outfit, and a cotton-stitched crotch that was far more comfortable than the restrictive polyester of traditional pantyhose.

If she had any hope of selling her idea, she needed a real prototype. So she traveled to the pantyhose mecca of North Carolina to pitch butt-thinning, pantyline-eliminating shape-wear to manufacturers. She drove factory to factory, only to be dismissed by the bewildered old men who owned them. But she'd faced this before: As a fax machine salesperson, she'd reg-ularly watched people rip up her business card and call security on her. She knew how to deal with no. She just needed a yes.

That's when Sara Blakely met Sam Kaplan.

Kaplan wasn't a fashion visionary. He was the seventy-year-old owner of a hosiery factory called Highland Mills. He was a con-servative man not accustomed to taking risks, but he had daugh-ters, so he was kind to Blakely and heard her out. That night, he ran the idea by his daughters. It was a brilliant idea, they told him. Where could they buy it? That's all Kaplan needed to hear. The next day, he called Blakely and told her he'd make her prototype.

Blakely told this story to Diane as she stood outside the bathroom stall, like she was on an episode of *Shark Tank* spon-sored by Charmin. She stood tall, showcasing the sleek fit of her cream-colored pants, courtesy of her new invention.

Diane looked at the bright red packaging with sleek illustra-tions of a woman that vaguely resembled Blakely and consid-ered the catchy name: Spanx. There was a ring to it. She looked back up at this twenty-something fax machine salesperson with no track record in retail, who'd pulled her into the strangest meeting of her life. She considered the cream pants. How good Blakely looked. And the deeply relatable story she'd just heard.

Then Diane decided to make a big gamble. "I totally get it," she said. "Let's do it. Let's try Spanx in seven stores."

Twelve years later, when Blakely had turned Spanx into an empire and become the youngest female self-made billionaire in history, she reflected on the secret superpowers that propelled her to wild success: tenacity, perseverance, and, most important, her ability to connect with people through her story.

Blakely's storytelling superpower helped her every step of the way. Why did Sam Kaplan, the pantyhose manufacturer, decide to help Blakely out? Because her story stuck with him so much that he recounted it to his daughters over dinner. Why did Diane, the Neiman Marcus buyer, decide to greenlight a premium product from a young fax machine salesperson? The product made sense, sure, but the science of persuasion tells us the biggest factor was Blakely's vulnerable story, which ignited mirror neurons in Diane's brain and triggered a flood of oxytocin, creating an instant bond of trust.

And before long, Blakely's storytelling superpowers would help her reach millions.

On November 17, 2000, Sara Blakely was sitting in Spanx's headquarters—aka her two-bedroom apartment in Atlanta, Georgia—at a crossroads. Dozens of boxes were piled up in her living room, overflowing onto her front stoop. The Neiman Marcus deal was going well, thanks to Blakely's creative tactics. She'd personally worked the Spanx displays from opening to closing each day, and even set up an unauthorized display at the checkout to juice sales. She even paid off friends and family to buy pairs. However, competition was looming, and Blakely had no funds to advertise. Everything she made from Neiman Marcus had been reinvested back into production and paying her rent. Blakely needed a win, or else she'd be crushed by her corporate competitors, like so many challenger brands before her.

Blakely turned on the TV. A middle-aged man in a green elf costume dashed through the studio audience, handing out presents. The camera panned to the stage. There, again, was Oprah.

"Now my next favorite thing is a great invention," Oprah said. "It's the result of one woman's determination to make her dream come true."

Oprah cut to a pre-recorded segment. On the screen, Blakely watched herself strutting through a department store, wearing her cream pants and open-toed shoes. In a voiceover, she began to tell the story of the cream pants and how they inspired her to invent Spanx.

As Blakely's segment ended, the audience went wild for her underdog story. They eagerly snatched Spanx from the elves who dashed through the crowd. At that moment, it seemed like nothing could stop Spanx, anointed as one of Oprah's Favorite Things. But in a corporate headquarters in the suburbs of Chicago, executives at Sara Lee were plotting to crush Blakely and steal the market she'd created.

Sara Lee, owner of the Hanes and L'eggs brands, had 48 percent of the pantyhose market, but they were struggling. Sheer pantyhose and tights were in decline, down from 1.8 billion units in 1994 to 1.2 billion units in 2000, as the new millennium ushered in a trend toward bare legs, casual dress at work, and open-toed shoes—like the ones that inspired Blakely and Oprah to cut the feet off their pantyhose.

To Sara Lee, Spanx wasn't a threat. It was an opening. They'd leverage the second-comer advantage—a popular business school strategy in which a company capitalizes on the innovations of the "first mover" in a new market, avoiding initial missteps and costs. They'd undercut Spanx, which retailed at $20, and blow it out of the water with its advertising and distribution advantages. Sara Lee had billions at their disposal. Blakely had a two-bedroom apartment and a landlord pissed about her boxes creating a fire hazard.

Sara Lee began with a conventional, data-driven approach, conducting extensive market research into what women wanted from this new class of shapewear. They decided to launch a new product line, Barely There, to compete with Spanx, undercutting them on price. They'd also launch a line of bras and panties using the same technology. They lined up a celebrity spokesperson, Jennifer Love Hewitt, who was red hot after starring in *Party of Five* and *I Know What You Did Last Summer*, and planned a marketing blitz across TV, print, billboards, and online ads.

As Sara Lee launched the Barely There line in the spring of 2001, it seemed like the perfect plan. Spanx could never keep up. A feature in Forbes portended Spanx's demise.

As Blakely faced down the charging Sara Lee army, she made a bold move: She applied to appear on QVC and got accepted after the producers remembered seeing her on Oprah. Her friends and advisors told her it was an insane idea. Spanx was a premium product available in Neiman Marcus and Bergdorf Goodman stores nationwide. QVC was for hawking microwave decals and cheap emerald jewelry.

"I had a lot of people who said, 'Sara, you can't also sell on QVC. You'll kill your brand,'" Blakely told Guy Raz on the *How I Built This* podcast. "I just said, 'Guys, I'm gonna be the one on QVC. I'm going to control the message and I'm going to have the chance to explain what this is.'"

On a warm day in May 2001, Blakely traveled to QVC's eighty-acre glass fortress in West Chester, Pennsylvania, and waltzed into its broadcast studios. She had five minutes to sell Spanx. When her time came, she smiled confidently into the camera and told the story of how she'd created Spanx to help women like her, a narrative she'd honed to perfection over the past year.

As she walked off the stage, the producers told Blakely there was a problem. A lump welled in her throat.

It was a good problem, they explained. Blakely had just sold 8,000 pairs in five minutes. QVC had only ordered 4,000. She was floored. "That was after a year of standing in department stores across the country, and on a really good day, I'd sell between thirty-five and seventy," she recounted.

From that moment, Spanx was in the zeitgeist. By the end of 2001, Spanx would hit $10 million in revenue. By 2006, it had hit $100 million. By 2014, it had eclipsed $400 million. In 2021, Blakely sold Spanx to the private equity firm Blackstone with a valuation of $1.2 billion. Because she had bootstrapped Spanx from the start and resisted taking on outside investors, it made Blakely the youngest self-made female billionaire of all time.

Despite their extensive market research, advertising blitz, and celebrity stars, Sara Lee was never able to keep up.

That's because Blakely knew something that entrepreneurs since Benjamin Franklin have held as gospel: There's nothing more powerful than a great story.

We are all in sales

Blakely is part of a prominent tribe. The most successful marketers, salespeople, and entrepreneurs have one thing in common: they're great storytellers. Ironically, this trend has only accelerated since the release of ChatGPT. As consumers unfollow brands and publications while flocking to individual creators, the most successful people are skilled storytellers who build trust with their target audience on LinkedIn, TikTok, Substack, and other channels where their audience spends their time.

Today, 70 percent of consumers feel more connected to a brand when the CEO creates content on social media. A LinkedIn study found that traffic generated from the posts of people convert at 2.5 times the rate of traffic generated by company posts.

As a deluge of AI content and bots makes it harder to trust what's real, people will gravitate toward the stories and perspectives of people they trust.

If you don't think you're in sales, you probably are. As part of the research for his best-selling 2012 book, *To Sell Is Human*, Daniel Pink surveyed over 9,000 workers across the globe and found that we spend "about 40 percent of our time at work engaged in non-sales selling—persuading, influencing, and convincing others in ways that don't involve making a purchase." Even if you're not on the marketing or sales team at your company, you spend much of your workday persuading others of your ideas and recommendations. And if you want to advance in your career and secure that dream job or promotion, you need to be skilled at selling yourself.

If the idea of being in sales gives you the ick, I get it. When I joined Contently as editor-in-chief, I scoffed at the idea; I was a writer, reporter, and editor, not a salesperson. My job was to write about the rise of the content marketing industry and help people do it well. Two years in, our founders revealed that the majority of our revenue came from customers who discovered us through our blog, newsletter, and the events I hosted. Then it hit me: I was, in fact, in sales. Except my job wasn't to push software on people. It was to sell them on an idea I believed deeply: Great content and storytelling are the best ways to attract customers and build your brand.

Since that moment, I've embraced my inner Sara Blakely. Over the past few years, I've focused more on becoming a more persuasive storyteller—particularly over the past year, as I've gone off to build my own consulting and media business. After all, we now live in a world where AI conducts product analysis and recommendations the moment you Google something. The real differentiator is the emotional bond you form with prospects.

We falsely assume that purchase decisions are based on rational decision-making, but Gallup's research has found that 70 percent of all purchase decisions are based on emotional factors, while only 30 percent are based on rational considerations. Harvard Business School professor Gerald Zaltman puts that figure even higher. His research estimates that 95 percent of purchasing decisions take place in the subconscious mind, driven by emotion, intuition, and implicit association. And as we explored in chapter 2, Dr. Zak's team found that storytelling is the most effective way to influence those emotion-based decisions. In his study with the ad agency BBDO, his team was able to predict purchase decisions with an 83 percent accuracy based on how engaged people's brains were with a brand's story.

The real challenge of sales—whether you're selling yourself to your boss and potential employers for a new role, or selling your product to potential customers—is to tell a story that's so sticky that your potential champion will remember and retell it to their fellow decision-makers when you're not in the room. So how do you do that? There's a simple framework I've come to rely on.

How to tell a great sales story

See if you can guess which story this is: The story starts with a character in humble beginnings. But soon they're called on an epic adventure. They leave home, receive training from a wise mentor, meet their enemy, and face all sorts of crazy obstacles. They almost fail, but at the last moment, they overcome the obstacles, save the day, and return home—having changed forever. Is it...

A. *Lord of the Rings*

B. *The Hunger Games*

C. *Harry Potter*

D. *Star Wars*

If you're saying "F*ck you Lazer, it's all of the above," you'd be right! All of these stories follow a template for storytelling that was first documented by author Joseph Campbell. It's called "the hero's journey." The hero's journey has long served as a go-to storytelling framework for novelists and screenwriters. It's always effective because it mirrors the narrative we tell ourselves about our own lives—about the adventures we go on, the obstacles we face, the rewards we reap, and how each journey changes us.

In all its glory, the hero's journey has twelve parts, broken into a three-act structure. Here it is broken down through the lens of one of the most famous stories of all time: *Star Wars Episode IV: A New Hope* (aka the first one).

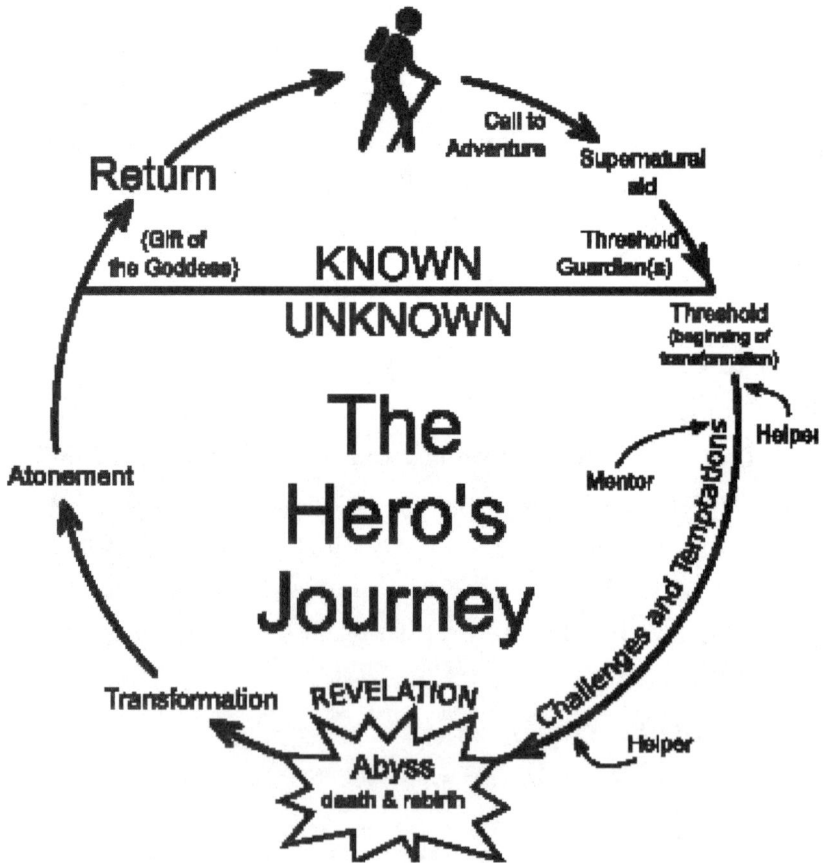

Act 1	
1. **Ordinary World:** Hero lives in an ordinary world.	Luke is living on a desert planet.
2. **Call to Adventure:** Hero is thrust out of the ordinary world.	Luke meets R2-D2 and triggers a hidden message from Princess Leia.
3. **Refusal of the Call:** Hero refuses the call.	Luke refuses, saying that he can't leave his aunt and uncle.
4. **Meeting with the Mentor:** Hero meets a magical guide.	Luke meets Obi-Wan Kenobi. (Sometimes the steps aren't in perfect order; that's okay.)
Act 2	
5. **Crossing the Threshold:** Hero enters the unknown.	Luke discovers that the Empire killed his aunt and uncle; goes to an alien bar and gets hammered.
6. **Tests, Allies, Enemies:** Hero is introduced to new world.	Luke is joined by his full crew of allies; we see Darth Vader's world, too.
7. **Approach to Innermost Cave:** Hero approaches a key battle.	Luke and company get sucked into the Death Star.
8. **Ordeal:** Hero faces a showdown.	He rescues Leia; Kenobi sacrifices himself.
9. **Reward:** Hero emerges victorious.	Luke escapes with the plan and princess.
Act 3	
10. **The Road Back:** Hero realizes challenge isn't over.	Luke realizes that the Galactic Empire is tracking them.

11. **Resurrection:** Hero emerges with a new power.	Luke wants revenge, blows up the Death Star, and emerges with new powers.
12. **Return (Transform-ation):** Hero returns home transformed.	Luke and Han return to the Rebellion stronghold victors.

You might have noticed that at its core, the hero's journey mirrors Vonnegut's "Man in a Hole" arc: Someone gets in trouble and gets out of it again. As Vonnegut said, "We love this story."

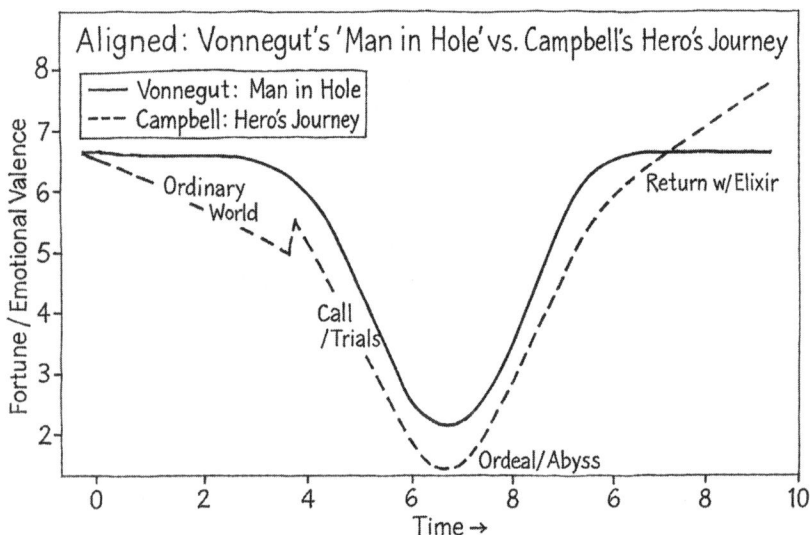

The one challenge with the hero's journey is that it works best for longer stories. I love using it when working on in-depth story-telling projects, like creative nonfiction essays and *Resignation*, the TV pilot and series I co-created with my *Storytelling Edge* co-author, Shane Snow. However, with business storytelling, it's challenging to incorporate all twelve steps. Unless you barricade the conference room door, you're probably not going to be able to turn your sales pitch into a two-hour feature.

That's why I adapted the hero's journey into a simpler struc-ture for persuasive sales storytelling. It's split into six steps instead of twelve, using the same three-act structure, and mirrors how the most successful founders and brands—from Apple to Spanx to Airbnb to Dollar Shave Club—tell their stories, communicate their mission and purpose, and create a mythology around their brand. It's called the Hero's Journey for Sales.

The Hero's Journey for Sales is tailored to win attention in a world where people want to follow people, not brands. If you're going to stand out and build trust, you need to introduce a protagonist people can root for and trust. As a result, the Hero's Journey for Sales focuses on telling the story of the people behind the brands, like Sara Blakely and Steve Jobs. It's perfect for crafting the "origin story" behind your personal brand.

The Hero's Journey for Sales

ACT 1

1. The ordinary world

We begin in the same place as the traditional hero's journey—establishing the relatable world in which our hero lives.

When Sara Blakely told the story of Spanx on TV, she always began in the same place: her ordinary world, selling fax machines door-to-door as she approached her thirtieth birthday—feeling like she was "in the wrong movie."

Think back to other leaders we've explored in this book. They all start here. The mythology of Airbnb begins with Brian Chesky and Joe Gebbia living in a very ordinary and relatable world—two broke creatives in San Francisco who can't even pay the rent. The mythology of Steve Jobs's return to Apple begins with him in an "ordinary world" (by Steve Jobs's standards) as the CEO of NeXT, a struggling computing company. Establish yourself as a vulnerable, relatable hero that your audience wants to root for.

Key questions to ask: Where did you begin? How can you frame your roots in a way that'll make you a relatable character to your target audience? What's a vulnerable moment you can reveal to build trust?

Key element of storytelling to prioritize: Relatability.

2. The call to adventure

An event occurs that gives the hero a purpose and calls them toward a new adventure.

For Blakely, this was the moment she was getting ready for a party and cut the feet off her pantyhose, and got the idea to create a better kind of shapewear for women like her. In the lore of Apple, this was when Jobs returned to Apple, realized that only he could save the company, and executed a boardroom coup. For Chesky and Gebbia, it was when they desperately rented air mattresses on the floor of their apartment, which led to the idea for Airbnb. The call to adventure should make your mission—the "why" behind the work you do—vivid. It introduces a novel idea and amps up the tension.

This structure is so ingrained in me that I used it at the beginning of this book to sell you on its premise. I began in an ordinary world, having my first child, trying to make it as a writer and marketer in New York. I then introduced the call to adventure: the release of ChatGPT, which sent me on a quest to figure out what it meant for me and my son. If you think back to Principle 7, Identify Your Big Idea, this is where you introduce the unique lens through which you see the world.

Key questions to ask: What was the "Eureka!" moment when you realized your calling? What were you feeling, seeing, and sensing in that moment? What was running through your mind? Describe the moment in vivid detail.

Key elements of storytelling to prioritize: Novelty, Tension.

ACT 2
3. Obstacles
This is where we establish the stakes for our hero.

Blakely initially refused her call to adventure, but she relented once she saw Oprah on TV talking about how she cut the feet off her pantyhose. With only $5,000 in savings, Blakely had to find someone to manufacture her Spanx prototype. No one would return her calls, so she drove to North Carolina and began showing up at manufacturing plants, asking to speak with the owner. No one was interested in buying her product—or helping her make it.

At Apple, this was when Jobs initially returned and realized the company only had a few months of runway left in the bank and a disastrously convoluted product line. This stage is the "hole" in your story arc.

Key questions to ask: What big challenges did you have to overcome to get where you are? What stakes did those challenges present? What threats did they pose?

Key element of storytelling to prioritize: Tension.

4. The meeting of the mentor/magical helper

Next, our hero meets the mentor who will help them on their journey.

Blakely's narrative actually introduces two key mentors/ magical helpers, emphasizing different ones based on the context in which she's telling her story. The first was Kaplan, the North Carolina manufacturer whose daughters convinced him to make Blakely's prototype. The second was Diane, the hosiery buyer at Neiman Marcus, who took a chance on Blakely after hearing her story. The magical helper is a surprise twist; you're playing on novelty here.

In Apple lore, Jobs met two magical helpers upon his return: art director Craig Tanimoto and the team at Chiat/Day, which helped develop the "Think Different" campaign, and designer Jony Ive. Jobs fell in love with Ive's work from the moment they met, and he tasked Ive with designing the iMac, the new product that would save the company. For Airbnb, it was when Silicon Valley legend Paul Graham accepted Chesky and Gebbia into his Y-Combinator Accelerator and became their mentor. This is the person, or people, who came to you at a key moment in your life and helped you get out of the "hole."

Key questions to ask: Who are the key people that you met when you were struggling to get your career or big idea off the ground? How did they help you?

Key element of storytelling to prioritize: Novelty.

ACT 3
5. Tests, allies, and enemies

With the mentor by their side, our hero faces a series of tests and competitors that prove their mettle.

When Blakely got the Neiman Marcus deal from Diane, her work had only begun. If it didn't sell in the seven-store trial, she'd be cooked. So she pulled out all the stops: paying friends in different markets to buy Spanx, spending all day in the store selling customers on the product, and even rigging up unauthorized Spanx displays at the checkout. Blakely also introduces Sara Lee as the "enemy" at this stage, ramping up the tension.

This part of the story serves a key purpose: It shows Blakely's grit and resourcefulness, boosting her relatability and making you want to root for her even more. Jobs faced numerous trials as he attempted to lift Apple out of its financial hole; he battled adversaries like Michael Dell and turned old enemies into allies, convincing Bill Gates to invest $150 million in Apple to save the company from bankruptcy. With a push from Paul Graham, Chesky and Gebbia visited Airbnb's guests and hosts one by one to learn what they could do better. Further struggle makes our hero more relatable and introduces greater tension.

This is where many business storytellers go wrong; they shy away from revealing their conflicts and challenges. Show your perseverance and vulnerability. Make it human.

Key questions to ask: What trials and tribulations tested your abilities and resolve? What actions did you take to persevere? Where did you find unlikely allies, and how did you build a relationship with them?

Key elements of storytelling: Relatability, Tension.

6. The transformation

The hero passes the test and emerges transformed.

Blakely faced existential threats from corporate competitors, when she got two big breaks. The first when Blakely mailed a pair of Spanx to Oprah, and thanks to the divine intervention of Oprah's hairdresser, Andre Walker, they ended up in her dressing room. Oprah tried them on, loved them, and ultimately chose them as her favorite product of the year—prompting her to invite Blakely on the show to share her incredible story. The next came when Blakely went on QVC and her story immediately resonated. As she beamed into the living rooms of millions of people across the country, her transformation from door-to-door fax machine salesperson to beloved entrepreneur was complete.

End your story with that final moment of transformation. Jobs's hard-earned run of product successes (iMac, iBook, iPod, iPhone) that put Apple on top, transforming him from a troubled visionary to the greatest technologist of his generation. Chesky and Gebbia's rocket-ship ride to unicorn status transformed them from unemployed designers into widely admired entrepreneurs.

Key questions to ask: What success came from your trials and tribulations? How have you changed compared to when you began your journey?

Key elements of storytelling to prioritize: Relatability.

Try this framework the next time you're . . .

- Pitching a new product
- Crafting your brand's founding story
- Developing a keynote talk
- Pitching media
- Refining your investor deck or sales deck
- Honing your career narrative
- Writing a social media post about your career journey

As AI makes ideas infinite and prototypes cheap, the products, ideas, and people that win will be the ones with the best story. We may not all become self-made billionaires. But with the right narrative, we can be the heroes of our own stories and bring our dreams to life.

Chapter 14

PRINCIPLE 11:
Build an Audience

Until 2018, I'd never built an audience for myself.

It just didn't cross my mind. My job was always to grow the audience of whatever company or publication I worked for. In high school, I grew the readership of *The Academy News* by writing an edgy back-page humor column that earned me several disciplinary trips to the dean's office. (He particularly did not like it when I attempted to rename the paper *The Academy Jews* for the April Fool's Edition.)[8] I ran the same humor playbook as editor-in-chief of my college newspaper, *The Phoenix*. Although the real laughs came from my straitlaced reporting on our student senate, which was like an episode of *Portlandia* come to life. Next came *The Faster Times*, the digital news site I helped found during my senior year of college and grew to millions of readers. I'd love to say it was for our hard-hitting tech coverage, but if I'm being honest, my shockingly popular live blogs of

---

8   In our defense, our newspaper staff was 95 percent Jewish. We really do run the high school media.

Gossip Girl kept our traffic afloat. After we sold that when I was twenty-five, I started from scratch again at Contently, growing our newsletter to hundreds of thousands of subscribers. At each stop, I had no idea what I was doing—no SEO or social media certification, no MBA, not even a journalism degree, since my crunchy arts school didn't believe in majors. But I figured out that if you could grab your audience's attention and make them laugh, it'd buy you enough time to figure out the rest.

Along the way, I found myself constantly building audiences that I had no real ownership over. When I moved on, I'd start again from zero. But I didn't think twice about it. As a writer and editor, it's just what you did. The brand ruled supreme.

Then Contently cofounder Shane Snow and I got a book deal for *The Storytelling Edge*, and as part of our marketing plan leading up to its launch, we offered a free storytelling course and newsletter. It spread on LinkedIn and Twitter. Thousands of people signed up. Suddenly, I had an audience that wasn't the property of my employer. It was mine.

I also got serious about posting on LinkedIn regularly and saw my followers grow. The book became a favorite among content marketing nerds and sold well. I went on dozens of podcasts. I gave a "Talk at Google," which is like a TED Talk for tech outcasts, and spoke at Web Summit, SXSW, Content Marketing World, and over fifty other conferences. Looking back, some of those early talks were humiliatingly bad, yet people continued to follow me on LinkedIn and sign up for my mailing list. Then, in early 2020, LinkedIn invited me to beta test its new newsletter program. I started publishing a biweekly column about content strategy and the science of storytelling. Over the next five years, my audience grew to over 150,000 LinkedIn newsletter subscribers.

As my audience grew, I noticed a shift in power. I had a direct line to the potential customers for Contently. I could send an email to over 100,000 people at any given moment, and many of them would open it and take action—attending events, joining a community, and even becoming customers. I had my own marketing channel, which was incredible because ever since I was a little boy, I told my mom, *"When I grow up, I want to have my own marketing channel."*

My professional value increased in turn. I negotiated a 50 percent raise and promptly subletted a downtown Manhattan apartment with a rooftop pool. Bobbing in chlorine and staring at the Brooklyn Bridge on a cloudless June morning, my hair slicked back in Patrick Bateman cosplay, I realized something I couldn't believe I hadn't seen before: Audience is power.

So far in the **Unleash** part of this book, we've learned how to develop a big idea, build connections through vulnerable story-telling, lead through stories, and sell through stories. Now that we know how to tell those powerful stories, it's time to build an audience for them, giving ourselves a powerful platform we can leverage over the course of our careers.

If there was one piece of advice I'd give anyone interested in content and storytelling, it would be this: Build an audience for *yourself*. Don't just do it for other people. And as much as you can, *own* that audience. Get their email addresses. Yes, you need to use social media to reach people, and I'll discuss in depth about how to do that. But don't be completely at the mercy of social media platforms that can delete your account with one click or annihilate your reach with one algorithm tweak.

If you're an entrepreneur, an audience will enable you to build attention and momentum for ventures throughout your career.

If you're a marketer, it will help you negotiate a raise.

If you're a sales or account person, it will make it much easier to land new clients and keep those commission checks growing.

If you work in product, engineering, finance, or HR, it will boost both the quantity and quality of job offers that slip into your DMs.

And across roles, an audience will give you the flexibility to say, "Screw it!" to the 9–5 and go work for yourself.

The first step is to understand how the digital media game has changed. Most people waste time and effort following best practices that worked five years ago—the most successful anticipate what comes next.

The new rules of content

In early 2025, one big story dominated my LinkedIn feed.

No, it wasn't a sociopathic billionaire trying to dismantle the federal government and casually breaking out a Nazi salute like he was dabbing at a white-power wedding. It's this graph, first posted by Ryan Law, the Director of Content Marketing at SEO platform Ahrefs, showing that Hubspot's search traffic had fallen off a cliff:

Everyone in my weird network of content geeks had something to say about this drop. In the 2010s, Hubspot wrote the playbook for inbound marketing, built upon a huge foundation of content designed to rank well in search engines and drive traffic, coupled with PDF-based e-books and playbooks, newsletters, and webinars to drive leads. For years, it worked. People adored and envied Hubspot for their success. So it became big news when their traditional playbook stopped working and their traffic plummeted.

It wasn't an isolated incident. HubSpot's decline was part of a wave of change upending the way we distribute content and build an audience today.

Three forces of change transforming the content game

There are three big forces changing the way that content will work over the next few years:

The SEO apocalypse and the rise of AI search

For two decades, marketers have been obsessed with creating generic blog posts like "What Is Content Marketing?" in hopes of driving easy traffic from anyone vaguely interested in what they do. This is the misguided advice that many VCs and advisors give marketers and entrepreneurs: Start by creating a bunch of content for search. Don't worry too much about the quality as long as it ranks.

What many people still don't realize is that AI has rendered that strategy obsolete. In 2024, Google introduced AI Overviews, a feature that provides AI-generated answers to users' questions instead of the traditional ten blue links. In 2025, Google introduced AI Mode, which automatically directs users to a ChatGPT-like chat experience whenever they search for something. This is the biggest change in a decade to how content gets distributed on the web. According to SEO platform Ahrefs, over 99 percent of "informational" Google searches—like "What is content marketing? Or "How does generative AI work?"—return an AI-generated answer, giving users little reason to click on a link. This is why HubSpot's traffic fell off a cliff. It created thousands of informational blog posts, but no one was finding those posts on Google and clicking on them anymore. That content no longer has any value.

The Substackification of media

People want to follow people, not brands.

The first era of the internet was largely dominated by brands. Within corporations, nearly all digital marketing efforts were channeled through the corporate blog and corporate social media accounts. In media, the publication reigned supreme: BuzzFeed, Vox, Quartz, Upworthy, Axios. That's changed. Increasingly, people want to follow people, not brands. This makes sense—we crave connection to other people, not logos. Technology has also made it much easier for individuals to build their own media brands. We now have entire video studios inside our phones, and platforms like Substack have made it easy to launch a revenue-generating media business in hours. It's why we're seeing everything from a video game writer leaving Axios and earning $100,000 on his Substack within his first year to Paul Krugman leaving the *New York Times* and racking up 150,000 subscribers within his first month.

The social algorithms know this, which is why company page posts only reach 1 to 2 percent of followers. If brands want to reach people efficiently, they need to go through creators their audience trusts, which is why influencer marketing has grown fourteen times since 2016 to $24 billion. Brands aren't just paying external influencers; they're also paying popular "creators" who work inside their companies as full-time employees two-three times their normal salaries to keep them around. Each year, individual creators and storytellers who can build an audience are gaining more and more power.

The rise of the For You algorithm

For much of the 2010s, it seemed like no new social media platform could break through. But then, as we touched on in Principle 6, Develop Taste, TikTok entered the chat. In 2019, TikTok caught fire in the United States thanks to a simple innovation: an algorithm that didn't care who you were friends with.

TikTok's addictive For You algorithm made it the fastest-growing social media app of all time, and over the past few years, every major social media platform has been copying it. It's like a virus, spreading over every corner of the social web. These algorithms are deeply addicting, but the upshot is that you can reach a large number of people very quickly, even if you're just starting out, since they prioritize highly engaging content above all else.

For years, I avoided TikTok because I have as much self-control as a twenty-year-old frat bro let loose in Ibiza for the first time. My willpower is no match for its crackorithm. However, I recently tried an experiment: posting on TikTok while still banning myself from watching TikToks. Despite having only twenty followers, the first video I posted got 7,500 views and 340 likes; the next one got over 60,000 views and 3,000 likes. With the right approach, you can reach millions when starting from zero.

Just look at Zohran Mamdani. The thirty-four-year-old New York State Assemblyman began his long-shot bid for the Democratic Party nomination for New York City Mayor with only a few thousand followers and less than 1 percent support in the polls. But he understood the grammar of vertical video, the strange syntax of the TikTok and Instagram algorithms. He launched his campaign with a common TikTok format, the man-on-the-street video. It begins with him asking New Yorkers who they voted for, revealing the surprising number of New Yorkers who voted for Trump. But then he twists it, announcing his candidacy at the end. The video went viral, as did most everything he put out afterward, earning hundreds of millions of free impressions as he rocketed up the polls. Mamdani would go on to upset former Governor Andrew Cuomo in a rout, 56 to 44 percent. After Cuomo ran on an independent line, Mamdani pummeled him again in the general election, winning by nearly ten points to become New York City's first Muslim mayor and its youngest mayor since 1892.

These three forces of change—the SEO apocalypse, the Substackification of media, and the rise of the For You algorithm—are creating a new content funnel that should guide the way you build an audience moving forward.

The new content funnel

If you've never heard of the funnel before, I envy you. It's one of the most durable marketing frameworks of all time, and I've been writing and talking about it for the past fifteen years.

The old content funnel—pioneered by Hubspot—was focused on brands. You'd invest heavily in SEO to scale traffic and then prompt people with pop-ups to sign up for a webinar or playbook. Afterward, twenty-three-year-old junior salespeople would inundate them with emails and phone calls until they bought something. Hubspot pioneered this funnel, and for a long time, it worked shockingly well.

The new content funnel looks similar, but it's built around people and embraces the dominant channels today. I think about it in three stages:

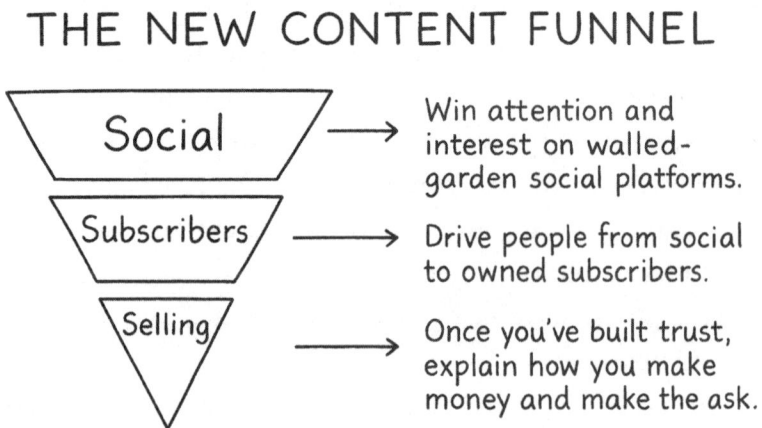

THE NEW CONTENT FUNNEL

Social → Win attention and interest on walled-garden social platforms.

Subscribers → Drive people from social to owned subscribers.

Selling → Once you've built trust, explain how you make money and make the ask.

1. **Social**: Generating attention and demand for your personal expertise

2. **Subscribers**: Driving subscribers or community members

3. **Selling**: Making the ask that really matters to you

I'm going to walk through this framework through the lens of building an audience for yourself, but it can also be easily adapted to build an audience for your company by showcasing a thought leader or personality who represents the brand that people want to follow.

Social

The most valuable and fleeting resource today is attention. The most efficient way to get it is to reach people within walled-garden social media platforms designed to capture most people's time and attention. The average person now spends nearly two and a half hours on social media each day. I have a fraught relationship with social media. Research shows these addictive, algorithm-driven platforms are pretty bad for us, but if you want to build an audience, they're also a necessary evil, since they're the primary place that most people consume and discover content. We can make it our mission, though, to contribute thoughtful ideas and well-crafted stories, drowning out the brain-rotting slop.

Take Ryan Law's LinkedIn post about Hubspot's traffic collapse. He's a content marketing geek marketing his expertise to other content marketing geeks, and his post examining Hubspot's traffic drop (which was mysteriously deleted afterward) got thousands of people debating the future of content.

Think back to Principle 1. I'd recommend that your storytelling practice include a social media component, like posting twice a week on LinkedIn or creating a vertical video for TikTok and Instagram each week. We tend to stereotype vertical video as nothing but dumb dance videos and memes, but pretty much every kind of content succeeds in that format: tech news, marketing tips, neuroscience explainers, and increasingly, episodic content that mirrors the kind of storytelling we see on Netflix and HBO Max. (Or as the Gen-Z calls it: "Slow burn content.")

Start with the social platforms you enjoy the most. You likely already understand the grammar of the content there, the strange syntax that dictates each platform's algorithm. The truth is that all kinds of content work on every platform. Political content is shockingly popular on LinkedIn; #BookTok is almost single-handedly keeping the publishing industry alive. Popular Gen Z economics writer Kyla Scanlon regularly goes viral on Instagram, TikTok, and YouTube.

Study the creators in your field. Then start posting with your own stories and big ideas. As much as possible, make your big idea message memetic and focus on the hook. This was Mamdani's secret to translating his success on TikTok to the polls. I was a dedicated Kamala Harris supporter in 2024, but I would have struggled to rattle off her top three campaign promises. Everyone in the city knew Zohran's top promises—freeze the rent, free childcare, free buses, city-run grocery stores—because he turned them into memes. For example, he introduced his "freeze the rent" promise by diving into the waters of Coney Island on New Year's Day in a full suit.

Key action: Identify one or two social media platforms you enjoy where you want to start creating content. Don't feel pressure to succeed overnight. Give yourself 6–12 months to experiment and fail. Be voicey and opinionated. Be human. Be real.

Subscribers

As you start to create demand within the walled-garden of social media platforms, you want to get them to subscribe to your content so that you have ownership over your audience.

Once I started growing my newsletter subscribers on LinkedIn, I realized something horrifying: even though my newsletter went directly to my subscribers' inboxes, I didn't actually own my subscriber list. I couldn't access it, download it, or take it to another platform. If LinkedIn decided to shutter their newsletter program tomorrow, I'd lose everything. So I changed course: in every edition, I began asking my LinkedIn newsletter subscribers to subscribe to my email newsletter, which I hosted first on Mailchimp and then on Substack. Slowly, I grew my owned newsletter list to over 35,000 subscribers. Even if LinkedIn shuts off its newsletter program tomorrow, I have a large audience that I can take with me wherever I want. My pitch is simple: I'm honest. I tell my audience that I don't want to build my house on the rented land of a social media platform, and that they'll get more in-depth content if they subscribe.

Millions of other creators had a similar epiphany in early 2025, when a congressionally mandated TikTok ban briefly went into effect. They'd spent years building an audience of millions of subscribers, and in a moment, their audiences appeared to vanish. President Trump promised to give TikTok a ninety-day extension, which he has continually extended. Although the TikTok ban didn't take effect (and probably never will), it was a boon to Substack and other newsletter-based platforms. The entire drama highlighted the screwed-up truth about traditional social media platforms: Your audience can vanish at any moment. Amid the TikTok saga, hundreds of prominent TikTok creators migrated their audiences to Substack. Popular Gen Z news commentator Aaron Parnas, for instance, urged his 1.6 million followers to subscribe to his new newsletter on Substack, where he shares in-depth news reports and commentary, growing to over 600,000 newsletter subscribers in less than a year. London chef Laila Mirza drove her 359,000 TikTok followers to follow her on Substack, where she provides a searchable catalogue of all her recipes. AI influencer and Penn professor Ethan Mollick runs a similar playbook on LinkedIn, teasing insights that he elaborates on further on Substack. I try to ensure that at least one to two of my LinkedIn, Instagram, TikTok posts each week are designed to explicitly tease in-depth content in my newsletter, accompanied by a link to the newsletter in the comments or in my bio.

Key Action: Once you start getting your groove on social, create a home where your followers can subscribe for more in-depth content. Substack is the easiest platform to get started on, but competitors like beehiiv and Ghost are great as well. Ask people to subscribe regularly and provide a clear value prop.

Selling

Building an owned list of subscribers is a worthy end goal. You'll have an audience that you can take with you and allow you to operate from a place of power and influence in your career. And we're all selling something—whether that's our job candidacy, services, book (hi!), paid newsletter, product, or access to a members-only Harry Potter fan-fiction community.

Once you've built trust with your audience and delivered valuable content and stories to them, you've earned the right to offer your services.

Technology and culture writer Max Read opens every edition of his *Read Max* newsletter with a note reminding readers that paid subscriptions are what allows him to pay the bills and stay caffeinated. "If you've been reading this newsletter and enjoying it without paying, I'm really glad to hear that! But perhaps you are also thinking to yourself, 'I would buy Max a beer and/or coffee to thank him for the entertainment (?) he has provided through his writing.' Here is the good news: You can effectively do so by upgrading your subscription, for the price of about one beer a month or ten a year," he wrote in a recent edition.

My *Storytelling Edge* co-author Shane Snow ends each newsletter by promoting his courses and keynote speaking with a simple call-to-action and banner ad at the end of each edition. Others promote a product. At Contently, I regularly promoted our events and content marketing platform in my personal newsletter, driving valuable customers. Today, I follow Shane's lead and promote my workshops, speaking, and consulting services. If you're publishing high-quality content that serves your audience's needs, you'll be shocked by how well it works.

It's a trope that the best salespeople are like consultants; increasingly, they're storytellers and creators.

Key action: Earn the right to make the ask with high-quality content. Then explain to your subscribers how you make money in plain English and give them a reason to take the action you want them to take.

Audience > AI

The most successful people I know invest heavily in their storytelling skills and spend time building an audience. If you're an entrepreneur, it gives you a powerful way to stay top-of-mind with customers. If you're an employee, it boosts your value and leverage in the job market. Anyone can learn how to use AI; only skilled storytellers can build a high-value audience. And they've figured out something that took me years to untangle: Audience is power. And in the AI age of work, those who tell the stories really do rule the world.

Part IV:
UPGRADE

I had a problem: a story I wanted to tell . . .
So I went and found the technology to do it.

— George Lucas

Chapter 15

PRINCIPLE 12:
Beware the Vortex of Mid

While writing this book, I had the help of a tireless assistant.

When I'm stuck on a chapter, he indulges me in long, late-night talks. He briefs me with background research on neuroscience and anthropology; I'm often in awe of how much he knows. He researches stories and examples that support my arguments, although he often makes shit up in hope of pleasing me. He's incredibly bad at coming up with names for things, but he'll try anyway, and his bad ideas unblock my brain. And most important, he takes on much of the tedious work in my business, allowing me to have more time to write and think than I've had since college.

I'm talking, of course, about Claude—Anthropic's popular ChatGPT competitor.

Every new technological advance ushers in a new era of storytelling, and while I certainly can't predict every new tool that will be available when you pick up this book, I can provide some frameworks for how to think about using generative AI in your storytelling practice.

Now that we've mastered our storytelling foundations and learned how to apply them to the most important areas of our work, we can use AI to amplify our abilities. The last part of this book will explore how to master the three levels of storytelling innovation in the AI Age:

Level 1: Automate. Use AI as an assistant to automate tedious busywork and free yourself up for deeper and more meaningful creative work.

Level 2: Iterate. Use AI ethically and responsibly to expand your creativity and tell stories that you couldn't otherwise.

Level 3: Innovate. Break the mold and push the limits of what's possible by using AI to shape new storytelling mediums and experiences.

The 3 Levels of Storytelling Innovation in the AI Age

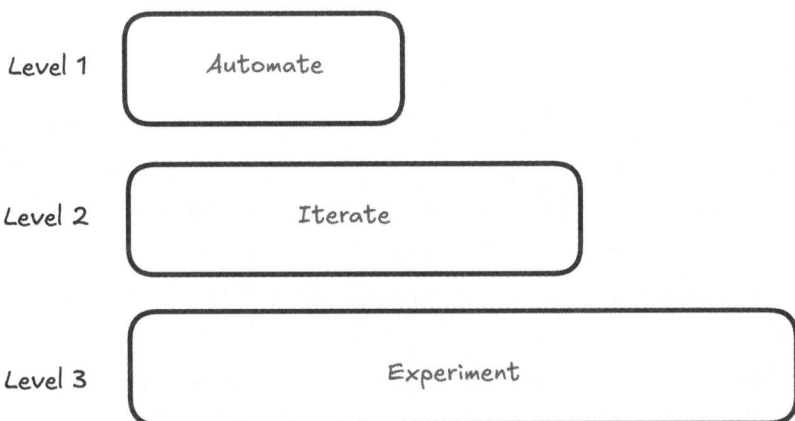

Level 1	Automate
Level 2	Iterate
Level 3	Experiment

The race to the middle

Recently, I found myself in a restaurant on the sixtieth floor of a Manhattan skyscraper, smack-dab in the middle of a giant Chief Marketing Officer therapy session.

The panoramic view was breathtaking. It was like we were cosplaying an episode of *Succession*. I was living out my Roman Roy fantasy. Except the power struggle wasn't with each other. It was with AI.

We went around the private dining room, sharing our biggest aspirations and concerns about this next age of work. A young CMO hoped that AI would execute what he'd been begging his team to do: Go on Instagram and TikTok, study what's working, and "copy the f*@%ing format—it's not f*@%ing hard." Others spoke of scale, one of CMOs' favorite buzzwords. "We'll scale content creation to maximize awareness and optimize lead gen," one Fortune 500 CMO added.

A few CMOs expressed concerns about using AI—particularly those from heavily regulated industries, such as healthcare and finance—and worried about hallucinations. Most in the room felt a top-down pressure to "lead the way" and use AI in all their content, from thought leadership to hyper-personalized ads. The majority were eager to outsource as much content creation as possible to AI.

When it was my turn, I couldn't help but pose a question that had been bugging me for months: Why were we so eager to hand over our content creation to AI when we know that it's a race to the middle?

The AI quandary

According to research from Ahrefs, 74 percent of content published in April 2025 was partially or fully generated by AI.

Love it or hate it, generative AI is here to stay. If you haven't already been instructed to use it at work, I can guarantee that it'll happen very soon. I've spent the past three years speaking with business leaders about AI—particularly how to use it in storytelling, content creation, and marketing—and I've learned that most executives think about AI the wrong way, following an outdated playbook.

For two decades, producing high quantities of content was seen as an easy way to create the illusion that you were doing a good job as a CMO. Create enough well-structured content on a topic, the theory went, and you'll see a spike in search traffic. Pump out mediocre webinars and downloadables and enough schmucks will fill out the form that you'll hit your superficial lead goal and survive another quarter.

This is why generative AI makes CMOs' eyes glisten more brightly than an open bar at Cannes. It looks like an easy button for content creation.

The only problem? This strategy was never very effective. Global research company Forrester found that 60 to 70 percent of business content is never used or seen by anyone. When Michael Brenner was the head of marketing and content strategy at tech giant SAP, he discovered that most of the demand generation content the company created failed to generate a single lead; they'd produce hundreds of e-books and guides that not a single person downloaded.

It's even less effective in the age of generative AI. When used thoughtfully, AI can drive down the cost of creating great content—boosting brainstorming and creativity, and automating time-consuming work (data visualization, research, interview transcription, social video editing, etc.). But it also allows people to make bad or mediocre content with zero effort, and there's already a backlash to the AI slop flooding the internet. As a result, the mediocre content most people pump out has minimal or negative value—it doesn't help your SEO, and sophisticated consumers will suspect you outsourced it to ChatGPT.

As a result:

- As the cost of creating mediocre content approaches zero, so does its value.

- The quality bar that people demand to capture their attention is rising; if you want to stand out, your content needs to be distinctly human and high-quality.

- As a result, the value of high-quality, distinctly human stories are rising with it—even as technology lowers the cost of telling those stories.

AI & Content Value

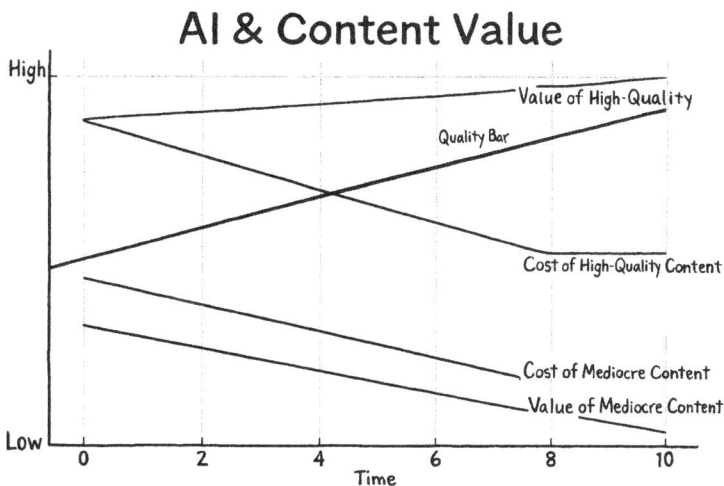

The winners of the next age will choose another path. Instead of *more*, we can choose *better*.

This age of generative AI can play out in one of two ways. There's a timeline in which generative AI pollutes the internet with so much crap that we can never go back. There's also a timeline where we use this technology to tell stories that we never could before. I'm fighting for that timeline. That's why I've run workshops to teach content and marketing teams how to use generative AI thoughtfully and responsibly, enhancing their own creativity and critical thinking. To scale quality, not quantity.

In those workshops, I always begin with the same message: Beware the Vortex of Mid.

Beware the Vortex of Mid

If you're going to use generative AI responsibly and effectively, you need to know how it works.

Popular chatbots like ChatGPT are called large language models (LLMs) because they learn to generate text from the most common patterns in their training data, which comprises everything their Silicon Valley overlords could scrape off the internet: YouTube video transcripts, blog posts, technical guides, community posts, news stories, social media posts, and allegedly, according to some active lawsuits, pirated books. According to one estimate by AI researchers, AI companies will have devoured all of the text training data on the internet by the time you read this in 2026.

One common misconception is that LLMs ingest these copyrighted works wholesale. They don't, which is why they rarely plagiarize existing works. Instead, the models use the content they've ingested as training data to predict the next word in a string of text. Each word (or technically, piece of a word) that an AI model produces is called a token, and every time it produces a token, it tries to generate a reasonable continuation of the text it has produced so far. It comes up with probabilities of what the next word should be and picks a new answer every time.

Stephen Wolfram gives a fantastic example in his guide to how ChatGPT works. Say if the text it's generated so far is: "The best thing about AI is its ability to . . ."

Then ChatGPT will generate probabilities for the next word:

- learn (4.5%)
- predict (3.5%)
- make (3.2%)
- understand (3.1%)
- do (2.9%)

The twist: ChatGPT doesn't always pick the highest probability word. It mixes things up. This is why you rarely get the same answer from ChatGPT two times in a row. This variation is what gives AI the veneer of creativity and originality.

However, because of this system, the content that LLMs like ChatGPT produce is mid by design. (If you don't speak Gen Z, "mid" means mediocre.) As we began exploring in chapter 3, while AI models have made giant leaps in technical areas like coding, math, and data analysis, their writing and storytelling capabilities have advanced more slowly due to a few reasons:

1. Much of the text that AI models are trained on is flat, jargony marketing and technical content. That's why so much AI writing is filled with meaningless babble like "groundbreaking," "game-changing," "landscape," "delve," and "holistic." AI writing isn't quite as bad as the data it's based on thanks to fine-tuning and training, but it still is not very good.

2. Before AI models are released to the public, they're finetuned through a process called Reinforcement Learning from Human Feedback (RLHF), in which humans rate the model's responses to fine-tune it. These human workers are trained to rate verbose answers more highly, which is why AI often rambles like it chased a six-pack of beer with 30 mg of Adderall.

3. When an LLM isn't sure of an answer, it's trained to hedge by spitting out extra text, basically like a student bullshitting his way through an answer.

This is why AI writing hasn't made the same leap as AI coding. AI is inherently an averaging out of all the crap on the internet, and as a result, it creates a vortex that sucks you back to the middle when you rely on it too heavily.

I call it the AI Vortex of Mid.

If you laid out all the content on the internet on a four-quadrant graph spanning low-high originality and low-high quality, most AI-generated or heavily AI-assisted content would fall in the middle. Not bad, but not good enough to make a significant impact.

This is due to AI's strong gravitational pull toward mediocrity. Outsource your outline to AI, and you'll be stuck with generic ideas. Outsource your prose, and it'll lack soul. With the right prompting and fine-tuning, you might get the veneer of originality (AI is skilled at connecting ideas) and produce slightly above-average content. But it won't be enough to win your audience's attention and break through.

Most people who use AI don't see the Vortex of Mid, and without realizing it, they get sucked in. Research shows that teams that over-rely on AI for ideation experience an overall decline in novelty and creativity. Additionally, research from MIT indicates that over-relying on AI can shut down certain parts of our brains.

But there's a flipside to that. The same research found that when you think and write on your own *first*, and then use AI as an amplifier, you can reach a higher level of cognitive engagement.

The last three chapters of this book will show you how to find that balance. You'll discover how AI can enhance your storytelling abilities and open new possibilities. It can automate the busywork that consumes our days, keeping us from doing the kind of deep work that nourishes our souls. It can help us tell the kind of stories we never could before.

As you read those chapters and incorporate generative AI into your storytelling practice, I want you to remember this principle: Beware the Vortex of Mid. It will always be there, threatening to suck you in. But as long as you keep your eye on it, you can take your stories to new heights.

Chapter 16

PRINCIPLE 13:
Automate the Busywork

A year and a half ago, I found myself in an existential crisis.

I'd never been busier. My calendar was stacked like a never-ending game of Tetris, and I was knocking items off my to-do list with manic intensity. Yet every night that I lay down, exhausted, the same thought haunted me: I hadn't gotten anything meaningful done. My storytelling practice was in shambles. Sure, I was eking out a newsletter every week or two, but this book was gathering digital dust in a forgotten corner of Google Docs. And the TV pilot scripts I'd promised my producer friends? They were stuck on page two.

I felt like a total failure. Sure, I had a baby and a full-time job, but Tolstoy had thirteen freakin' kids! And a gambling addiction! And he made it work. Jane Austen secretly scribbled her great works in short bursts between visits in her parlor. So why couldn't I get my shit together and write between meetings? Why couldn't I shrug off the soot from the email mines and knock out a chapter or two after my son went to bed?

A few days later, I was listening to *The Ezra Klein Show* while getting a $70 haircut, the perfect caricature of an insufferable Brooklyn dad. The show's guest was Cal Newport, author of a new book called *Slow Productivity*. By the time I walked out of the salon with a grossly overpriced fade, I realized that everything I thought I knew about productivity was wrong.

Technology and productivity

Pop quiz: Which period in US history had the fastest rise in worker productivity?

A. The Post–WWII Industrialization Era (1950–1970)

B. The Service Economy Era (1970–1994)

C. The Early Internet Era (1994–2004)

D. The High-Speed Internet Era (2004–2022)

It's got to be D, right? High-speed internet was transformative. It gave birth to a trillion-dollar software industry. Suddenly, we didn't need to be in an office to work together; we could collaborate with anyone across the globe, with awe-inspiring tools at our fingertips. The most complicated aspects of our jobs became trivial. A good friend of mine is an executive search consultant. Twenty-five years ago, contacting candidates was espionage-level work. If she wanted to get in touch with the VP of Design at Google about a new opportunity at Apple, she would have had to call Google's headquarters and lie her way into getting the VP of Design on the phone. Search consultants regularly pretended to be family members, vendors, or doctors calling with urgent medical news. It'd take hours. Today, she spends thirty seconds messaging that person on LinkedIn or looking up their contact information in a database.

But here's the shocker: From 2004 to 2022, our labor productivity dropped by half compared to the early-internet era (1994–2004).

US labor productivity growth, 1950-2023

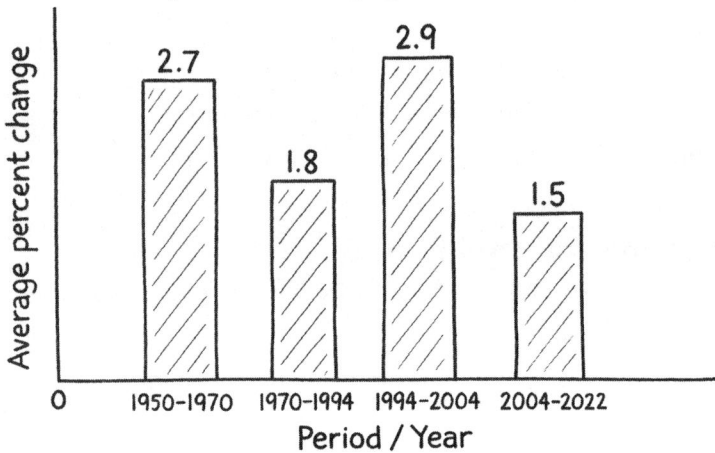

A bar chart titled "US labor productivity growth, 1950-2023." The y-axis is labeled "Average percent change" and the x-axis is labeled "Period / Year." The bars are:
- 1950-1970: 2.7
- 1970-1994: 1.8
- 1994-2004: 2.9
- 2004-2022: 1.5

The digital revolution was supposed to make us hyper-productive, but as it turns out, it's just made us hyper. All the frictionless communication tools—Slack, email, WhatsApp—that promised to create synergy by allowing us to collaborate in real time have actually just created a clusterfuck of distractions and unnecessary tasks.

In *Slow Productivity*, Cal Newport explains how we ended up in this digital hellscape. At the turn of the century, factories could easily measure worker productivity on assembly lines. Once we entered the knowledge work age, we kept the structure of factory work (9–5 days, blatant sexism, etc.) and measured productivity by whether the boss could see you physically working. This is why in *Mad Men*, Pete Campbell, Paul Kinsey, and Ken Cosgrove are always waiting for Roger and Don to leave the office before they head to the bar to commit misdemeanor sexual harassment. You can't let the boss see you slacking.

In the 2000s and 2010s, we added another measure of work productivity: how fast you respond to emails and Slack messages, and how many tasks you check off on work management boards like Trello and Monday. When COVID hit and remote work proliferated, we added a third measure of productivity: a calendar full of Zoom meetings.

In the remote work era, we show that we're working by bothering each other with dumb messages, responding as quickly as possible, and then scheduling a Zoom meeting to explain the confusing messages we just sent. In *Slow Productivity*, Newport calls this pseudo-work. It feels like work because it makes us stressed and exhausted, but we're not actually accomplishing anything meaningful. A global 2025 Microsoft study found that knowledge workers are interrupted every two minutes by meetings, emails, or messages. Research from the University of California Irvine has found that every time we get distracted, it takes us twenty-five minutes to recover—meaning that every thirty-minute Zoom and "quick Trello task" is stealing an hour from our lives. Honestly, it's a shock we get *anything* done.

The result is that we all feel overworked and underproductive, and push our "focus work" to nights and weekends. In another 2025 study, Microsoft found that knowledge workers are stuck in an "infinite workday," increasingly working after 10 p.m. at night and on weekends. The trend started during the pandemic as a way to finish the deep work that got delayed because of all our psuedo-work, but in the past year, messages have crept into the evening too, with workers getting over fifty messages in the evening.

In late 2024, DHR Global surveyed 1,500 knowledge workers and found that 82 percent were experiencing some degree of burnout, with a third feeling "very" or "extremely" burned out. One marketing exec described their team's job as "creating decks for sales teams that they never use and reports for leadership that they never read."

Unconsciously, we're sabotaging ourselves and making it impossible to get deep work done, which is very bad news if you want to tell great stories.

The biggest storytelling myth

But what about Jane Austen secretly writing her great works in short bursts between meetings in her parlors? Or Jack Kerouac churning out *On the Road* in just three weeks? Does great storytelling *really* require long blocks of deep work? Can't we just knock out some quick videos in between Zoom meetings? Write that viral essay in thirty minutes?

It turns out that those stories about magical creative productivity were lies.

In reality, Austen rarely took visitors; she was too busy running around doing chores. Her family wasn't actually rich; her father ran a boys' school out of her home—plus a farm. Her writing languished, unfinished, for decades. There were chickens and teenage boys to clean up after.

Austen's writing didn't take off until 1809 when her family closed the school and retired to a modest cottage in the country. After making breakfast for her family in the morning, she was free to write the rest of the day. Over the next few years, Austen went on a heater. She finished her half-finished manuscripts for *Sense and Sensibility* and *Pride and Prejudice* and wrote *Emma* and *Mansfield Park*.

As a teenager, I was enthralled with Kerouac. The legend of the sexy rebel writing *On the Road* in three weeks made me always believe that with enough amphetamines and willpower, I too could write the Great American Novel during Christmas break. (I never did locate enough amphetamines or willpower to give it a shot.) So when Newport revealed that this, too, was a lie—Kerouac actually spent *nine years* writing *On the Road*, although did type up the manuscript in three weeks—I felt both crushed and freed. Crushed by a teenage dream extinguished, but freed from the feeling that there was something wrong with me.

My inability to write a book or TV show in tiny bursts amid a frenetic schedule wasn't a personal deficit. Almost every storyteller who produced great works did so over an extended stretch of time, creating the space to think, imagine, and iterate on their work.

So this is what I've come to believe: If you want to tell great stories, one of the most important things you can do is automate and eliminate the distractions that plague us in the digital age.

How to make time

I recognize the irony in suggesting that generative AI can help us get the time back to do the work we love. After all, technology got us into this mess in the first place. The last tech revolution made us less productive. Why wouldn't AI do the same?

This is yet another scenario where technology can be used for good or evil, and generative AI is uniquely positioned to take busywork off our plates. And there are five key steps you can take:

1. Audit your workday.
2. Automate the overhead.
3. Eliminate "shallow work."
4. Rethink your job around outcomes, not tasks.
5. Run the research.

1. Audit your workday

During my creative crisis, the turning point came when I decided to sit down and review my workday. What the hell was I actually *doing* with my life?

So I tracked my time for one week in thirty-minute intervals and discovered that I spent most of my day bogged down in what Newport calls "administrative overhead." I'm a people pleaser and avoid conflict like it's a Phish cover band. I say yes by default when people ask for my help. As a result, I'd gotten myself involved in over a dozen projects simultaneously—both at A.Team, where I led marketing, and with my side hustles. Every new project added administrative overhead: emails, Slacks, and texts I needed to answer. Project boards I had to update. Meetings that clogged my calendar.

I wasn't doing work, exactly. I was doing *work about work*. It turns out I'm not alone. In 2021, work management platform Asana conducted a study of over 10,000 workers and found that, on average, people spent 58 percent of their day on administrative overhead—communicating about work, searching for information, switching between apps, rearranging priorities, and asking for status updates. This is the plague of projects; every time you say yes to something new, it adds more administrative overhead tasks, to the point where you're not getting any actual work done. The result? An "overhead tax."

What's worse: All of this task switching makes it nearly impossible to think clearly. University of Washington professor and researcher Sophie Leroy calls this "attention residue." As we switch from task to task—or Slack to Zoom to Slack—a little bit of our attention remains focused on each task, meaning that we can't fully focus on anything we're working on. It's like every unfinished task gives birth to a hyperactive toddler who follows us around muttering, "What about me?" In addition to interruptions, this is another reason we feel so burnt out at work.

The third reason is video meetings. If you've ever sat in back-to-back video meetings and felt like your brain was on fire, that's because it probably was—at least it would look that way if you were strapped to an EEG scanner. Microsoft studied scanned workers' brains using an EEG cap while they sat through four back-to-back thirty-minute video meetings without a break—a common occurrence for me, as well as pretty much every other knowledge worker I know. Stress levels peaked. On the imaging software, their brains were bright red, lit up with stress. And research shows that stress is a creativity killer.

My audit made me realize it was time for an intervention. I followed Newport's simple advice: "Do fewer things." I began by divorcing myself from as many projects as possible—wrapping them up, delegating them to someone on my team, or simply saying, "You guys don't really need me on this" and bowing out.

Key questions to ask: What tasks occupy most of your day? Track them over the course of a week. Which ones fall into the category of administrative overhead? How can you reduce that administrative overhead by strategically divorcing yourself from projects?

2. Automate the overhead

On the remaining projects, I explored how to lower the overhead tax I was paying by automating administrative tasks using AI.

One of my favorite workflows came from my friend Luke, who runs a consultancy advising startup founders and CEOs on how to better manage and grow their sales teams. His busy clients most valued the detailed follow-ups he provided after their weekly calls; they discussed so many things during their weekly sessions that they were often unsure about the next steps they needed to take. These follow-up emails also benefited Luke, since they helped him identify where he needed to pick up the next session.

However, writing these follow-ups and reviewing his notes to prepare for his next call consumed most of his workday, keeping him from growing his business. So he turned to Claude, Anthropic's LLM.

For each client, Luke set up a "Project" within Claude, which is essentially a contained workspace where he can train Claude to perform a specific task. He used it as a "second brain" to take on administrative overhead, treating it like an executive assistant. For each project, he gave Claude the background on his client—who they were, their goals, and why they were using him. Each week, he'd upload the call transcript (generated with another AI tool, Otter.ai, which records and summarizes calls) and train Claude to generate the first draft of his follow-up email to clients.

Surprisingly, Claude often did a better job than he did. It combed through the transcripts, identifying key moments from the calls and linking them to the soundbites in Otter so his clients could listen back. It learned his voice and writing style, and mimicked him reasonably well. Luke went from spending two hours putting these follow-ups together to fifteen minutes; he'd just double-check Claude's work for hallucinations and send it off. Claude also proved to be an excellent assistant. He automated a prompt so that Claude generated a prep doc before each call, saving another hour. Claude also automatically reviews all of his calls with clients each month and flags any reason the client might not be happy.

"It's insane," he told me. "It allows me to spend more time on high-value activities like strategy and direct client interaction." With much of the administrative overhead off his plate, Luke doubled his client base and launched a small sales recruiting agency called Repeatability, as many of his successful clients were asking for his help with hiring.

Afterward, I took Luke's advice and set up similar workflows with Claude for projects that I was leading. For an AI product launch, for instance, I trained Claude to generate meeting agendas ahead of time and recaps with key action items. Within a month, I had five hours back to write each week. If you want to figure out the best way to do this, you don't need to hire an AI consultant. AI tools are very, very good at telling you how to use them.

Key questions to ask: Write two paragraphs explaining the administrative overhead plaguing your workday. Send that explanation to ChatGPT, Claude, or Gemini and say: "Act as an AI advisor. Here is the administrative overhead that's keeping me from doing deep work. What actions would you recommend that I take to use generative AI systems to automate this overhead?"

3. Eliminate "shallow work"

In his 2016 book *Deep Work*, Newport popularized the term "shallow work" for tasks that don't require much cognitive engagement—the types of things you can do on autopilot while listening to a podcast. Many administrative overhead tasks fall under the category of "shallow work," but it also encompasses all the other small tasks that don't require your unique perspective or expertise.

If you work on a marketing team, you've likely encountered at least one of these: finding and sending case studies to the sales team.

At every B2B company I've ever worked for, the same dynamic plays out. The marketing team spends hundreds of hours creating case studies about successful customers and organizing them into neat folders in an internal portal, which no one ever visits. Instead, someone from the sales team pings the entire marketing team on Slack almost every day with a message like this: "URGENT—I have a call in 20 minutes. Do we have any case studies with Fortune 500 healthcare companies?" Then half the marketing team immediately stops what they're doing to find it.

I spent the first ten years of my career presenting the case study portal to the sales team every few months, begging them to use it. Eventually, I just gave up and accepted it as one of the laws of nature inside revenue teams. If you make a case study, the sales team will always need you to find it.

At A.Team, I challenged my overworked team to identify the dumbest work we were wasting time on and explore whether we could use generative AI to solve it. After a long weekend, a marketing strategist on my team, May, made an announcement in our weekly team meeting. She'd spent the weekend building a CustomGPT in ChatGPT; whenever the sales team asked for a case study, ChatGPT would immediately deliver it to them, along with email copy about the case study that they could send to clients.

Within a week, the case study requests for our sales team were gone. Inspired, our creative director built a similar system to handle ad-hoc design requests, using a Slack integration to automatically turn desperate pleas for last-minute design help into project management tasks.

With AI handling so much of our shallow work and communications, I challenged my team to spend two to three hours every day with Slack completely turned off, focused on deep work. Within days, I noticed an uptick in their productivity and moods. They were no longer haunted by shallow work.

Key questions to ask: Go back to your work audit—how much time is spent in deep work vs. shallow work that could be automated? If you're a manager, what are common distractions for your team that you wish you could eliminate if you had a magic wand?

4. Rethink your job around outcomes, not tasks

Modern knowledge work is driven by performative productivity —actively showing that we're *doing things*. As a result, workers are increasingly precious about their tasks—like Gollum clutching the ring—even if the tasks themselves have little impact or require any particularly special skill.

Many marketing jobs are bloated with shallow tasks. Making landing pages. Writing follow-up emails. Setting up webinars. Writing formulaic performance ad copy, nurture email sequences, and creative briefs. This content isn't designed to be entertaining, original, or particularly insightful. But it serves a function in the corporate machine, making it hard to eliminate.

The truth is that generative AI has gotten pretty good at this stuff, and it's getting better. If you train a model like ChatGPT or Claude with the right data, guidelines, and past examples to mimic, it'll do these tasks at a B+ level. It's very good at taking a big, original research report and producing all the derivative assets, like landing page copy and key takeaways one-sheets. When prompted well, its writing is concise and clear. It's good at putting all the gross little CTAs where the gross little CTAs need to be.

Many employees resist giving up these tasks. There's a sense of identity. *I write the landing page copy. I make the sales decks.* But the people increasing their value most are those who reorient their jobs not around the tasks they accomplish, but the outcomes they drive.

The employees who have learned to use these tools effectively—as automators of busywork and enhancers of creativity—have exponentially increased their value. Take May, the content strategist on my team who used ChatGPT to automate 90 percent of her shallow work. She reinvested that time in launching new original research and field marketing campaigns that generated thousands of new leads. It earned her three promotions in just eighteen months.

As it turns out, these employees are also happier. A study by researchers from MIT and George Mason University had 444 knowledge workers use ChatGPT for formulaic business writing tasks like writing press releases, analysis plans, and email copy. AI decreased the time they spent on these tasks by 40 percent, and independent evaluators judged the AI-assisted work to be 18 percent better than that done by humans alone. (While generative AI struggles with storytelling, it's very good at templatized writing.) Participants also enjoyed their work more in the process; deep down, we don't really like doing boring, shallow work. It's much more cognitively rewarding to focus on ambitious projects and in-depth storytelling.

It's not surprising, then, that people who regularly use generative AI at work feel more positively about its long-term impact. A 2024 Deloitte study found that 84 percent of millennials and 80 percent of Gen Z who frequently use generative AI at work say it will free up their time and improve their work-life balance, which is about 25 to 30 percent higher than that of all respondents. Similarly, 86 percent of millennials and 79 percent of Gen Z who frequently use generative AI at work say that it will improve the way they work.

The challenge is to use it intentionally: Outsourcing shallow work to make room for the kind of deep work that matters, allowing you to escape the dreaded Vortex of Mid. Increasingly, there are out-of-the-box AI tools that can help you do that. I use Opus.ai to edit and clip videos for social media, and Gamma.ai to design presentations and landing pages. Fast-improving agentic workflows in these tools are making it so that you don't even need to manually upload files anymore for repeated workflows; AI tools like Claude will just pull them automatically. For less than $50/month combined, these tools give me 20–30 hours back that I can reinvest in meaningful, long-term projects like this book.

Key questions to ask: How much of your time is spent doing tasks out of habit instead of because it's crucial to an outcome? Which ones follow a template or formula that require minimal original thinking or storytelling and could be easily replicated by AI tools?

5. Run the research

When I sold my media company and left the media world to be editor-in-chief of Contently, my mom could not explain to anyone what I did. I told her to just say that I googled things for a living.

That wasn't entirely true. I also interviewed people while googling, wrote articles and newsletters while googling, and half-paid attention in meetings while googling. If I wasn't googling, I was searching Google Drive or another internal database for information. A 2021 survey of 1,000 knowledge workers conducted by the Harris Poll for work optimization platform Glean found that, on average, we spent 25 percent of the workday searching for information, a figure that's likely much higher for anyone whose job involves creating content.

The most useful feature offered by LLMs like ChatGPT, Gemini, and Claude today is Deep Research. It's transformed the way I work and saved me ten plus hours each week. Even if you're reading this book two years from now, I'd wager that Deep Research will remain one of generative AI's killer applications.

Deep Research operates like a research assistant; you give it a tightly scoped assignment, like, "Find academic studies and reputable industry reports that explore the time savings that knowledge workers receive from using generative AI tools." The large language model goes off, breaking the query into several smaller questions simultaneously while searching hundreds or thousands of sources to generate a structured, in-depth report with links and citations. You can also give it access to your email, Google Drive, Dropbox, Sharepoint, Hubspot database, and more to securely bring first-party data and information into your search. It's like having a team of Ivy League research assistants working for you for just $20 per month, with the caveat that those research assistants are occasionally on acid and will hallucinate a piece of information. But since every claim comes with a citation and link, you can double-check its work. And increasingly, AI is laying off the psychedelics. While GPT-4 hallucinated over 20 percent of the time, GPT-5-Thinking, the most advanced version of ChatGPT available as I write this, hallucinates less than 5 percent of the time when using web search to find an answer, instead of just relying on its training data. Recently, OpenAI researchers have identified a new method of fine-tuning AI that promises to reduce hallucinations even further.

For writers like me, the impact is small yet profound. Last night, I left my desk at 5:30 p.m. to buy my son Max the bougie pasta sauce he likes and pick up my dog from daycare; when I got home, I made Max pasta and put him to bed. All the while, three different AI agents were conducting Deep Research for the next chapter of this book. Thanks to my AI researchers, I finished the outline for that chapter in three hours instead of staying up all night. I woke up this morning a rested, competent parent instead of a tweaked-out trainwreck.

Most AI use cases get overhyped, but this is one they've gotten right. When used the right way, that's the feeling that technology can give you as a storyteller. Like you have a secret army of helpers by your side. Over the past eighteen months, AI has transformed the way I work, giving me the time to do the kind of deep work that brings me meaning and joy.

As we'll explore next, it can help you tell better stories too.

Chapter 17

PRINCIPLE 14:
Iterate with Intention

One hundred eighty-four years before ChatGPT, another technological leap sparked widespread panic in the creative world.

The year was 1839. Puffy sleeves were IN. Shoulder pads were OUT. And on a cold January morning in Paris, members of the French Academy of Sciences were shocked when an artist named Louis-Jacques-Mandé Daguerre revealed his new invention, which captured images with shocking precision and detail.

It was a massive leap forward, and for members of the Academy, it came out of nowhere. Sure, primitive photography had been around since 1826, when Joseph Niépce invented the heliograph, but it wasn't very impressive. Niépce's process involved using asphalt on a pewter plate and required eight hours of exposure time. The end result was a negative image. It was a curiosity but no threat to the dominant visual art form of the day: painting. Why sit for hours for a grainy photo when you could get a baller portrait painted of you instead?

Daguerre was known as a showman, famed for his Diorama displays, which mixed theatrical painting with clever lighting to create the illusion of moving pictures. But he'd secretly grown obsessed with photography. In 1829, he began collaborating with Niépce to crack the challenge of creating images through light and chemistry. When Niépce died in 1833, they'd made little progress. But Daguerre kept going. After years of tinkering, Daguerre reimagined the heliograph. He used silver-plated copper sheets, iodine, and mercury to reduce exposure times and create positive images, making photography far faster and crisper. He christened it the daguerreotype. Immediately, the art world was shook.

As soon as the famous French painter Paul Delaroche saw the daguerreotype, he declared, "From today, painting is dead!" (Probably while smoking a cigarette in an incredibly sexy fashion.) Nearly two centuries later, we're having another daguerreotype moment.

Over the past eighteen months, we've all had a little Delaroche whispering inside of us: Is my creative practice dead? It started with ChatGPT, and every time a new AI advancement emerges—such as GPT-5, Claude 4.5, or Google's Nano Banana and Veo 4 image-generation and video-editing tool—that whisper gets a little bit louder. I'm sure that by the time you're reading this, there will be a new tool of the week creating hysteria in media land.

But the camera didn't kill painting; it changed it. As customers flocked to daguerreotype studios in Paris, London, and New York in the ensuing decades, vibrant new art movements came in quick succession—Impressionism, Post-Impressionism, Cubism, and Surrealism—that went beyond simply depicting reality.

The Lucas Cycle

The camera wasn't an isolated phenomenon; every storytelling technology goes through this kind of cycle.

When reporting on the good, bad, and ugly of AI content, I often think back to an interview that George Lucas gave at the

"All Things D" conference in 2007, which Kara Swisher recapped in her memoir, *Burn Book*. Lucas is arguably the greatest modern thinker on the intersection of technology and storytelling. His production company, Lucasfilm, ignited the special effects revolution with *Star Wars* and *Indiana Jones*. Lucasfilm also pioneered computer graphics. In 1986, Jobs financed the spinout of Lucasfilm's computer division to create an independent company that would reimagine movies, Pixar.

"Painting, music, any kind of art form is essentially technological. The most important part is to be able to communicate emotions," he told All Things D cofounders Swisher and Walt Mossberg. "Digital technology is a tool. Whatever you do, it's going to get abused. Sound was abused. Color was abused, everything gets abused. But that's just the nature of human nature. When you get a new toy, you want to use it until it breaks, and then you start to calm down."

I've come to think of this as The Lucas Cycle: A new technology emerges, gets abused, and innovative new forms of storytelling emerge once people focus back on what's important—great storytelling that drives emotional connection.

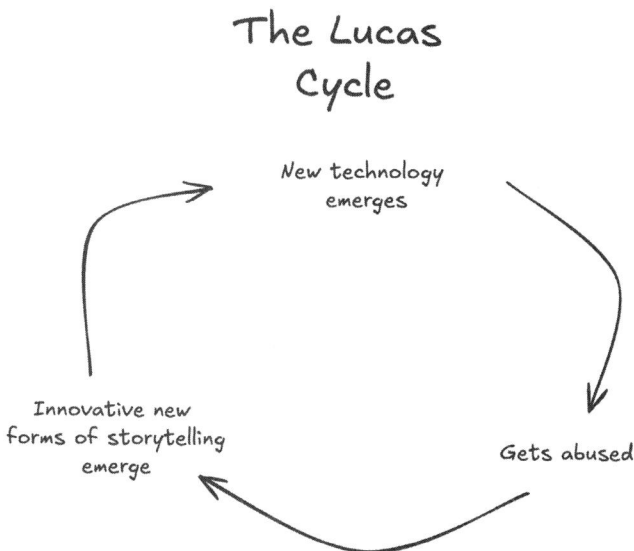

The Lucas Cycle

New technology emerges

Gets abused

Innovative new forms of storytelling emerge

With generative AI, we're already seeing this cycle play out. We're currently in the abuse phase: Growth hackers and hustlepreneurs are flooding the internet with AI-generated slop, and most AI users are creating deeply mediocre content. Short-sighted executives will try to replace writers and creatives with AI, often with disastrous results. But we're also beginning to see AI's potential as a storytelling tool, with thoughtful storytellers leveraging generative AI to spark their creativity, shape new mediums, and tell stories they never could before.

What separates those abusing generative AI from those using it as a tool to tell better stories? Intention. Abusers outsource the creative process to AI; they aimlessly prompt and publish slop. Storytellers use AI thoughtfully and deliberately. They ensure their hands are always in the wheel, and they're transparent and intentional about when and how they use it.

In Principle 14, Iterate with Intention, we'll explore the second level of storytelling with AI. Once you use AI to automate the busywork and free up time and space to do deep work, it's time to examine the role that AI can play in your creative and storytelling process. How can you use AI to iterate on your creative process with intention, unlocking new levels of creativity and productivity? How can you use AI in a way that increases your cognitive engagement, amplifies your foundational storytelling skills, and keeps the choices that make art and storytelling meaningful in your hands?

How to use AI to amplify your creativity

In 2014, researchers from the University of Pittsburgh set out to better understand creativity by studying engineers developing new products.

We tend to think that creativity comes in big leaps, the dramatic "Eureka!" moments we see in movies. But in reality, creativity comes in small steps—small iterations on ideas until you hit on something big. As the researchers wrote: "Idea A spurs a new but closely related thought, which prompts another incremental step, and the chain of little mental advances sometimes eventually ends with an innovative idea in a group setting."

For instance, one group in the study was designing a hand-held printer for kids and trying to figure out how the door should close. One participant suggested it could work like a VCR tape flap. Another suggested a garage door. Finally, a third landed on the idea of a roller door.

As you'll see in the transcript below from the study, each team member uses each other's analogy as a springboard to a better idea, until they hit on a winner:

> Todd: I'm thinking of something a bit like the flap on a video tape
> (Pause)
> Alan: What the flap?
> Todd: Yeah.
> Tommy: Like a garage door type of thing.
> Todd: Yeah you push the button, then it goes open.
> Tommy: Yeah.
> Todd: But that's probably overly complicated.
> Rodney: Garage door… well it could be a roller
> Todd: A roller door!

The art and science of brainstorming effectively

Although people have been gathering in a room and coming up with ideas for millennia, the term "brainstorming" originates exactly where you'd expect: an ad agency. BBDO's Alex Osborn coined it in 1939 to describe the meetings where he'd bring together a bunch of people from the agency to come up with ideas for clients.

This method is surprisingly ineffective. Dozens of studies over the years have found that group brainstorming often yields middling results because introverts tend to stay quiet, and people hold back ideas for fear of being judged, unless there's strong psychological safety in the group. But there is a method that *does* work reliably: Have people come up with their own ideas *first*, then share them with the larger group.

This is where AI comes in. The magic of generative AI tools is that they give us unlimited ideas to jolt our creativity; it's like having a hundred brainstorming partners on standby inside your computer at all times. You start by coming up with ideas on your own, get stuck, and then turn to AI for prompts that trigger the "chain of little mental advances" that end with a breakthrough.

For instance, British researchers ran an experiment comparing writers who wrote a short story alone to writers who used AI to help generate story ideas. The writers who used AI as a creative springboard wrote much higher-quality and novel stories than those who did not, as judged by a blind panel of evaluators. The more story ideas they were able to generate with AI, the better their final output.

Using AI this way might give some writers the ick, but it's the same basic mechanism as creative writing prompts. A simple catalyst for creativity, fighting back against the tyranny of the blank page.

This principle also applies to creative problem-solving. A recent study of Procter & Gamble employees found that an individual with an AI teammate was better at solving a business challenge than a team of two humans without AI.

Logically, this makes sense—you can get a lot more information and ideas out of an AI teammate in a few hours than you can from a human partner. In many ways, AI is the ideal brainstorming partner, especially since its ideas don't even have to be good. Bad ideas can just as easily catalyze those small steps of creativity that lead to a brilliant one.

The AI Thought Leadership Loop

Throughout the process of writing this book, AI has been an incredible help in the research, brainstorming, and editing process. ChatGPT's Deep Research tool has saved me countless hours by doing detailed, well-cited background research. Claude has talked me through tricky issues with the book's structure and served as a tireless editor, pointing out flaws I couldn't see. Even though every single suggestion Claude has given me for a chapter title has been hilariously awful, those bad suggestions have consistently inspired me to think of better ones. Every word I've written in this book has been my own, and I've worked through the structure and ideas for each chapter before turning to AI. But still, these tools have revolutionized my creative process, consistently keeping me going when I'd otherwise get stuck.

For business writing, I call this process the "AI Thought Leadership Loop" with a simple progression: Ideate → Research → Write → Refine.

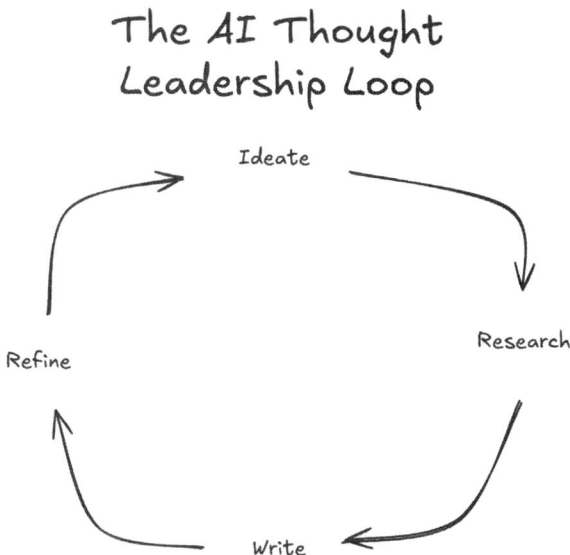

The AI Thought Leadership Loop

Ideate

Research

Write

Refine

Ideate

I'll start by writing a summary of my thesis for my newsletter or a chapter of my book completely on my own. Then, I'll present it to Claude, Anthropic's chatbot, and ask it to act as a critical editor and dissect the flaws in my argument and logic. (I prefer Claude for this because it's been much less sycophantic than ChatGPT.)

I then ask Claude to provide feedback from the perspective of my target audience from my book—specifically, my muse for this book, the creative looking to take control of her future amid a hurricane of AI hype.

I make this easy by using Claude's "Projects" feature, which allows you to upload documents, files, and instructions for a specific use case. I describe my ideal reader in detail, provide full context on my book, and then ask for critical feedback, using this prompt recommended by Anthropic's Lani Assaf:

> "You embody [Person/Role]'s perspective. Review my work through their specific lens. Flag what they'd notice. Suggest what they'd recommend. Be direct—I'm here to level up."

You can take this process one step further. Say you want AI to act like a real person to review your work, such as your boss. Assaf recommends uploading their public writing (blog posts, LinkedIn posts, newsletters, etc.) as well as the written feedback they've given you in the past. You can do this with public figures as well. Say you're a glutton for punishment and you want Kara Swisher to tear apart your work. You could upload her writing and podcasts and get her feedback on your ideas. Assaf calls this building your "Board of Brains." (This made me picture Richard Nixon's head in a glass jar on *Futurama*, but it's a good idea nonetheless.)

Research

Once I've strengthened my outline, I turn to ChatGPT's Deep Research tool. I'll ask it to investigate lesser-known academic papers, podcast interviews, and YouTube interview transcripts—the kind of sources that would normally take me dozens of hours to comb through on my own.

I'll start by giving it my outline and asking ChatGPT to research each specific section, with clear citations from academic and high-quality journalistic sources, as well as podcasts and media interviews. After reviewing the research and the source material it cites, I'll usually ask ChatGPT to do further research on specific sections. Take the Sara Blakely story in Principle 10, Sell Through Stories. Blakely was one of the entrepreneurs I listed in my outline; I knew that I'd likely want to write about her. When ChatGPT returned its first research brief, I asked it for deeper research on specific sections where I needed more detail. For example, it surfaced Blakely's podcast interview with Guy Raz, where she told the story of going on QVC in exquisite detail that I hadn't heard anywhere else.

The magic here is in the prompting. The term "prompt engineering" terrifies most people. It's up there with "synergy," "ping," and "smarketing" as the worst business buzzwords today. If I could, I'd raze it in a glorious field of fire. It's designed to make AI sound unapproachable, but there's nothing technical about prompting. If you know how to communicate with a colleague, you know how to prompt. Just imagine that you're working with a research assistant and tell it how you want it to refine each part of your research in detail.

Write

More specifically, YOU write. The primary tool at this stage? Your fingers.

This is where you cement your unique advantage over others who use AI. Every AI influencer in the world will push you to outsource your first drafts to AI, and I get the temptation: First drafts suck—the procrastination, the self-flagellation as you grope for a hook, the early thesis that turns out to be nonsensical. But that process is important.

First drafts are a creative journey; they're how you learn new things, question your hypothesis, and explore rabbit holes that stood invisible just seconds before. They're a portal to flow. To untangle an idea until you see a golden thread that makes you perk up in wonder. They're the catalysts of long walks where your own arguments play in your head like a podcast, rearrange a story twenty different ways, and earn the delicious high that comes from creating. They're where you discover the story you shouldn't be writing and find the one you should.

As beloved American historian and author David McCullough once said: "Writing is thinking. To write well is to think clearly. That's why it's so hard." A few years ago, a group of German neuroscientists discovered the wonderful truth in that statement. When the researchers connected writers to fMRI machines as they were working on a draft, the parts of their brains in charge of information retrieval, visual processing, problem solving, and speech all lit up. When you outsource your writing to AI, you forgo that wonderful cognitive symphony, but there's also a more subtle risk: Without even knowing it, you'll become anchored to the recycled ideas that AI puts in front of you, reducing your chances of generating something truly novel.

You *can* use AI at this stage, but within strict limits. For instance, best-selling author Daniel Pink told me that he uses it to get unstuck. "Sometimes, I might write a phrase like, 'It sent shockwaves through Baba,'" he explained. "Okay, that's a cliché. So what's an alternative? Give me ten alternatives to the cliché 'shockwaves.' It'll give me ten, and nine will be horrible.

I'm like, 'Oh, wait a second, I can take that one as a jumping-off point to something else.'"

I resist it to the last second, but I use AI similarly, asking for suggestions when I'm stuck on a phrase or transition. I've never actually used its suggestion, but it jars my creativity, and I come up with the answer faster.

I've written this book roughly 60 percent faster than my last one—nearly 70,000 words in the past eight weeks (although I spent eight lazy months researching and outlining before that). I attribute that speed to two primary factors: AI drastically accelerating the pace of my research, getting me unstuck when I might otherwise get up, eat a snack, and get distracted for forty minutes.

Refine

Once I have the first draft, I'll invite AI back to provide feedback as my muse—again, using the Claude Project I've built. You can also use your "Board of Brains."

You want to give AI permission to be blunt and critical in its feedback, the same way you would a colleague or friend who veers on the side of acting too nice. And specificity wins. I often use prompts that relate to the storytelling principles in this book:

Principle	Feedback Questions to Ask Your AI Persona
Principle 2: Master the Elements	Relatability: Does this story and perspective feel relatable to you? Identify specific areas where it does, and areas where it might not.
	Ease: Is the hook of this story engaging? What would you change, if anything?
	Novelty: Do the ideas here feel novel? Did this story give you something new, or did it feel like I was repeating a cliché?
	Tension: Am I maintaining tension throughout this narrative? Where does it lose your attention?

Principle 3: See the Shapes	Which story shape does this narrative most resemble, and does the arc feel satisfying? Are there points where the pacing lingers too long on a plateau in the shape? Does the emotional rise-and-fall match the journey I want the audience to feel?
Principle 5: Find Your Muse	Does this feel as if it was written for one specific person [your muse], or for everyone? If you imagine yourself as [target muse], what would you want clarified or expanded? Where does the writing lose focus on the muse and become too self-serving?
Principle 7: Identify Your Big Idea	How would you define the lens and promise that I have in this piece? What's the most provocative or contrarian idea in this draft? Is it clear? Does this feel bold and original, or more like a remix of conventional wisdom?
Principle 8: Be Vulnerable	Where do I open up with genuine vulnerability, and where do I hold back? Which detail made you laugh, wince, or empathize most? Where does my voice shine through? Where does it sound generic?
Principle 9: Lead Through Stories	If you were on my team, would this story make you feel part of a shared journey? Does this story clearly define the stakes and the transformation ahead? How would you map the Story Spine leadership arc? Where does it deliver, and where does it fall flat?

Principle 10: Sell Through Stories	If you were a skeptical buyer, what part of this story would persuade you most? Least?
	Which obstacle or moment of tension makes the product/idea most compelling?
	Would you retell this story to someone else, and if so, which part?
Principle 11: Build an Audience	Which parts of this story would make you want to follow me for more?
	What detail feels most shareable or meme-able?
	Do I come across as a real human with a point of view, or like brand copy?

You choose

In April 2024, Shy Kids, a trio of Toronto-based filmmakers Walter Woodman, Sidney Leeder, and Patrick Cederberg, released a short film called *Air Head,* created using OpenAI's video generation model, Sora. They were part of a select group of filmmakers that OpenAI had given early access to the tool.

I assumed the film would absolutely suck. My feed had been flooded with AI-generated videos that were only grotesquely interesting because they were created by AI, the content equivalent of an old Victorian freak show.

But *Air Head* didn't suck. It was strangely captivating. It tells a story. It *felt like art,* which shook me, challenging my prior assumption that anything made using AI video and image-generation tools could never be artistic.

The eighty-second short film follows Sunny, a young man with a yellow balloon for a head, as he narrates the story of his life. It's tongue-in-cheek funny. "Windy days are particularly troublesome," he explains, as we see him chase his head past a fountain. "One time my girlfriend asked me to go to the cactus store to get my Uncle Jerry a wedding present—ugh," he deadpans, strolling through rows of prickly cacti. It also has heart, in its own absurdist way, as we hear Sunny explain his unique perspective on the world as he floats over concerts, Formula 1 races, and a majestic pod of whales.

On social media, the film elicited responses that echoed Delaroche: "From today, film is dead!" But Woodman, Leeder, and Cederberg saw it much differently. In an interview with *The Hollywood Reporter*, they explained the intricate storytelling process behind *Air Head*, comparing OpenAI's Sora to traditional video editing tools like Adobe After Effects or Premiere.

"It's something where you bring your energy and your talents and you work with it to make something," Woodman explained. "There's a lot of hot air about just how powerful this is and how this is going to replace everything and how we don't need to do anything. That's really undervaluing what a story is and what the components of a story are and the role of storytellers."

Much like the camera democratized visual art, *Air Head*'s creators see generative AI as a tool with the potential to democratize film and break down barriers to access in the film industry, where it's capital-intensive to get projects going. They also think the social media hype about Sora is ridiculous.

"You read the Twitter comments, and they're like, 'Oh my God, this was so easy,'" Woodman said. "If you only knew how many psychotic balloon-faced things I've seen, you would know that it wasn't just, 'Here you go, here's the movie.' It still requires tons of work and tons of molding."

After reading Woodman's perspective, I realized *Air Head* felt more artistic than other AI-generated videos because he and his team were still making thousands of choices in the creation of the film, in the same way they would without the help of generative AI.

In a 2024 *New Yorker* article, award-winning novelist Ted Chiang presented a wonderfully simple theory: "Art is something that results from making a lot of choices." When you're writing a story, each word is a choice. If you outsource the writing to AI, you're moving from thousands of choices to just one—the prompt you give ChatGPT. And when ChatGPT produces text, the choices it makes are simply an averaging out of all the mediocre text on the web. What could be more boring?

When using generative AI—and whatever sci-fi technologies come after it—in storytelling and art, this is the fundamental litmus test: Are you the one still making the choices? Are you exercising your unique taste in each of those decisions? So much of using AI well is tied to taste—the ability to know which ideas are good, and when you're using AI as a tool for creation, choosing which outputs are worth using.

The other key is transparency. Ninety percent of people say they want transparency on whether AI created an image; 71 percent say they're worried about being able to trust what they see or hear because of AI; 83 percent say it should be required by law to label AI-generated content. Transparency isn't just the right thing to do—it has upside. In one recent study, brands that disclosed the use of AI in their ads saw a 96 percent lift in brand trust. Like Shy Kids with *Air Head*, you want to be completely transparent with your audience about your use of AI.

Your intentional use of generative AI doesn't have to mean making an entire film using the tool. Take CARE, one of the world's leading nonprofits fighting global hunger. The primary way they drive donations is through storytelling—telling the stories of the people the organization helps. CARE's marketing team spends much of their time on a plane, flying all over the world, interviewing subjects and telling their stories.

"Most of the time, we're holding the story of someone who might be living in the most hardest-to-reach places," CARE CMO Monica Rowe told me. "They don't have photos, they don't have the things to bring those stories to life."

One way that CARE has filled in the gaps is through the use of generative AI, in thoughtful collaboration with the subject. Take a piece that CARE's team told through the perspective of Dalmar, a Somali refugee, to illuminate the devastating impact of famine.

As a child in the early 1970s, Dalmar's family fled their pastoral home as a drought turned to famine. He traveled to Uganda, where they had to flee a bloody civil war. It's a gripping and heartbreaking story, and Rowe's team wanted to bring it to life with images. The only problem is that Dalmar didn't have any photos or artifacts from his childhood. So Rowe's creative director worked with Dalmar to bring the memories of his youth to life with the AI image generation tool Midjourney. He'd describe scenes from his life like the night when his parents left, and he remembered staring up at the stars and moon, forlorn. "He was blown away at how accurately it showed his experience," Rowe said.

Like the team behind *Air Head*, CARE's content team was using AI thoughtfully as a tool talented storytellers can use, but not a replacement for the storyteller. The choices and stories remain yours. Much like the camera, it's simply a pathway to new possibilities, allowing storytellers to bring their story to life and tell stories that would be financially and logistically impossible otherwise. By lowering the barrier to entry for visual effects, generative AI has the potential to allow us to independently create stories that we couldn't otherwise. The use of generative AI in video is also an ethical minefield. As I write this, my feeds are flooded with videos and short films made with Nano Banana and Veo 3 image and video generation tools. Previous tools had a crippling constraint; the images and video they produced didn't stay consistent from frame to frame. That's why the trio behind *Air Head* chose a protagonist with a yellow balloon for a head. It was easier to keep consistent than a character whose face is changing from scene to scene.

Nano Banana and Veo 3 are the first tools that create consistent images and video from frame to frame, which means you can generate a protagonist that looks the same in every shot. It's already obvious that it's going to transform content in ways that are both incredible—allowing us to create proof-of-concepts for films in mere hours—and terrifying—ushering us into a dangerous new era where deep fakes are indistinguishable from reality.

The genie is out of the bottle, and this technology is only going to keep getting better. As storytellers, the important thing is that we use it authentically, transparently, and with intention. Use AI to amplify your creativity, not replace it. Hold on to the choices you make with AI; don't outsource them.

Like with the daguerreotype, the motion picture camera, CGI, and every technological advancement in storytelling that's come before it, there's no going back. The question is whether we'll use it for good or evil. Intention or outsourcing. Art or abuse. There are two timelines ahead of us. It's our job to pick the right one.

Chapter 18

PRINCIPLE 15:
Innovate Boldly

Most PhDs in computer research from Stanford University go into academia or to work at Google, Microsoft, Meta, OpenAI, or another one of Silicon Valley's prominent AI research labs.

Holly Herndon decided to become a groundbreaking EDM star.

Herndon wasn't new to music. She grew up in East Tennessee singing in her church choir. As a teenager, she fell in love with electronic dance music (EDM). She released her debut EDM album, *Movement*, in 2012, while finishing her undergraduate degree at Mills College, and a second album, *Platform*, in 2015, while pursuing her PhD. In 2017, Herndon was planning her third album, *Proto,* with her husband, Mat Dryhurst, a fellow musician and tech researcher. One day, the couple had an idea. Herndon had long been derided as a "laptop girl" by other musicians who denigrated the computer as a musical instrument. She wanted to show how the computer could push the boundaries of human-computer collaboration to make the most radically human electronic music in history. Her studies at Stanford gave her the idea of working with an AI model, training it on her own voice to collaborate with her on stage. She could sense that AI was going to be big business. And she wanted control.

So Holly Herndon decided to build her own AI.

In June 2017, Herndon and Dryhurst gave birth to Spawn, an early AI model trained on both of their voices, as well as a group of "willing collaborators" they invited to further refine the model. "Spawn is our AI baby," Herndon said in her documentary, *Birthing Proto.*

Herndon decided to build her own AI model and train it herself because she wanted to use the technology intentionally. "How can this technology be used in a way that's not this kind of retro mania where we're just regurgitating the past? That's not how music develops," she explained in an interview in *Vogue.* "Instead of outsourcing my composition to an AI [model], I'm still the composer. I'm the director of the ensemble, and the AI is an ensemble member that is improvising and singing and performing alongside us."

Herndon trained the model through call-and-response training sessions, and on *Proto,* it blended in with a choir of other voices, harking back to Herndon's days in a Tennessee choir. On tour, she wanted to see how she could push past the limitations of her physical body, singing on stage through Spawn, which came to develop a unique voice of its own, thanks to the melting pot of voices she trained it on.

At each tour stop, she'd lead the audience through additional call-and-response singing and then use that recording to train Spawn; it gave her more training data, and in each case, she'd then share a unique model made in collaboration with each audience. Attribution was crucial to her; she credited all the collaborators that gave Spawn her voice.

"That's one of the biggest problems of AI; it's this kind of opaque, black box technology, and when we have this glossy press release where it's like 'the machine just wrote this song' you're totally discounting all the human labor that went into the training set that the thing learns on," she presciently told *Jezebel* in 2019. "That was a really important part of how we set up the project and the way that we did it. We wanted the people training Spawn to be visible, to be audible, to be named, to be compensated, because I think that's a huge part of what we're facing with this thing today."

In 2021, Herndon decided to push that collaboration further. She released Holly+, an AI model that served as Herndon's vocal twin. Holly+ allows fans to sing through her voice by simply uploading an audio file of them singing, which helps train the neural network. It also works live. In a TED Talk by Herndon, the musician Pher picked up a mic and started singing in Herndon's voice, like a Greek god who'd stolen her vocal chords. In 2023, this idea went mainstream when pop artist Grimes released her own AI model, Elf.Tech, which fans could use to create music using her voice. Herndon and Grimes presented collaborators with the same financial deal: any profits made from new art made using the model get split with its creators 50/50.

"There's a narrative around a lot of this stuff that it's scary dystopian," Herndon told *Wired*. "I'm trying to present another side—this is an opportunity." By building her own model, she got ahead of any future deep fakes of her voice, creating a communal tool for her fans to create art alongside her.

A musician cross-training as an AI researcher, Herndon saw one of the biggest challenges of the twenty-first century coming.

When ChatGPT debuted a year after the release of Holly+, it sparked a crisis over fair use, copyright law, and IP. LLMs like ChatGPT are trained on the writing, videos, and images of millions of writers, storytellers, musicians, and visual artists without compensation. Google, Anthropic, OpenAI, Meta, Nvidia, and Perplexity are all entangled in unresolved copyright lawsuits, but one thing is clear: Artists are losing.

As of October 2025, the most interesting development on this crisis was a class-action lawsuit by a group of authors, which alleged that Anthropic trained its model by downloading millions of pirated books.[9] Anthropic settled for $1.5 billion, agreeing to pay out roughly $3,000 each to 500,000 authors. It was the largest payout for a copyright lawsuit in history. On the surface, it was a win for writers, but a very temporary one. The judge in the case ruled that Anthropic's use of the books was "transformative" under the fair use doctrine, meaning that when copyrighted works are used for training data, the model "transforms" them enough that their use isn't considered copyright infringement. The penalty was imposed because the books were pirated from sites like LibGen and PiLiMi, rather than obtained legally.

As storytellers, we can wait for others to rip off our work using generative AI. Or we can take control. Instead of waiting for corporate giants to ingest our IP into their models, we can build solutions of our own and create interactive, communal storytelling experiences.

Imagine James Cameron opening the *Avatar* universe to fans, allowing them to iterate and expand on it through a GenAI model, while licensing his visual style, voice, and pacing. Or George R. R. Martin doing the same with *Game of Thrones*. Imagine a new generation of storytellers building their own worlds, governing and guiding their character development and style through custom GenAI models. All of this is already possible and both financially and creatively inevitable. Emerging startups, like the Story Foundation, an AI rights platform, are working to build the infrastructure to make it easy for artists and storytellers to operate like Herndon and Grimes and get paid when people license and remix their work.

---

9 Anthropic has an additional open copyright lawsuit from a group of major music publishers.

All around us, we see artists using generative AI to push boundaries and innovate. During COVID, British media artist Jake Elwes created *The Zizi Show*, a deep-fake drag cabaret where AI performers learn how to do drag by watching human performers. His goal is to "queer the AI" and turn deep fakes from an exploitative tool to a collaborative experience, where audience members are invited to interact and guide the AI dancers. French artist Pierre Huyghe worked with neuroscientists to create an AI that brings to life images imagined in people's minds while undergoing an fMRI scan, literally bringing imagination to life. German artist Mario Klingemann created a robot dog that literally poops out art critiques, a commentary on the "endless barrage of A.I.-created art to consume, critique, or rather, endure." Hollywood visual effects shop Metaphysic is using generative AI to reimagine CGI, producing IMAX-level films at a fraction of the cost and enabling small movies to produce big effects, like a 2024 film called *Here*. The film tells the story of a baby-boomer couple at various stages of their lives, using AI to make a sixty-eight-year-old Tom Hanks look eighteen. "You couldn't have made this movie three years ago," director Robert Zemeckis told the *New York Times*, explaining that with traditional CGI, it would have cost tens of millions of dollars. "There's no capes or explosions or aliens or superheroes or creatures. It's people talking, it's families, it's their loves and their joys and their sorrows. It's their life."

The opportunity afforded to us by any transformative technology—whether it's generative AI, virtual production, or whatever comes next—is that we can find new solutions from scratch. Can't break through the Hollywood gatekeepers? Build your own model of production. Want to use AI artistically and maintain control? Build your own model.

I often think back to the renegade approach that George Lucas took to making *Star Wars*, which he explained at the

Sundance Film Festival in 2015. Lucas believed that making movies on your terms meant being able to "have your imagination go wherever it wants to go."

"I had a problem: a story I wanted to tell," he explained. "So I went and found the technology to do it. In the process of making *Star Wars* there weren't any visual effects houses so I had to invent one."

Rethinking the book

As I outlined this book in the spring of 2025 and reached this final principle, I wanted to take my own advice.

I've read voraciously since I was five years old, starting with *Goosebumps* and *Animorphs* in elementary school before graduating to Kafka and Vonnegut in high school. I had a tumultuous childhood, and I always loved the magical way that books transport you to a new world that's unique to each reader. The way stories come to life in your imagination, a rendition unique to your mind's eye. When my entire grade was nose-deep in *Harry Potter* in middle school, it was a collective experience that bonded us, but it was also unique to each of us. Each character took a different form in each of our minds, which is why we all screamed, *"That's what Hermione looks like?!"* when the first *Harry Potter* movie hit the big screen. We were all betrayed in our own special way.

Narrative nonfiction books, like the one you're reading, are an interesting beast. They're filled with stories, and as an author, I want those characters to come to life in your imagination. But this book is also backed by a more explicit premise: I want you to embrace storytelling as your super skill. I want to give you the gift of great storytelling. In each chapter, there are key actions I hope you'll take. But I know from experience how hard it is to always take those lessons and actually apply them successfully. (If I'd done so with every pop business/narrative nonfiction book on my shelf, I'd be living on a superyacht and coaching the New York Giants over Zoom—a company I personally founded.)

I'm a writer, but I've spent the past decade cross-training as a tech executive inside AI and content technology companies. I've learned how to develop tools that help marketers and creatives tell better stories. So I wondered, how can I tap into my inner Holly Herndon and build a companion product that would make it easier for you to develop a successful storytelling practice and apply the 15 Principles in this book?

As any of the CTOs I've worked with will tell you, I am not an engineer; my coding prowess stops at HTML. My first thought was to start with a simple iterative approach and provide prompts you could use to get ChatGPT to coach you through each Principle of this book. But I quickly ran into a problem: The advice ChatGPT gave would be based on its training data, not the lessons in this book.

I realized that what I really wanted to do was build an AI version of myself.

Now, by the time my son Max is my age, having an AI clone might be as common as having an email address or a Ziploc bag of wires you carry from apartment to apartment. But no one I know has an AI clone. I worried I'd developed a case of AI-tinged egomania. But screw it, I thought, if Holly Herndon can do it, so can I. Sure, she's an international EDM star with a PhD from Stanford and I'm a Brooklyn newsletter writer with an intolerance to lactose. But doesn't she always preach taking control of how AI uses your IP?

So I tried building my AI clone with a "CustomGPT," ChatGPT's tool that allows you to build custom versions of its chatbot, fine-tuned with your own training data. There, I ran into another problem: ChatGPT is an awful coach. It's trained to be helpful to a fault. After a few prompts, it would give up coaching and insist on writing for me, like an overbearing parent who just can't watch their kid struggle.

I met with a half-dozen AI engineers to see if they could help. "Why wouldn't you want the AI to write for you?" they asked, looking at me as if I'd said I wanted to build an AI that gives Swedish massages to chickens. They were baffled. Why wasn't I trying to automate content creation like everyone else in the AI gold rush? I started to wonder if this was a stupid idea, a deviously self-centered form of procrastination. Then, an old colleague sent me a message on LinkedIn. Her friend Lim was building an AI tool for nonfiction authors. Would I be willing to speak with her and give some feedback?

I met with Lim over Zoom and explained what I wanted to build; shockingly, she understood completely. She'd been speaking with other nonfiction authors, and they too wanted to build an AI coach that could help readers apply their principles in an environment where they'd have total ownership and control. So I became an early design partner for her platform. In the ensuing months, I sent Lim hundreds of pages of training data, and tried to imagine how to teach an AI model to ask questions and guide people the way I would. I remember the first time I tried it out; Lim had designed an AI version of my headshot that made me look like the missing nerd elf from *Lord of the Rings*. I imagined Max chatting with this version of me in a few years when he could use a computer, strangely preferring Elf Dad to the real one. Then I started chatting with it. It responded like a friend parodying my own writing. It reminded me of the early versions of Herndon's Spawn: scratchy, distorted, disorienting, like looking at yourself in a funhouse mirror.

But we continued to train and tweak Elf Joe, and over time, it improved. Getting the first exercise practices ready, which explored Principles 2 and 3 of this book, was fascinating. The process of chatting with my AI clone, testing how it would answer certain questions, how it would tell certain stories, made me rethink how I was writing about the Principles themselves. It raised questions people might ask that I hadn't thought to answer.

I've since rolled out the AI clone to some of my newsletter readers as beta testers; a few were able to crack stories and personal narratives that they'd been stuck on for months. You can try it out at joelazer.com/superskill. I don't know if this is the version that will work—I'm actively testing an alternative approach as well—but I do know that I want to continue to push myself to reimagine what's possible. For instance, I'm also working on a companion audio product that's more native to the medium of audio than a traditional audiobook. Five years ago, it would have been dauntingly expensive and complicated for me to build companion experiences like this. Now, it's relatively trivial. Given a week and a case of sugar-free Red Bull, I could likely figure out how to turn this book into a film as well. We no longer need to accept the limits of how things have always been done. We don't have to wait for the AI giants to take control of our work and ideas. We can build our own.

I wrote my first book when I was three years old. It was about a cat chasing a dog, a subversion of the traditional cat-dog genre, inspired by my nana's cat, Nookie, and her reign of terror over my mom's dogs. I've been telling stories ever since, and as I finish this book, I have the joy of watching my son as he approaches his third birthday. He lives each day in Neverland, telling stories of his own, intricate dramas between cars come to life, usually as they make their way to the beach. Often, he picks up his ukulele guitar and enacts them in song. The fears I had the day he was born have subsided; no technology could dampen his storytelling superpowers. For him, stories are like air.

I don't know what the job market will look like when he graduates college in twenty years, but I'm certain the storytelling skills he's honing now will serve him well. As I look at my own career, I believe there's never been a better time to be a story-teller. Sure, the world is a little fucked, and the business models around content are too. But we have more power to tell stories than anyone in history. In our pockets are recording studios and movie cameras; with a $30 green screen, we can transport our audience anywhere in the world. Any scene we can imagine, we can bring to life. We can bring all our strange and wonderful experiences from other art forms and industries, and use our unique perspective to tell stories in ways that have never been told before.

So be curious. Experiment. The winners of tomorrow will be open to the possibilities of what's to come.

SUPER SKILL CHEAT SHEET

Get more storytelling resources and strategies at **joelazer.com/superskill.**

Subscribe to Joe's popular storytelling newsletter at **storytellingedge.substack.com.**

PART I: The Storytelling Economy

Three Magic Questions (to ask yourself monthly)

- ☐ **Is 25 percent or more of my day spent doing repeatable tasks that AI can do at an acceptable quality?** (If yes, outsource those tasks and reinvest the time in strategic work.)

- ☐ **Is my judgment, domain expertise, and taste crucial to my company making smart strategic decisions?** (If no, aggressively acquire domain expertise or move to a role that leverages your strengths.)

- ☐ **Do my relationships and influence with people (offline or online) deliver surplus value compared to the average worker in my role?** (If no, invest aggressively in your storytelling skills and ability to influence others.)

PART II: Unlock

Principle 1: Build a Storytelling Habit

☐ Commit to a storytelling identity.

☐ Define your storytelling medium (LinkedIn posts, videos, newsletters, etc.).

☐ Set a consistent frequency (twice a week, daily, biweekly, etc.).

☐ Create your cue-craving-response-reward system for your storytelling habit.

Principle 2: Master the Elements (RENT Framework)

☐ **Relatability:** Ensure your audience sees themselves in your story.

☐ **Ease:** Hook your audience in the first three seconds and eliminate jargon.

☐ **Novelty:** Share something unexpected or counterintuitive.

☐ **Tension:** Establish the gap between "what is" and "what could be."

Principle 3: See the Shapes

☐ Draw the shapes of your favorite stories (Man in a Hole, Boy Meets Girl, etc.) to trigger multimodal encoding and supercharge your storytelling processing.

☐ Work backward from the emotional journey you want your audience to go on to identify the right story shape.

☐ Use these shapes to get your team on the same page when crafting brand narratives.

Principle 4: Become an Active Listener

☐ **Synchronize:** Use body language and facial expressions to create comfort.

- ☐ **Trust:** Create psychological safety with stories and reassurance.
- ☐ **Opening questions:** Focus on feelings, not facts.
- ☐ **Reflect:** Paraphrase emotions back to the interviewee to invite deeper exploration.
- ☐ **Yield space:** Be fully present, embrace silence, and let the subject's story emerge.

Principle 5: Find Your Muse

- ☐ Identify one specific person who represents your ideal audience.
- ☐ Conduct "muse interviews" with your target audience to get inspired.
- ☐ Use the "Letter to a Friend" technique to unlock the muse.
- ☐ Before creating, ask: "What promise am I making? Would this help/delight/teach my muse something new?"

Principle 6: Develop Taste (TASTE Framework)

- ☐ **Take back the wheel:** Reclaim control from the algorithms. Choose one thing to consume each day on your own.
- ☐ **Attune your taste:** Record which stories resonate with you and why.
- ☐ **Study the masters:** Mimic the storytellers you love.
- ☐ **Try and fail:** Do the work and keep telling stories consistently to close the taste-talent gap.
- ☐ **Embrace the gap:** Use the taste-talent gap as a north star to guide you.

PART III: Unleash

Principle 7: Identify Your Big Idea

- ☐ Define your unique lens—the unique way you see the world.

☐ Develop your promise—how will people's lives transform if they adopt your lens?

☐ Craft a signature story as a delivery mechanism for your big idea.

☐ Test your idea—score its resonance using the six-point scale.

Principle 8: Be Vulnerable

☐ Mine your personal experiences to find authentic, vulnerable stories.

☐ Build trust and connection by sharing those stories and instigating the Vulnerability Loop.

☐ Leverage the four elements of storytelling (RENT) to tell vulnerable stories that resonate.

Principle 9: Lead Through Stories

☐ Use the Story Spine to craft the story of your team's shared journey (Once upon a time . . . Every day . . . Until one day . . . Because of that . . . Until finally . . .)

☐ Paint a vivid picture of the stakes and the transformation ahead.

☐ Build a culture of storytelling where teammates naturally tell these stories to each other.

Principle 10: Sell Through Stories

☐ Use the Hero's Journey for Sales to craft compelling sales stories (Ordinary World → Call to Adventure → Obstacles → Magical Helper → Tests, Allies, and Enemies → Transformation).

☐ Obsess over showing how you've transformed—and how that transformation changed customers' lives for the better.

☐ Make your story so memorable that your champion will tell it when you're not in the room.

☐ Use the same template to craft and "sell" your career narrative.

Principle 11: Build an Audience

☐ Choose one or two social platforms you actually enjoy using and start telling stories with a strong hook.

☐ Convert from Social → Subscribers, building an owned channel (email list, newsletter) to have a direct relationship with your audience.

☐ Obsess over serving your audience. What do they need to learn or experience?

☐ Earn the right to "sell" and ask your audience to take action.

PART IV: Upgrade

Principle 12: Beware the Vortex of Mid

☐ Before using AI, understand how it works and where it's flawed.

☐ Think and write on your own first, and then use AI as an amplifier and creativity partner.

☐ Always beware the Vortex of Mid: AI's gravitational pull toward mediocrity and sameness.

Principle 13: Automate the Busywork

☐ Audit your work: identify "administrative overhead" that AI can handle (research, copyediting, organizing notes).

☐ Set up AI workflows to automate "shallow work" (email summaries, meeting notes, first-draft editing).

☐ Reinvest the time saved into deep creative work that only you can do.

☐ Reorient your job around outcomes, not tasks.

Principle 14: Iterate with Intention

☐ Initiate the AI Thought Leadership Loop: Ideate → Research → Write → Refine.

☐ Always ideate and write on your own first, then turn to AI as a brainstorming partner to get unstuck and find lateral leaps of creativity.

☐ Don't outsource the creative choices you make to AI. Constantly stay in control.

Principle 15: Innovate Boldly

☐ Explore how AI can help you tell stories in entirely new mediums, inviting your audience as collaborators.

☐ Take control of how your work is using AI by building your own models and tools.

☐ Use AI as a tool to democratize storytelling forms previously accessible only to elites.

☐ Focus on creating art that reflects intentional human choices, not algorithmic outputs.

REMEMBER...

✓ Storytelling is humanity's superpower—you already have it in you.

✓ AI won't replace storytellers; it will make storytelling more valuable, supercharging the soft skills that matter most in the new world of work.

✓ AI can write, but it can never be a storyteller. Your unique experience is what makes your story special.

✓ Build the habit, master the foundations, then unleash your storytelling superpowers on the world.

ACKNOWLEDGMENTS

The night before I was supposed to send the final manuscript of this book to the publisher, I got pneumonia.

My first thought: *Is this Vonnegut from the grave telling me that I secretly wasn't writing for one person?*

In a small way, Vonnegut would be right. If I'm being honest, I had a secret second muse while writing this book: my son Max.

I didn't write this book for him—it would be absurd for Max to ask three magic questions about how AI will affect his career. He's two years old! But I wrote this book because of him. He sparked my obsession with the central question of this book: *What will be the super skill of the AI Age?* And he lit a fire under my butt to write it because I want him to grow up with a father who lives by example and does what he loves. And I love telling stories. So thank you, Max, for constantly reminding me what matters.

And then there's my wife, Nicole, who supported this book from the start. You're the perfect case study in the power of storytelling—a Tisch-trained actress who parlayed her storytelling skills to become wildly successful in the corporate world. You're incredible to watch, and I love traveling to Neverland with you and Max. Thank you.

This book wouldn't have been nearly as polished or coherent without my editor, Jordan Teicher. (It also would have been at least 20 percent more offensive.) It's wild to think we've worked together for fifteen years, homie. There is no one I trust more. You're a fantastic editor and an even better friend.

Thank you to my mom for always supporting me, even when I told her I wanted to go to arts school and be a writer. To Shane Snow, thank you for shaping my ideas here. You've been an incredible mentor, creative partner, and friend. My career never would have happened without you. And thank you to the rest of our nuclear, found family of creative misfits—Brandon, Brian, Sylvia, Jess. I love you, and you give me the confidence to try crazy shit.

Several other friends heavily influenced my thinking and challenged my point of view: Kyle, Raphael, Anirudh, Kishan, May, Dan, Brad, Margaret, plus many more I can't remember right now because I actually do still have pneumonia, and this acknowledgments note is overdue. Special shoutout to Eric Solomon, who endured some unhinged outlining sessions with me, and we feel destined to write a book together one day. And to David at Prospecta for shepherding this book wonderfully. Thank you to the teachers and professors who nurtured my love of storytelling—Steve Valentine, Rachel Cohen, Jeff McDaniel, and Melvin Bukiet. You gave me the greatest gift.

Finally, thank you to all of you who read my work—whether on Substack, LinkedIn, or my books. All I've ever wanted to do is tell stories and help people think about the world in a new way, and it's so fucking magical that I've carved out a career doing it. So thank you for reading, commenting, and emailing—it really brings me so much joy. You have no idea. I'm living the dream.

SOURCE NOTES

Introduction

Goldman Sachs predicted that 300 million creative jobs would soon be lost: Joseph Briggs and Devesh Kodnani, *The Potentially Large Effects of Artificial Intelligence on Economic Growth*, Goldman Sachs Global Economics Analyst, March 26, 2023, **https://www.ansa.it/documents/1680080409454_ert.pdf.**

McKinsey projected that generative AI was poised to add $2.4–$4.4 trillion to the global economy: Michael Chui et al., *The Economic Potential of Generative AI: The Next Productivity Frontier*, McKinsey Global Institute, June 14, 2023, **https://www.mckinsey.com/~/media/mckinsey/business%20functions/mckinsey%20digital/our%20insights/the%20economic%20potential%20of%20generative%20ai%20the%20next%20productivity%20frontier/the-economic-potential-of-generative-ai-the-next-productivity-frontier.pdf.**

"Some creative jobs will go away . . . ": Shanti Escalante-De Mattei, Artists and Creatives Are Working with AI Companies, But Should They? https://www.artnews.com/art-news/news/openai-nvidia-runway-artists-creatives-beta-testing-residencies-1234716406.

"Art is dead, dude . . .": Kevin Roose, "An A.I.-Generated Picture Won an Art Prize. Artists Aren't Happy," *New York Times*, September 2, 2022. https://www.nytimes.com/2022/09/02/technology/ai-artificial-intelligence-artists.html. studocu.com.

The majority of U.S. workers are worried about how AI will affect their careers: Luona Lin and Kim Parker, "U.S. Workers Are More Worried Than Hopeful About Future AI Use in the Workplace," Pew Research Center, February 25, 2025, **https://www.pewresearch.org/social-trends/2025/02/25/u-s-workers-are-more-worried-than-hopeful-about-future-ai-use-in-the-workplace/.**

Overrelying on AI shuts off parts of our brains: Nataliya Kosmyna et al., "Your Brain on ChatGPT: Accumulation of Cognitive Debt when Using an AI Assistant for Essay Writing Task," *arXiv* (June 10, 2025), https://arxiv.org/abs/2506.08872.

You spend 75% of your waking hours consuming, exchanging, or daydreaming in story: Simon Kemp, "Digital 2025: Global Overview Report," DataReportal, February 5, 2025, https://datareportal.com/reports/digital-2025-global-overview-report; and Matthew A. Killingsworth and Daniel T. Gilbert, "A Wandering Mind Is an Unhappy Mind," *Science* 330, no. 6006 (November 12, 2010): 932, https://www.science.org/doi/10.1126/science.1192439

Chapter 1: Storytelling Sapiens

Neanderthals vs. Homo sapiens (superbrain/gigabrain): Rutger Bregman, *Humankind: A Hopeful History* (New York: Little, Brown, 2020).

Humans and Neanderthals co-existed: Ian Sample, "Humans and Neanderthals Co-Existed in Europe Far Longer than Thought," *The Guardian*, May 11, 2020, https://www.theguardian.com/science/2020/may/11/humans-and-neanderthals-co-existed-in-europe-far-longer-than-thought.

Toddler–ape cognition comparison: Esther Herrmann et al., "Humans Have Evolved Specialized Skills of Social Cognition: The Cultural Intelligence Hypothesis," 2007, https://evolutionaryanthropology.duke.edu/sites/evolutionary-anthropology.duke.edu/files/site-images/Herrmann%20et%20al,%202007.pdf.

Joseph Henrich study: Rutger Bregman, *Humankind: A Hopeful History* (New York: Little, Brown, 2020)

Earliest human writing: *The Evolution of Writing*, University of Texas at Austin, https://sites.utexas.edu/dsb/tokens/the-evolution-of-writing/.

Stories improve memory (classic 1969 Stanford study): Gordon H. Bower and Michael C. Clark, "Narrative Stories as Mediators for Serial Learning," *Psychonomic Science* 14 (1969): 181–82. https://www.researchgate.net/publication/232549160_Narrative_stories_as_mediators_for_serial_learning.

Immersive stories and memory encoding: Joe Lazer, "We Strapped Neurosensors to Voters and Showed Them 2020 Campaign Ads," *GEN* (Medium), 2020, https://gen.medium.com/we-strapped-neurosensors-to-voters-and-showed-them-2020-campaign-ads-6af534e2e875.

Dunbar's number / social group size: "Bonds and Communities: The 150-Layered Structure," *Biology Letters* 17, no. 7 (2021), https://royalsociety-publishing.org/doi/epdf/10.1098/rsbl.2021.0158.

Storytellers in Agta hunter-gatherers: Daniel Smith et al., "Cooperation and the Evolution of Hunter-Gatherer Storytelling," *Nature Communications* 8, no. 1853 (2017), https://www.nature.com/articles/s41467-017-02036-8.

Harari on imagined orders ("monkey heaven") and other *Sapiens* quotes and references: Yuval Noah Harari, *Sapiens: A Brief History of Humankind* (New York: Harper Collins, 2015).

Reading fiction and empathy: Raymond A. Mar, Keith Oatley, and Jordan B. Peterson, "Exploring the Link between Reading Fiction and Empathy: Ruling Out Individual Differences and Examining Outcomes," Communications 34, no. 4 (2009): 407–28, https://doi.org/10.1515/COMM.2009.025.

Chapter 2: The New Science of Stories

Social trust and economic growth: Stephen Knack and Philip Keefer, "Does Social Capital Have an Economic Payoff? A Cross-Country Investigation," *Quarterly Journal of Economics* 112, no. 4 (1997): 1251–88.

Neuroscience of narrative (Dr. Zak 2015 paper): Paul J. Zak, "Why Inspiring Stories Make Us React: The Neuroscience of Narrative," *Cerebrum: The Dana Forum on Brain Science*, February 2, 2015, https://pmc.ncbi.nlm.nih.gov/articles/PMC4445577/.

Narrative reflection and team effectiveness: Anne Marie Lohuis, Anneke Sools, Mark van Vuuren, and Ernst T. Bohlmeijer, "Narrative Reflection as a Means to Explore Team Effectiveness," *Small Group Research* 47, no. 4 (2016): 406–37, https://journals.sagepub.com/doi/10.1177/1046496416656464.

Predicting sales from immersion (BBDO case): Immersion Neuroscience, "Case Study: BBDO Ad Test," https://www.getimmersion.com/v4/case-study-bbdo-ad-test.

Chapter 3: Welcome to the Storytelling Economy

Karpathy coins "vibe-coding": Andrej Karpathy, post on X (n.d.). https://x.com/karpathy/status/1886192184808149383?lang=en.

Humanities majors down: American Academy of Arts & Sciences, "Bachelor's Degrees in the Humanities," *Humanities Indicators*, https://www.

amacad.org/humanities-indicators/higher-education/bachelors-degrees-humanities#31600.

UW-Madison humanities decline: "The Great Recession Continues to Drive Major Choices," *Badger Herald*, May 10, 2024, https://badgerherald.com/news/campus/2024/05/10/great-recession-continues-to-drive-major-choices/.

STEM enrollment grew during the recession: "Study Finds Increased STEM Enrollment in the Recession," *Inside Higher Ed*, April 7, 2014. https://www.insidehighered.com/news/2014/04/07/study-finds-increased-stem-enrollment-recession.

GPT-4 technical report (includes HumanEval figure): OpenAI, "GPT-4 Technical Report," 2023. https://cdn.openai.com/papers/gpt-4.pdf.

Audience response to AI-labeled content: Article on *PubMed Central* (n.d.). https://pmc.ncbi.nlm.nih.gov/articles/PMC11332189/.

J. Crew AI-image backlash case: "J. Crew Used A.I. to Counterfeit Their Own Vibes," *Blackbird Spyplane*, https://www.blackbirdspyplane.com/p/jcrew-used-ai-to-counterfeit-their-own-vibes.

Claude coding usage: Anthropic, "The Anthropic Economic Index," 2025, https://www.anthropic.com/news/the-anthropic-economic-index.

ChatGPT writing usage down: Aaron Chatterji, Thomas Cunningham, David J. Deming, Zoe Hitzig, Christopher Ong, Carl Yan Shan, and Kevin Wadman, *How People Use ChatGPT*, NBER Working Paper No. 34255 (Cambridge, MA: National Bureau of Economic Research, September 2025), https://www.nber.org/system/files/working_papers/w34255/w34255.pdf.

"AI will write 90% of code in 3–6 months": "Anthropic CEO: AI Will Write 90% of Code in 3–6 Months," *Business Insider*, 2025, https://www.businessinsider.com/anthropic-ceo-ai-90-percent-code-3-to-6-months-2025-3.

Brian Armstrong on 40% of Codebase Code being written by AI: Brian Armstrong (@brian_armstrong), *X post*, September 3, 2025, https://x.com/brian_armstrong/status/1963315806248604035.

"Most of Meta's code written by AI within 12–18 months": Igor Bonifacic, "Mark Zuckerberg 'Predicts' AI Will Write Most of Meta's Code Within 12 to 18 Months," *Engadget*, n.d., https://www.engadget.com/ai/mark-zuckerberg-predicts-ai-will-write-most-of-metas-code-within-12-to-18-months-213851646.html.

Altman says AI will soon be just as good as an engineer: "OpenAI CEO Sam Altman Says AI Is Ready for Entry-Level Jobs," *MSN* (syndicated), https://www.msn.com/en-us/news/technology/openai-ceo-sam-altman-says-ai-is-ready-for-entry-level-jobs-but-unbothered-gen-z-have-made-it-their-new-work-friend/ar-AA1G9Y7T.

Andy Jassy on AI agents and job cuts (reported remarks): "Amazon CEO Andy Jassy: AI Job Cuts and 'Agents,'" *ITPro*, https://www.itpro.com/business/business-strategy/amazon-ceo-andy-jassy-ai-job-cuts.

Benioff: "No more software engineers in 2025": "Salesforce Will Hire No More Software Engineers in 2025, Says Marc Benioff," *Salesforce Ben*, https://www.salesforceben.com/salesforce-will-hire-no-more-software-engineers-in-2025-says-marc-benioff/.

Unemployment by major: Federal Reserve Bank of New York, "The Labor Market for Recent College Graduates—Outcomes by Major," n.d., https://www.newyorkfed.org/research/college-labor-market#--:explore:outcomes-by-major.

AI companies targeting all technical skills: *The Information*, "Anthropic, OpenAI Developing AI 'Co-Workers',," https://www.theinformation.com/articles/anthropic-openai-developing-ai-co-workers.

Research by LinkedIn economists on most valuable skills: "The A.I. Economy Is Coming for Higher Education," *New York Times* (Opinion), February 14, 2024, https://www.nytimes.com/2024/02/14/opinion/ai-economy-jobs-colleges.html.

WEF jobs report stats: World Economic Forum, *The Future of Jobs Report 2025* (2025), https://reports.weforum.org/docs/WEF_Future_of_Jobs_Report_2025.pdf.

Attention as capital: Kyla Scanlon, "Trump, Mamdani, and Cluely," *Kyla* (Substack), June 25, 2025, https://kyla.substack.com/p/trump-mamdani-and-cluely.

"Flow of capital concentrates around good stories": Scott Galloway, "See What Others Miss: The Prof G Storytelling Playbook," *No Mercy / No Malice*, n.d., https://www.profgalloway.com/see-what-others-miss-the-prof-g-storytelling-playbook/.

Creators earning outsized comp in brand roles: Rachel Karten, "Brand Social Trend Report," *Link in Bio* (Substack), n.d., https://substack.com/@rachelkarten/p-160270013.

Chapter 4. Principle 1: Build a Storytelling Habit

Vonnegut's writing routine: Maria Popova, "'I Numb My Intellect With Scotch and Water': Kurt Vonnegut's Daily Routine," *The Atlantic*, November 5, 2012, https://www.theatlantic.com/entertainment/archive/2012/11/i-numb-my-intellect-with-scotch-and-water-kurt-vonneguts-daily-routine/264561.

James Clear's *Atomic Habits* (referenced throughout): James Clear, *Atomic Habits: An Easy & Proven Way to Build Good Habits and Break Bad Ones* (New York: Avery, 2018).

Pink on writing inspiration: Daniel H. Pink, "How I Write 500 Words a Day (and Why)," *YouTube* video, https://www.youtube.com/watch?v=6om9nd-A8dyc.

Creator habit-building, Nas Daily: Jay Clouse (host), "#159: Nuseir Yassin—The Price of Growing Nas Daily to 12 Million Subscribers," *Creator Science* (podcast), August 8, 2023, https://podcast.creatorscience.com/nuseir-yassin/.

80% of our workday communicating: C. C. Brumback, "Measurement of Time Spent Communicating," *Journal of Communication* (via ResearchGate), https://www.researchgate.net/publication/229753860_Measurement_of_Time_Spent_Communicating.

"We have to continuously be jumping off cliffs and then developing our wings on the way down.": Kurt Vonnegut Jr., *If This Isn't Nice, What Is?: Advice for the Young* (New York: Seven Stories Press, various eds.).

Chapter 5. Principle 2: Master the Elements

Mirror neurons (foundational discovery): "Reflections on Mirror Neurons," *APS Observer*, Association for Psychological Science. https://www.psychologicalscience.org/observer/reflections-on-mirror-neurons.

Ohio State jargon study: Hillary C. Shulman, Graham N. Dixon, Olivia M. Bullock, and Daniel Colón Amill, "The Effects of Jargon on Processing Fluency, Self-Perceptions, and Scientific Engagement," *Journal of Language and Social Psychology* 39, nos. 5–6 (2020): 579–597, https://doi.org/10.1177/0261927X20902177.

"The use of difficult, specialized words is a signal": Jeff Grabmeier, "The Use of Jargon Kills People's Interest in Science, Politics—Even When Specialized Terms Are Defined, the Damage Is Done," *Ohio State News*, February 12, 2020, https://news.osu.edu/the-use-of-jargon-kills-peoples-interest-in-science-politics/.

Attention hasn't collapsed (meta-analysis overview): Lydia Denworth, "People Pay Attention Better Today Than 30 Years Ago—Really?" *Scientific American*, March 12, 2024, https://www.scientificamerican.com/article/people-pay-attention-better-today-than-30-years-ago-really/.

Cameron Gidari quote: Rachel Karten, "14 Creative Video Hooks: A Non-Gimmicky Guide to Those First Few Seconds," *Link in Bio* (Substack), September 16, 2025, https://www.milkkarten.net/p/brand-video-hooks-social-media.

Curiosity-gap hook (Yale Cleaners viral case): Yale Cleaners, "Have we ever had a wedding dress we couldn't save?," *TikTok*, May 2024, https://www.tiktok.com/@yalecleaners/video/7541181300573539598.

Novelty boosts learning: Nico Bunzeck and Emrah Düzel, "Absolute Coding of Stimulus Novelty in the Human Substantia Nigra/VTA," *Neuron* 51, no. 3 (August 3, 2006): 369–79, https://pubmed.ncbi.nlm.nih.gov/16880131/.

Chapter 6. Principle 3: See the Shapes

Vonnegut at GE (early "content marketer"): Rance Crain, "Meet GE's Content Marketer: Kurt Vonnegut," *Ad Age*, April 11, 2014, https://adage.com/article/news/meet-ge-s-content-marketers-kurt-vonnegut/295375.

Vonnegut on his rejected thesis ("one must not be too playful"): Kurt Vonnegut, *Palm Sunday: An Autobiographical Collage* (New York: Delacorte Press, 1981), https://www.penguinrandomhouse.com/books/184340/palm-sunday-by-kurt-vonnegut/.

Vonnegut lecture: Kurt Vonnegut, "Kurt Vonnegut on the Shapes of Stories," *YouTube* video, n.d., https://www.youtube.com/watch?v=oP3c1h8v2ZQ.

Chesky quotes: "Brian Chesky: From Airbed to Airbnb," *Masters of Scale* (podcast). https://mastersofscale.com/brian-chesky/.

AI analysis of story shapes in popular literature (2k-book NLP study): Andrew J. Reagan et al., "The Emotional Arcs of Stories Are Dominated by Six Basic Shapes," *arXiv* (2016), https://arxiv.org/pdf/1606.07772.pdf.

Chapter 7. Principle 4: Become an Active Listener

Stanton origin story: *The Tim Ferriss Show*, "Brandon Stanton—The Story of Humans of New York," podcast episode, 2015.

"I've been green for 15 years": *Humans of New York*, Facebook photo post, https://www.facebook.com/photo.php?fbid=215399998534108&id=102099916530784&set=a.102107073196735.

Active listening reward system: Hidenori Kawamichi et al., "Perceiving Active Listening Activates the Reward System and Improves the Impression of Relevant Experiences," *Social Neuroscience* 10, no. 1 (2015): 16–26, https://pubmed.ncbi.nlm.nih.gov/25188354/.

Approaching strangers: Eric Kim, "How to Approach Strangers on the Street: Brandon Stanton (Humans of New York)," blog post, April 30, 2014, https://erickimphotography.com/blog/2014/04/30/how-to-approach-strangers-on-the-street-brandon-stanton-from-humans-of-new-york/.

Oprah quotes at Forbes Summit: *Forbes Women*, "Oprah: What Every Person I Interview—Including Beyoncé—Asks Me After We Speak On Camera," https://www.youtube.com/watch?v=Y9-CPlEW4WU.

Oprah's "What's your intention?" (Forbes Summit recap): "What Is Your Intention? Oprah's One Question that Changes Everything," *Medium*, https://medium.com/p/e785799a3e52.

Terry Gross's reflection technique: National Press Club Journalism Institute, "Terry Gross . . . Interview Tips," July 20, 2020, https://www.pressclubinstitute.org/2020/07/20/terry-gross-and-michael-barbaro-share-interview-tips-and-techniques/.

Ira Glass on sharing his story to guests: "To Get Things More Real: An Interview with Ira Glass," *The New York Review of Books*, August 8, 2019, https://www.nybooks.com/online/2019/08/08/to-get-things-more-real-an-interview-with-ira-glass/.

Edmondson's landmark psych-safety paper: Amy C. Edmondson, "Psychological Safety and Learning Behavior in Work Teams," *Administrative Science Quarterly* 44, no. 2 (1999): 350–83, https://web.mit.edu/curhan/www/docs/Articles/15341_Readings/Group_Performance/Edmondson%20Psychological%20safety.pdf.

How Stanton gets people to share for HONY: ABC News, "Humans of New York Creator Reveals Why People Share Life's Intimate Details," Sept. 2015, https://abcnews.go.com/US/humans-york-creator-reveals-people-share-lifes-intimate/story?id=34410836.

Ethnographic interviewing (feelings, facts): "Ethnographic Interviewing," *The ASHA Leader* (American Speech-Language-Hearing Association), https://leader.pubs.asha.org/doi/10.1044/leader.FTR3.08082003.4.

Chapter 8. Principle 5: Find Your Muse

Stephen King on his wife, Tabitha, being his muse: Stephen King, *On Writing: A Memoir of the Craft* (New York: Scribner, 2020, 20th-anniversary ed.), https://www.simonandschuster.com/books/On-Writing/Stephen-King/9781982159375.

"Please write for one person" (Vonnegut): Kurt Vonnegut, *Bagombo Snuff Box: Uncollected Short Fiction* (New York: G. P. Putnam's Sons, 1999).

Steven Pressfield's *The War of Art* (creative "Resistance" and Muse frameworks): Steven Pressfield, *The War of Art: Break Through the Blocks and Win Your Inner Creative Battles* (New York: Black Irish Entertainment LLC, 2012), https://blackirishbooks.com/product/the-war-of-art/.

Empathy boosts creative output (study): Yang Cao et al., "Cognitive Empathy Predicts Creative Performance Across Domains," *Personality and Individual Differences* (2024), PubMed 39691954, https://pubmed.ncbi.nlm.nih.gov/39691954/.

Empathy boosts productivity & creative engagement: Greater Good Science Center, "Can Empathy Help You Be More Creative?" (interview with Matthew Pelowski), 2025, https://greatergood.berkeley.edu/article/item/can_empathy_help_you_be_more_creative.

Dopamine and creativity research: Arne Dietrich, "The Cognitive Neuroscience of Creativity," *Psychon Bull Rev* 11 (2004): 1011–1026; see also PMCID overview, https://pubmed.ncbi.nlm.nih.gov/15875970/.

Chapter 9. Principle 6: Develop Taste

Ira Glass on the "taste–talent gap" (video): Ira Glass, "Ira Glass on Storytelling (The Gap)," *YouTube*, 2009, https://www.youtube.com/watch?v=5p-FI9UuC_fc.

Teens wish TikTok never existed: The Harris Poll, "Gen Z & Social Media/Smartphones," 2024–2025 findings, https://theharrispoll.com/briefs/gen-z-social-media-smart-phones/.

Sedaris on tuning your ear: "Tips for Improving Your Writing by Reading Aloud with David Sedaris," *MasterClass* (article), https://www.masterclass.com/articles/tips-for-improving-your-writing-by-reading-aloud-with-david-sedaris.

Tarantino on learning from films: "Quentin Tarantino: BBC News Interview (1994)," summary via BBC archive reporting, https://www.bbc.com/articles/c4g40ndzpe0o#:~:text=He%20immersed%20himself%20in%20the,collection%20or%20a%20still%20collection.

How the video store shaped Tarantino's taste: Aimee Ferrier, "How did working at a video store shape Quentin Tarantino?," *Far Out Magazine*, 2021, https://faroutmagazine.co.uk/how-did-working-at-a-video-store-shape-quentin-tarantino/.

Joe Frank's influence on Ira Glass: Ira Glass, "Joe Frank," *This American Life* (site announcement/tribute), 2013, https://www.thisamericanlife.org/about/announcements/joe-frank.

Ira Glass on his admiration for Didion: "Ira Glass Brings 'Seven Things I've Learned' to San Diego," *San Diego Magazine*, 2023, https://sandiegomagazine.com/everything-sd/people/ira-glass-brings-seven-things-ive-learned-to-san-diego/.

TAL / "Harper High School" case study and accolades: "Harper High School (WBEZ Chicago 91.5)—Award Profile," *Peabody Awards*, 2013, https://peabodyawards.com/award-profile/harper-high-school-wbez-chicago-91-5/.

Tarantino on how he learned how to make a movie (ComicCon panel): "Crucial Filmmaking Advice from Quentin Tarantino and Sam Raimi," *Far Out Magazine*, Oct. 23, 2021, quoting 2006 ComicCon remarks, https://faroutmagazine.co.uk/quentin-tarantino-sam-raimi-filmmaking-advice-comic-con/.

Chapter 10. Principle 7: Identify Your Big Idea

Time reporting there was a deathwatch on Apple: *Time*, "Steve's Job: Restart Apple," September 1997 (archive edition), https://time.com/archive/6731292/steves-job-restart-apple/.

Apple marketshare 4%: "Jobs's Second Act at Apple," *Commoncog* (case study), https://commoncog.com/c/cases/jobs-second-act-apple/.

Short job tenure in tech: Kaylee Fagan, "Average Employee Tenure at Top Tech Companies," *Business Insider*, Apr. 2018, https://www.businessinsider.com/average-employee-tenure-retention-at-top-tech-companies-2018-4.

Think Different ad: Apple Computer, Inc., "1984," television commercial, directed by Ridley Scott, 60 sec, aired January 22, 1984 (Super Bowl XVIII, CBS), video, YouTube, https://youtu.be/2zfqw8nhUwA

Gated content drives 90% of buyers away: AMRA & ELMA, "Gated Content Conversion Statistics," 2023, https://www.amraandelma.com/gated-content-conversion-statistics/.

Cognitive diversity fuels problem-solving and innovation: Alison Reynolds and David Lewis, "Teams Solve Problems Faster When They're More Cognitively Diverse," *Harvard Business Review*, Mar. 30, 2017, https://hbr.org/2017/03/teams-solve-problems-faster-when-theyre-more-cognitively-diverse.

Chapter 11. Principle 8: Be Vulnerable

Kevin Hart's early-career struggles: Nina Metz, "Interview: Kevin Hart Not Shy About Past Flubs," *Chicago Tribune*, January 22, 2012, https://www.chicagotribune.com/2012/01/22/interview-kevin-hart-not-shy-about-past-flubs-2/.

Robinson mentoring Hart: Kevin Hart bio-doc, "Don't Fuck This Up," 2019 https://www.netflix.com/title/81010817?fromWatch=true

"I was trying to be everybody": Dave Itzkoff, "Kevin Hart Learns to Tell the Truth," *New York Times*, September 2, 2012, https://www.nytimes.com/2012/09/02/arts/television/kevin-hart-learns-to-tell-the-truth.html.

Hart film opens in box-office Top 10: Darren Franich, "Kevin Hart's *Laugh at My Pain* Cracks Box-Office Top 10," *Entertainment Weekly*, September 13, 2011, https://ew.com/article/2011/09/13/kevin-hart-laugh-at-my-pain-top-10-box-office/.

"Vulnerability creates trust" (leadership science): Daniel Coyle, *The Culture Code: The Secrets of Highly Successful Groups* (New York: Bantam, 2018), https://www.penguinrandomhouse.com/books/546350/the-culture-code-by-daniel-coyle/.

"Look for the ouch" (Moth story coaching framework): The Moth, *How to Tell a Story: The Essential Guide to Memorable Storytelling from The Moth* (New York: Crown, 2022), https://themoth.org/books/how-to-tell-a-story.

Brené Brown TEDx talk, "power of vulnerability": Brené Brown, "The Power of Vulnerability," TEDxHouston (2010), YouTube video, https://www.youtube.com/watch?v=iCvmsMzlF7o,

Brené Brown on courage and vulnerability (On Being podcast): Krista Tippett (host), "Brené Brown—The Courage to Be Vulnerable," *On Being*, originally aired November 22, 2012; updated January 29, 2015, https://onbeing.org/programs/brene-brown-the-courage-to-be-vulnerable-jan2015/.

Sedaris quote on the relatability of embarrassment: Annabel Gutterman, "David Sedaris and Andrew Sean Greer Fight for the Last Laugh," *TIME*, September 21, 2022, https://time.com/6215416/david-sedaris-and-andrew-sean-greer-interview/.

Chapter 12. Principle 9: Lead Through Stories

Micha Kaufman memo about AI and jobs: Micha Kaufman (@michakaufman), posted on X (formerly Twitter), https://x.com/michakaufman/status/1909610844008161380.

Job tenure trend (U.S., by decade): USAFacts, "How long do Americans stay at their jobs?," https://usafacts.org/articles/how-long-do-americans-stay-at-their-jobs/.

Average employee tenure at top tech companies: Kaylee Fagan, "Silicon Valley techies get free food and dazzling offices, but they're not very loyal—here's how long the average employee stays at the biggest tech companies," *Business Insider*, April 16, 2018, https://www.businessinsider.com/average-employee-tenure-retention-at-top-tech-companies-2018-4.

Employee engagement down to 31% (U.S./Canada): Gallup, *State of the Global Workforce 2024*, https://www.gallup.com/workplace/349484/state-of-the-global-workplace.aspx.

Employees' low alignment with mission inside their company: Gallup Workplace, "How to Build a Better Company Culture," section on mission/purpose, https://www.gallup.com/workplace/327371/how-to-build-better-company-culture.aspx.

3x growth rate when employees are aligned with mission: Korn Ferry, "People on a Mission," December 2016, https://cashmanleadership.com/wp-content/uploads/2016/12/KF_Summary-Report_People-on-a-mission_Dec2016.pdf.

Cowher whiteboard erasure scene: *The Athletic* (*NY Times*, "Untold Stories about Bill Cowher," July 30, 2021, https://www.nytimes.com/athletic/2736257/2021/07/30/untold-stories-about-bill-cowher-incidental-fluids-colorful-sweaters-and-racquetball-rage/.

Roethlisberger tackle + season background: *ESPN.com*, "Winning for Bettis Motivates Steelers," January 29, 2006.

"Just get me to Detroit!" (AFC title week): *The Spokesman-Review*, "Steelers Make Sure Bus' Final Stop Is in Super Bowl," January 23, 2006, https://www.spokesman.com/stories/2006/jan/23/steelers-make-sure-bus-final-stop-is-in-super-bowl/.

"He always said, 'If you need to trick 'em, you can't beat him!'": *Footbahllin with Ben Roethlisberger*, Episode 36 (YouTube), https://www.youtube.com/watch?v=7VZOm3Z_gac.

Brain sync helps learning and problem-solving: Lydia Denworth, "Brain Waves Synchronize When People Interact," *Scientific American*, https://www.scientificamerican.com/article/brain-waves-synchronize-when-people-interact/.

Teams with synchronized brains solve problems better: Diego A Rienerro et al., "Electroencephalographic Signatures of Team Flow State," *Social Cognitive and Affective Neuroscience* 16, nos. 1–2 (2021): 43–55, https://academic.oup.com/scan/article/16/1-2/43/5912973.

Chapter 13. Principle 10: Sell Through Stories

Blakely background and narrative: Guy Raz, "Spanx: Sara Blakely," *How I Built This With Guy Raz*, Sept. 12, 2016, https://podcasts.apple.com/us/podcast/spanx-sara-blakely/id1150510297?i=1000396023160.

How Oprah picked Spanx as a Favorite Thing: Sara Blakely, "How She Got Spanx on Oprah," *Inc.*,https://www.inc.com/sara-blakely/how-sara-blakely-got-spanx-on-oprah.html. Inc.com.

Spanx early history, manufacturing with Highland Mills (Sam Kaplan), market context for hosiery, and early retail expansion: John Colapinto, "Smooth

Moves," *The New Yorker* (March 28, 2011), https://www.newyorker.com/magazine/2011/03/28/smooth-moves.

Spanx growth milestones (bootstrapped origin, early revenue arc) and founder background: Polina Marinova Pompliano, "The Profile Dossier: Sara Blakely," *The Profile* (curated deep-dive), https://www.readtheprofile.com/p/the-profile-dossier-sara-blakely.

Spanx background: "Spanx Founder Sara Blakely: Billion-Dollar Idea Started with $5,000 in Savings," *Fortune*, https://fortune.com/article/spanx-founder-sara-blakely-billion-dollar-idea-started-with-5000-in-savings/.

Sale to Blackstone at a $1.2B valuation: "Blackstone to Acquire Majority Stake in Spanx, Inc." (press release, Oct. 20, 2021), https://www.blackstone.com/news/press/blackstone-to-acquire-majority-stake-in-spanx-inc/.

Traffic from employees social media posts converts ≈2.5× vs. company posts: *The Official Guide to Employee Advocacy* (LinkedIn Elevate/LinkedIn Marketing Solutions), https://business.linkedin.com/content/dam/me/business/en-us/elevate/Resources/pdf/official-guide-to-employee-advocacy-ebook.pdf

"70% of consumers feel more connected to a brand when its CEO/founders are active on social": *The Sprout Social Index*—Edition XV: "Empower & Elevate" (brand connection & executive social visibility), https://sproutsocial.com/insights/data/.

Purchase decisions are primarily emotional: Gallup, "The New Brainstorm: Why Most Customer Decisions Are Emotional," *Gallup Workplace* (analysis summary page), https://www.gallup.com/workplace/398954/customer-brand-preference-decisions-gallup-principle.aspx.

Pink: 40% of work is "non-sales selling" (9,057-person survey): Daniel H. Pink, *To Sell Is Human: The Surprising Truth About Moving Others* (New York: Riverhead Books, 2013 paperback ed.), https://www.penguinrandomhouse.com/books/309694/to-sell-is-human-by-daniel-h-pink/.

Purchase decisions are largely subconscious: Gerald Zaltman, *How Customers Think: Essential Insights into the Mind of the Market* (Boston: Harvard Business School Press, 2003), https://www.hbs.edu/faculty/Pages/item.aspx?num=13632.

Hero's Journey framework: Joseph Campbell, *The Hero with a Thousand Faces* (Princeton: Princeton University Press, 1949), https://press.princeton.edu/books/paperback/9780691183046/the-hero-with-a-thousand-faces.

Background on Blakely: Polina Marinova Pompliano, "The Profile Dossier: Sara Blakely," *The Profile*, n.d. https://www.readtheprofile.com/p/the-profile-dossier-sara-blakely and *Fortune*, "Spanx Founder Sara Blakely: Billion-Dollar Idea Started with $5,000 in Savings," n.d., https://fortune.com/article/spanx-founder-sara-blakely-billion-dollar-idea-started-with-5000-in-savings/.

Primary anecdotes and timeline (Blakely Facebook posts and LinkedIn posts): Sara Blakely, Facebook Page, n.d., https://www.facebook.com/sarablakely/ and Sara Blakely, LinkedIn profile, https://www.linkedin.com/in/sarablakely27/.

Chapter 14. Principle 11: Build an Audience

Ahrefs study of 300k keywords triggering AI Overviews: Louise Linehan, "I Analyzed 300K Keywords. Here's What I Learned About AI Overviews," *Ahrefs Blog*, October 31, 2024, https://ahrefs.com/blog/ai-overview-keywords/.

Influencer marketing growth: Statista Research Department, "Market size of the influencer marketing industry worldwide from 2016 to 2024 with forecast to 2025," *Statista*, 2025, https://www.statista.com/statistics/1092819/global-influencer-market-size/.

Creators making outsized salaries in marketing roles: Rachel Karten, "Brand Social Trend Report (Q1/Q2 2025)," *Link in Bio* (Substack), 2025, https://www.milkkarten.net/p/brand-social-trend-report-q1-2025.

Chapter 15. Principle 12: Beware the Vortex of Mid

The majority of new content is AI-generated: Ryan Law, "What Percentage of New Content Is AI-Generated?," *Ahrefs Blog*, May 7, 2025, https://ahrefs.com/blog/what-percentage-of-new-content-is-ai-generated/.

Most B2B content goes unused: Forrester, "It's Not Content—It's A Lack Of Buyer Insights That's The Problem," https://www.forrester.com/blogs/its-not-content-its-a-lack-of-buyer-insights-thats-the-problem/.

Brenner found most content didn't produce a lead at SAP: Michael Brenner, "The Cost of Bad Content," *Marketing Insider Group*, https://marketinginsidergroup.com/content-marketing/the-cost-of-bad-content/#:~:text=According%20to%20Forrester%2C%2060,content%20goes%20completely%20unused.

We'll soon exhaust high-quality text for AI training: Pablo Villalobos et al., "Will We Run Out of Data? An Analysis of the Limits of Scaling Datasets in Machine Learning," *arXiv* 2211.04325 (2022), https://arxiv.org/abs/2211.04325.

Wolfram how AI works explainer: Stephen Wolfram, "What Is ChatGPT Doing ... and Why Does It Work?" *Writings of Stephen Wolfram*, February

14, 2023, https://writings.stephenwolfram.com/2023/02/what-is-chatgpt-doing-and-why-does-it-work/.

Overreliance on AI can dampen neural engagement: Nataliya Kosmyna et al., "Your Brain on ChatGPT: Accumulation of Cognitive Debt when Using an AI Assistant for Essay Writing Task," *arXiv* (June 10, 2025), https://arxiv.org/abs/2506.08872.

AI usage can reduce creativity research: Arvin Duhaylungsod and Jason Chavez, "ChatGPT and Other AI Users: Innovative and Creative Utilitarian Value and Mindset Shift," *Journal of Namibian Studies: History Politics Culture* 33 (March 2023): 4367–4385, https://www.researchgate.net/publication/373169762_ChatGPT_and_other_AI_Users_Innovative_and_Creative_Utilitarian_Value_and_Mindset_Shift.

Chapter 16. Principle 13: Automate the Busywork

Slow Productivity, **referenced throughout**: Cal Newport, *Slow Productivity: The Lost Art of Accomplishment Without Burnout* (New York: Portfolio, 2024).

Labor productivity slowed by half (2004–2022 vs. 1994–2004): Economic Strategy Group, "In Brief: U.S. Labor Productivity," 2023, https://www.economicstrategygroup.org/publication/in-brief-us-labor-productivity/.

"Interrupted every 2 minutes," "infinite workday," and meeting overload: Microsoft Work Trend Index, "2025: The Year the Frontier Firm Is Born," *Microsoft WorkLab*, 2025, https://www.microsoft.com/en-us/worklab/work-trend-index/2025-the-year-the-frontier-firm-is-born.

25–30 minutes to get back on task after distractions: Daniel Goleman, "A Focus on Distraction," *New York Times*, May 5, 2013, https://www.nytimes.com/2013/05/05/opinion/sunday/a-focus-on-distraction.html.

Burnout among knowledge workers: DHR Global, "Workforce Trends Report 2025," 2025, https://www.dhrglobal.com/insights/workforce-trends-report-2025/.

"Work about work" time drain: Asana, *Anatomy of Work Global Index 2022*, https://www.cnbc.com/2022/04/06/people-spend-more-than-half-of-the-day-on-busy-work-says-asana-survey.html.

Attention residue: Sophie Leroy, "Why Is It So Hard to Do My Work? The Challenge of Attention Residue When Switching Between Work Tasks," *Organizational Behavior and Human Decision Processes* 109, no. 2 (2009): 168–81, https://www.sciencedirect.com/science/article/abs/pii/S0749597809000399.

Stress is a creativity killer: Weiwei Zhang et al., "Acute Stress and Decision Making: A Systematic Review," *Psychoneuroendocrinology* 104 (2019): 39–52,

AI speeds routine business writing (quality/time study): Shakked Noy and Whitney Zhang, "Experimental Evidence on the Productivity Effects of Generative Artificial Intelligence," *MIT Economics Working Paper*, 2023, https://economics.mit.edu/sites/default/files/inline-files/Noy_Zhang_1_0.pdf.

Stress signals in brain in back-to-back video calls: Microsoft WorkLab, "The Effects of Back-to-Back Meetings," 2021, https://www.microsoft.com/en-us/worklab/does-your-brain-care-what-meetings-look-like.

Gen Z and Millennials who use GenAI perceive time savings and better balance: Deloitte, *2024 Gen Z and Millennial Survey*, 2024, https://www2.deloitte.com/global/en/pages/about-deloitte/articles/genzmillennialsurvey.html.

Searching for information eats a quarter of the day (Harris Poll for Glean): Glean, *Hybrid Workplace Habits & Hangups* (survey of 1,000 knowledge workers), 2022, https://get.glean.com/rs/626-JWX-444/images/2022_Hybrid-workplace-habits-hangups_Glean-report.pdf.

Chapter 17. Principle 14: Iterate with Intention

Daguerreotype background: Daguerreotype overview (Library of Congress): Library of Congress, "The Daguerreotype Medium," *Daguerreotypes: Articles and Essays*, n.d., https://www.loc.gov/collections/daguerreotypes/articles-and-essays/the-daguerreotype-medium/; and The Franklin Institute, "Daguerreotype Photography," n.d. https://fi.edu/en/science-and-education/collection/daguerreotype-photography and Exhibition—*From Today, Painting Is Dead: Early Photography in Britain and France* : Barnes Foundation, "From Today, Painting Is Dead: Early Photography in Britain and France," exhibition page, February 24–May 12, 2019, https://www.barnesfoundation.org/whats-on/early-photography.

The Lucas Cycle: Kara Swisher, *Burn Book: A Tech Love Story* (New York: Simon & Schuster, 2024), 133, https://www.simonandschuster.com/books/Burn-Book/Kara-Swisher/9781982170921.

Creativity advances via small, iterative steps: University of Pittsburgh, "Study shows creativity emerges through incremental idea chains," EurekAlert! news release, 2014, https://www.eurekalert.org/news-releases/717957.

The science (and pitfalls) of classic brainstorming: Rachel Gillett, "The Science of Brainstorming," Fast Company, July 7, 2014, https://www.fastcompany.com/3032418/the-science-of-brainstorming.

Generative AI improves idea quality/novelty: Science Advances, "Generative AI improves creativity/novelty in ideation tasks," 2025, https://www.science.org/doi/10.1126/sciadv.adn5290.

Lani Assaf prompt: Assaf, Lani, LinkedIn Post, July 2025,https://www.linkedin.com/feed/update/urn:li:activity:7348024744849408001/.

Neuroscience of writing: Pam Belluck, "Researching the Brain of Writers," The New York Times, June 18, 2014. https://www.nytimes.com/2014/06/19/science/researching-the-brain-of-writers.html.

Shykids quotes: Etan Vlessing, "OpenAI's Sora: Beta Testers Share Their First Videos," *The Hollywood Reporter,* Feb. 18, 2024, https://www.hollywoodreporter.com/business/business-news/openai-sora-beta-testers-videos-1235866655/.

Ted Chiang on the importance of choices: Ted Chiang, "Why AI Isn't Going to Make Art," *The New Yorker,* 2024, https://www.newyorker.com/culture/the-weekend-essay/why-ai-isnt-going-to-make-art.

Audiences want transparency on AI images: Getty Images, "Nearly 90% of consumers want transparency on AI images," newsroom report, 2024, https://newsroom.gettyimages.com/en/getty-images/nearly-90-of-consumers-want-transparency-on-ai-images-finds-getty-images-report.

71% say they're worried about being able to trust what they see or hear because of AI: Quirk's Media, "Consumer Trust: Will AI Erode Authenticity in Marketing?," 2024, https://www.quirks.com/articles/consumer-trust-will-ai-erode-authenticity-in-marketing.

AI disclosure lifts brand trust: AdExchanger, "How Advertisers Can Unlock the Promise of AI with Transparency," 2024, http://adexchanger.com/content-studio/how-advertisers-can-unlock-the-promise-of-ai-with-transparency/.

Chapter 18. Principle 15: Innovate Boldly

"Spawn is our AI baby": *Birthing PROTO* (documentary), YouTube video, 2019, https://www.youtube.com/watch?v=v_4UqpUmMkg.

Herndon building Spawn: Rachel Hahn, "Holly Herndon on *PROTO*, AI, and Collaboration," *Vogue,* May 10, 2019., https://www.vogue.com/article/holly-herndon-interview-proto-dropbox-documentary-proto-ai-music-spawn-new-album.

Herndon on attribution: Hazel Cills, "A Chat With Holly Herndon About Making Music With AI," *Jeze.bel,* May 16, 2019, https://www.jezebel.com/a-chat-with-holly-herndon-about-making-music-with-ai-a-1834562691.

Herndon TED Talk: Holly Herndon, "What if you could sing in your favorite musician's voice?," TED Talk, posted September 2022, https://www.ted.com/speakers/holly_herndon.

Herndon framing AI as an opportunity: Amos Barshad, "Holly Herndon Is Building a Future for Human-AI Music," *Wired*, 2019, https://www.wired.com/story/holly-herndon-ai-deepfakes-music/.

Elwes Queer AI drag show: Sanjana Varghese, "Jake Elwes: 'Part of my role as an artist is demystifying AI technologies,'" *1854 Photography*, June 1, 2023, https://www.1854.photography/2023/06/jake-elwes-part-of-my-role-as-an-artist-is-demystifying-ai-technologies/; and Jake Elwes, "The Zizi Show," 2020, https://www.jakeelwes.com/project-zizi-show.html.

Huyghe human imagination image reconstruction: Hettie Judah, "The mind gardener: the machine that turns your thoughts into art," *The Guardian*, October 2, 2018, https://www.theguardian.com/artanddesign/2018/oct/02/pierre-huyghe-serpentine-gallery-london.

Metaphysic AI replacement for CGI: Devin Gordon, "What If AI Is Actually Good for Hollywood?," *The New York Times Magazine*, November 1, 2024, https://www.nytimes.com/2024/11/01/magazine/ai-hollywood-movies-cgi.html.

Lucas—build the tech you need to tell the story: Shipra Harbola Gupta, "6 Great Insights from George Lucas at the Sundance Film Festival," *IndieWire*, Jan. 30, 2015, https://www.indiewire.com/news/general-news/6-great-insights-from-george-lucas-at-the-sundance-film-festival-248345/.